K<small>THE</small>ASPAR HAUSER SYNDROME

OF "PSYCHOSOCIAL DWARFISM"

ALSO BY JOHN MONEY

Hermaphroditism: An Inquiry into the Nature of a Human Paradox, 1952.

The Psychologic Study of Man, 1957.

A Standardized Road-Map Test of Direction Sense (with D. Alexander and H.T. Walker, Jr.), 1965.

Sex Errors of the Body: Dilemmas, Education, and Counseling, 1968.

Man and Woman, Boy and Girl: The Differentiation and Dimorphism of Gender Identity from Conception to Maturity (with A. A. Ehrhardt), 1972.

Sexual Signatures (with Patricia Tucker), 1975.

Love and Love Sickness: The Science of Sex, Gender Difference, and Pairbonding, 1980.

The Destroying Angel: Sex, Fitness, and Food in the Legacy of Degeneracy Theory, Graham Crackers, Kellogg's Corn Flakes, and American Health History, 1985.

Venuses Penuses: Sexology, Sexosophy, and Exigency Theory, 1986.

Lovemaps: Sexual/Erotic Health and Pathology, Paraphilia, and Gender Transposition in Childhood, Adolescence, and Maturity, 1986; paperback, 1988.

Gay, Straight, and In-Between: The Sexology of Erotic Orientation, 1988.

The Breathless Orgasm: A Lovemap Biography of Asphyxiophilia (with G. Wainwright and D. Hingsburger), 1991.

Biographies of Gender and Hermaphroditism in Paired Comparisons: Clinical Supplement to the Handbook of Sexology, 1991.

The Adam Principle: Genes, Genitals, Hormones, and Gender: Selected Readings in Sexology, 1993.

The Armed Robbery Orgasm: A Lovemap Biography of Masochism (with R.W. Keyes), 1993.

EDITED BY JOHN MONEY

Reading Disability: Progress and Research Needs in Dyslexia, 1962.

Sex Research: New Developments, 1965.

The Disabled Reader: Education of the Dyslexic Child, 1966.

Transsexualism and Sex Reassignment (with R. Green), 1969.

Contemporary Sexual Behavior: Critical Issues in the 1970's (with J. Zubin), 1973.

Developmental Human Behavior Genetics (with W. K. Schaie, E. Anderson, and G. McClearn), 1975.

Handbook of Sexology (with H. Musaph), 1977.

Traumatic Abuse and Neglect of Children at Home (with G. Williams), 1980.

Handbook of Human Sexuality (with B. B. Wolman), 1980.

The Pharmacology and Endocrinology of Sexual Function (with H. Musaph and J. M. A. Sitsen), Vol. 6 of *Handbook of Sexology*, 1988.

Childhood and Adolescent Sexology (with H. Musaph and M. E. Perry), Vol. 7 of *Handbook of Sexology*, 1990.

KASPAR HAUSER SYNDROME

THE

OF "PSYCHOSOCIAL DWARFISM"

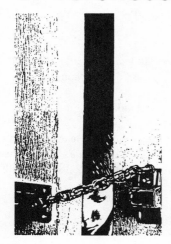

Deficient Statural,

Intellectual,

and Social Growth Induced

by Child Abuse

JOHN MONEY

Prometheus Books • Buffalo, New York

Published 1992 by Prometheus Books

96 95 94 93 92   5 4 3 2 1

Library of Congress Cataloging-in-Publication Data

Money, John, 1921–
    The Kaspar Hauser syndrome of "psychosocial dwarfism" : deficient statural, intellectual, and social growth induced by child abuse / John Money.
        p.   cm.
    Includes bibliographical references (p.   ) and indexes.
    ISBN 0-87975-754-X
    1. Failure to thrive syndrome. 2. Maternal deprivation—Health aspects.
3. Dwarfism, Pituitary. 4. Abused children—Health and hygiene. 5. Psychologically abused children—Health and hygiene. 6. Hauser, Kaspar, 1812–1833—Health.
I. Title.
RJ135.M66   1992
618.92—dc20   92-11008
                                                                  CIP

Printed in Mexico on acid-free paper.

Dedicated to my brother,
Donald Frank Light Money,
pioneer in basic veterinary and public health research
for the prevention of sudden infant death syndrome.

Contents

PART III: KASPAR HAUSER IN LITERATURE
            BY JOSHUA KENDALL, M.A.

Acknowledgments

The United States Public Health Service's National Institute of Child Health and Human Development has, for all twenty-nine years of its existence, continuously supported the Psychohormonal Research Unit (PRU) at the Johns Hopkins University and Hospital, and thus may claim kudos for this book as well as for the PRU research publications cited in it. Kudos rightfully goes also to William Wang, B.A., as manuscript director, and to Joshua Kendall, M.A., as humanities and history research specialist and author of Part III. Many people who, in the course of many years, have worked in the PRU have assisted in the long-term followup of patients who contributed data to publications quoted in this book. The same applies to the staff of the Pediatric Endocrine Clinic. Without them, and in particular Robert M. Blizzard, M.D., and Claude J. Migeon, M.D., directors of the clinic, this book would not have been able to exist. Needless to say, those on whom the book's existence is utterly dependent are the patients themselves, and their family members and case workers. Their reward, in addition to whatever personal benefit they may have received, is to have participated in the advancement of knowledge.

9

Preface

A century's worth of information is gathered together in this book, which begins with a retrospective glance at the nineteenth century, and ends in anticipation of the twenty-first. The mid-twentieth century was an era in which clinical investigation was esteemed. There was funding support for long-range outcome studies of human development in health and sickness. There was funding even for developmental clinical biographies from infancy to adulthood and beyond.

That era was brought to a close by a climate of antiscientism manifested, inter alia, as repudiation of the medical model, proliferation of excessively restrictive bureaucratic rules and regulations against breach of patients' rights, and expansion of litigation against research practitioners. The advancement of clinical science has been curtailed by patients' veto power over the use of case history material that might be emotionally upsetting even to a patient whose identity had been scrupulously disguised. Although not yet entirely extinct, clinical research has become a severely endangered species.

It is not yet possible to foresee whether or not this book will mark the end of an era of long-term, clinical outcome studies in child

11

development, and the onset of a descent into a dark age. The alternative is that it may foretell a new dawn in the twenty-first century, with a renewed recognition of the absolute indispensability of outcome research that is not only long-term, but very long-term. In order to avoid becoming the long-range victims of unforeseen outcomes of treatment, all patients should require, as a condition of undergoing any treatment, the guarantee of long-range, outcome research. Had such a guarantee formerly been in effect, it would not have taken the best part of the twentieth century to discover what is revealed in this book about the Kaspar Hauser syndrome.

Introduction

One of the ironies of altruism is summed up in the maxim that no good deed ever goes unpunished. For the virtuous founders of hospitals for giving birth and for the care of sick children, the punishment for their good deed was that hospital wards became incubators of lethal contagion and its epidemic spread. For the founders of orphanages for abandoned and homeless children, the punishment for their good deed was that these institutions exposed their inmates to the potentially lethal syndrome of institutionalism. The victims of institutionalism fail to thrive. Some of them waste away, and they may die. Those who survive fail to achieve full growth, staturally, intellectually, and socially.

Germ theory, formulated in the 1870s and antibiotics, clinically available initially in the late 1940s, made it possible to prevent and control the spread of infections in hospitals. It would, however, take an additional half century and more to formulate a theory that would make it possible to prevent and control the failure-to-thrive symptoms of the syndrome defined not only as institutionalism, but also as hospitalism.

13

Historically, the search for this syndrome is reminiscent of the allegory of three blind men palpating different parts of an elephant, and coming to divergent conclusions as to what manner of beast they had encountered. In the case of the syndrome of institutionalism or hospitalism, the counterpart of the three blind men is the three specialties of pediatrics, mental deficiency, and child psychiatry. In pediatrics it was recognized somatically as the syndrome of failure to thrive and of retardation of growth. In mental deficiency, it was recognized intellectually as the syndrome of environmental deprivation and decrease in IQ. In child psychiatry, it was recognized psycho-pathologically as the syndrome of maternal deprivation, anaclitic depression and/or personality disorder.

These three different versions of this allegorical elephant became convergent when a fourth specialty, pediatric endocrinology, bearing the gift of sight, joined the other three. Slowly, and with the help of pediatric psychoendocrinology, the allegorical elephant emerged as a syndrome of threefold failure of growth and development, namely the failure of physique age, intellectual age, and social age to increase in synchrony with chronological age.

At first, this threefold failure was attributed to maternal deprivation, emotional deprivation, or simply, deprivation. Subsequently, deprivation was recognized as being a euphemism for neglect and abuse. In the domicile of neglect and abuse, the velocity of all three dimensions of growth slows down and may come to a standstill. Thus a child of chronological age four may have the size and developmental age of a one year old baby. For catchup growth to begin, transfer to a nonabusive domiciliary environment is all that is needed. The sooner the transfer the better, for the longer the exposure to abuse and neglect, the greater the limitation on the amount of lost growth that can be retrieved, and the greater the degree of permanent residual loss in height, IQ, and social maturity.

There is a special feature of this domicile specific syndrome, namely that, when the velocity of growth is diminished in the home of abuse and neglect, the plasma level of growth hormone secreted by the pituitary gland also is diminished. Conversely, as growth velocity increases in a benign environment, so also does the plasma level of growth hormone. From data on newborn rats, it has been established that the plasma level of growth hormone is contingent upon stimulation of skin senses by vigorous maternal licking, or by the simulation of maternal licking with strokes of an artist's paint brush. Without stimulation, the babies die. In human babies born prematurely, stroking, patting, and massaging increases growth and shortens the period of hospital care. It is possible that the growth hormone response is mediated by endorphins, the brain's own opioid secretions.

In folklore and fairy tale, the character of the wicked stepmother who treats the child with cruelty is a reminder of the antiquity of parental abuse and neglect. It is, however, to the historical figure, Kaspar Hauser, that one turns for evidence of growth failure as a sequel to abuse and neglect, for his is the first case in which adequate documentation has survived. Thus his name is ideally suited as an eponym with which to name a syndrome that, until now, has not had its own definitive name.

The history of discovery of the etiology of Kaspar Hauser syndrome is a fascinating example of medical detectives sighting their quarry but being unable to capture it by reason of precommitment to a paradigm of the separation of body and mind. For future science, the syndrome offers the great challenge and research promise of being a syndrome in which body and mind are one and inseparable. That is why its history and present status are brought together in this book, for students of, in particular, child development, psychoneuroendocrinology, and brain science in the twenty-first century.

PART I

KASPAR HAUSER SYNDROME, 1800–1967

1

Eponym

The life and death of Kaspar Hauser (1812–1833) was wrapped in sufficient mystery to ensure that his name would not be forgotten in literature and science. It is not the mystery of who he was, however, that warrants the eponymic perpetuation of his name in the Kaspar Hauser syndrome. Rather, it is the mystery of how isolation, abuse, and neglect in childhood might induce a syndrome of overall physical and mental growth retardation, following which catchup growth would be at best only partial and incomplete.

The plight of Kaspar Hauser became known on May 26, 1828, when he was abandoned at the Haller Gate of the city of Nuremberg, Bavaria. He was carrying a written note from which his age could be calculated as sixteen. The note identified him as Kaspar Hauser, born April 30, 1812, a foundling whose deceased father had been a member of the Light Cavalry.

In her brief biography of Kaspar Hauser, Nicole Simon (1980) relied on von Feuerbach's account (translated and published in Boston, 1833). The following information is adapted from Nicole Simon's biography. When abandoned at the Haller Gate, the boy appeared not to know where he was. He showed neither fear, astonishment, nor confusion, but rather an almost animal-like dullness, either not noticing external objects, or staring at them, blankly. Detained as a vagabond, he spent hours seated on the floor playing with toy horses, this having been one of his pastimes, it was subsequently ascertained, while living in solitary isolation. His vocabulary was limited to a few, reiterated words. His height was 4 feet 9 inches (145 cm) (final height 4 feet 11 inches; 150 cm). Beard and moustache were beginning to show. There were no wisdom teeth until age nineteen.

The prison superintendent's eleven-year-old son, Julius Hietel, became Kaspar Hauser's tutor for the six weeks that he lived with the Hietels. After paying a visit on July 28, 1828, von Feuerbach described Kaspar's speech as telegraphic and deficient in syntax, especially conjunctions, participles, and adverbs. The pronoun I occurred very rarely; he usually referred to himself in the third person or as Kaspar. Formulation of coherent speech was still beyond his capabilities. Often he would repeat a phrase over and over.

In February, 1829, after continued personalized tuition by a young high-school teacher, G. F. Daumer, Kaspar Hauser wrote in the style of a beginner learning German. He recorded some of his own story. He had always lived in a small dark room. He was fed coarse dark bread and water. Sometimes he would have a clean shirt, and his fingernails would be cut. He had two toy horses and would run them back and forth. Shortly before being taken to Nuremberg, his custodian guided his hand until he could write his name, and taught him to say a few words. He practiced his new words and phrases on the way to Nuremberg. To walk was painful and tiring.

After the existence of Kaspar Hauser's written memoir was reported in the newspaper, an attempt was made on his life in October, 1829. In May, 1833, von Feuerbach died, the victim of suspected poisoning, presumably because he may have been close to solving the mystery of Kaspar Hauser's true identity. On December 14, 1833, Kaspar Hauser was himself murdered, stabbed to death in a public park by a stranger who had decoyed him on the pretext of having documentation of his true heritage. The most likely theory of his heritage is, according to Malson (1972), as follows.

> It is almost certain that Kaspar was in fact the son of Stéphanie Beauharnais, Josphine's niece, who had been married off by Napoleon to Prince Charles of Baden. So that the crown would revert to the children of a morganatic line, Kaspar, the son of Charles and Stéphanie, was taken away from them and entrusted to the care of Baron Griesenberg's game-keeper, Franz Richter, otherwise known as 'The Man.' The name of his murderer was Johann Jacob Muller. These revelations were made only sometime afterwards by Edmond Bapst (p.67).

Before he died, despite his overall achievements, Kaspar Hauser remained socially inept. Von Feuerbach wrote: "If he were to enter a mixed company without being known, he would strike everyone as a strange phenomenon, not capable of uttering a single pleasantry, or even of understanding a figurative expression. . . . He often utters things which, coming from any other person of the same age, would be called stupid or silly."

The case of Kaspar Hauser entered the annals of social thought as an object lesson on the influence of civilizing nurture over untamed nature. His was not, however, a full fledged case of untamed nature, that of a so-called feral child. He was not discovered wandering in the wild with no retrievable vestige of his prior history, and the fragments of prior history that were retrieved told a story of deprivation, neglect, and abuse.

2

Untamed Nature Versus
Social Deprivation

It goes without saying that it would be ethically impermissible to design an experiment to create feral children, first authenticating their prenatal and infantile history, and then releasing them into the wild, perhaps under the care of animals. In fortuitously occurring cases, no assumptions may be legitimately made about the prior history of a feral child who is rescued from the wild. Beginning in the 19th century, however, social theorists fell back on the assumption that, in those feral children who failed to become adequately socialized after having been rescued, the failure could be attributed to a history of congenital feeble-mindedness. The possibility of a history of congenital psychosis could not be raised, for the very existence of psychosis in childhood was not recognized until Leo Kanner described and named infantile autism in 1943. The notion that deprivation of socialization at a critical period of early development might itself induce irreversible impairment of not only social and behavioral maturation, but of intellectual and physical maturation as well, would remain unformulated for another century or more.

It was with Victor, the Wild Boy of Aveyron in central southern France, that congenital mental defect first became a diagnosis to explain a feral child's learning disability. In 1800, some months after leaving the wild, Victor had been examined in Paris by the famed French psychiatrist of the Bicêtre asylum, Philippe Pinel, who declared him a congenital idiot. Jean M. G. Itard (1774–1838) a physician at the Institution for Deaf-Mutes disagreed. As an heir to the scholarship of the French Enlightenment era, Itard considered Victor's case to be not congenital, but a product of lack of socialization, and socially remediable. Thus his education would be important for the issue of human nature versus social nurture. By order of the Ministry of the Interior, the boy's socialization was entrusted to Itard who personally designed the program of his training and implemented it together with the boy's house mother, Madame Gurin and her husband (Itard, 1962).

Itard wrote two lucidly detailed scientific reports of his work with Victor, of which the first appeared in 1801, under the title of *First Developments of the Young Savage of Aveyron*. It begins as follows.

A child of eleven or twelve, who some years before had been seen completely naked in the Caune Woods seeking acorns and roots to eat, was met in the same place toward the end of September 1799 by three sportsmen who seized him as he was climbing into a tree to escape from their pursuit. Conducted to a neighboring hamlet and confided to the care of a widow, he broke loose at the end of a week and gained the mountains, where he wandered during the most rigorous winter weather, draped rather than covered with a tattered shirt.

At night he retired to solitary places but during the day he approached the neighboring villages, where of his own accord he entered an inhabited house situated in the Canton of St. Sernin. There he was retaken, watched and cared for during two or three days and transferred to the hospital [orphanage] of Saint-Affrique, then to Rodez, where he was kept for several months.

While in Saint-Affrique, the boy was visited by the Abbé Pierre-Bonnaterre, professor of natural history at the Central School of the Department of Aveyron in Rodez (Lane, 1976). Bonnaterre kept extensive notes of his observations which Lane has translated. He reported the boy's height as four and a half feet, his physique as prepubertal, and estimated his age as twelve or thirteen years old (Lane, p.33).

Victor may, in fact, have been older, even as old as nineteen or twenty, for it is now known (Money and Wolff, 1974) that under prolonged conditions of extreme deprivation and abuse, failure of statural growth may be accompanied by failure of the onset of puberty. Following rescue, puberty may begin almost precipitously or, as Itard reported of Victor, precociously.

Victor's height and puberty are consistent with a diagnosis of abuse dwarfism. There is additional evidence of abuse in the multitude of scars on the boy's body.

There could be counted four upon his face, six along his left arm, three at some distance from the right shoulder, four at the margin of the pubis, one upon the left buttock, three on one leg and two on the other which makes twenty three altogether (Itard, 1962, p.9).

Bonnaterre (Lane, p.34) wrote that the greater part of the scars seemed to have been produced by burns, but Itard attributed them to animals' teeth and claws and to vegetation scratches. However, there was one other scar visible on the throat, of which Itard wrote (Malson, p.29):

In fact it looks like a wound made by a sharp instrument, but from its linear appearance one is inclined to believe that the wound was only a superficial one, and that it would have reunited [easily]. It is to be presumed that a hand with the will, rather than the habit, of crime had wished to make an attempt on the life of this child and that, left for dead in the woods, he owed the prompt recovery of his wound to the help of nature alone.

Itard was intent on deducing that the injury had not injured the vocal cords, and that Victor would eventually learn to talk. In fact, the boy's achievement with spoken and heard language was negligible, whereas he made some progress with visual language by signs and even in writing. One must consider, therefore, that, in addition to having his throat cut, he might have had an extensive history of violent abuse. Bonnaterre described a rotation of the right knee inward. It could have been the product of abusive trauma and have been fractured. He might have suffered traumatic head and ear injuries, as well, with perhaps a partial hearing impairment specific to the acoustics of the consonants. Bonnaterre noted the occurrence of "spasms, some kind of convulsive fits, which seems to indicate that the nervous system is affected" (Lane, p.36). Abandonment or escape into the woods would have brought an end to abusive violence, but not to deprivation, isolation and neglect, and their cumulatively irreversible sequelae.

After five years of disappointing effort, Itard's prediction that he could completely civilize the Wild Boy of Aveyron remained unfulfilled. Reluctantly he conceded the possibility of congenital mental deficit. His concession would haunt the literature for a full century or more after Victor's death at the age of 40 in 1828.

In the mid-20th century, for instance, David Levy, a child psychiatrist, known for his work on maternal overprotection as well as maternal rejection and, in the child, "affect hunger" (Levy, 1937), failed to recognize the significance of maternal underprotection when he wrote, as follows, of an unusual case from 1918.

World War I had depleted the staff. I was pressed into service as sole psychiatrist even before my general internship. At the Illinois Juvenile Psychopathic Institute . . . there appeared among my patients an idiot who presented interesting neurologic and psychologic behavior. He had been confined to the cellar of his father's bakery most of his ten years of life. He ate food like an animal, nuzzling his mouth into the dish. His spine was arched forward, and when he walked, his arms hung loosely in front of his body, the hands reaching a position below the knees. He slept curled up. Sometimes he loped on all fours. He looked like the "missing link." . . . He had an IQ of 30 (Levy, 1947, p.9).

In discounting the effects of ten years of abusive deprivation and neglect, Levy was in conformity with the nature/nurture doctrines of his era, according to which idiocy was an evolutionary regression or degeneration to the subhuman state of the "missing link."

In the social and developmental psychology of the 1940s, there was a minor revival of interest in reports of feral children, and their merit for theories of learning versus genetic endowment in child development. The term, feral, was used loosely to refer to children found literally in the wild, like Kamala and Amala, two girls known as the wolf children of India (Singh and Zingg, 1941; Gesell, 1942), as well as to those found living under appalling conditions of abuse, restraint, isolation, and deprivation, like Anna from Pennsylvania and Isabelle from Ohio, reported by the sociologist, Kingsley Davis (1940, 1947).

Anna and Isabelle were both illegitimate and were kept in enforced concealment by the mother's family. Both were rescued at age six. Both were retarded in growth and maturation staturally, intellectually, and socially. Both lacked language. After rescue, Anna's rate of catchup growth on all counts was dismally poor, whereas Isabelle progressed so rapidly that she appeared normal by age eight and a half. Davis labored over the pros and cons of congenital feeble-mindedness present in Anna, but not in Isabelle. He took note of the fact that Isabelle had been locked away with her deaf-mute mother and so had not been deprived of human contact, especially body contact, and motherly attention. He did not take the next intellectual step and formulate the proposition that body contact, as observed in mothering, might have been the decisive variable in Isabelle's rapid recovery—but that is precisely what subsequent research would eventually reveal.

3

Hospitalism

Galen, in the second century, had written a treatise, *De Marasmo* (Theoharides, 1971). Galen applied the term, marasmus, meaning wasting away or dying, to adults. It was only in the nineteenth century that the term marasmus was applied to the wasting away of infants and youth as well as the elderly. By the turn of the century, the prevalence of marasmic death amongst once healthy infants in institutional care was appallingly high. Chapin (1915) surveyed ten institutions in ten American cities. The death rate among infants under two years of age ranged from 32% in Philiadelphia to 75% in Baltimore. The overall rate of 50% was much higher among those under one year of age.

There were those who attributed marasmic death to nutritional deficiency or to susceptibility to chronic infection. Henry Dwight Chapin was not one of them. As early as 1902, he recalled, he had "instituted a plan for boarding out atrophic or abandoned babies" to supervised home care, so as to prevent the "cachexia of hospitalism." He summed up his philosophy of prevention as follows (Chapin, 1915, p.3).

The unit of civilization is the family which offers the healthiest physical environment. The most susceptible member of the family to all external conditions is the infant. When transplanted from natural and normal conditions, the little ones quickly droop and suffer most.

We must see to it that relief is afforded in the most natural and effective way to these unfortunates who come under our care. For this reason the infant asylum must go.

Cottages must take the place of barracks. An increased knowledge of the real needs of infant life will not tolerate the old methods much longer, for a larger and wiser human spirit is at work on these problems, which is not content to put up with evils that can be avoided.

Chapin's teachings eventually bore fruit in the widespread acceptance of foster care as a substitute for institutionalization, but the magic of the success of the foster home placement would remain unexplained, as would the phenomenon of hospitalism itself, until after pediatrics had become established as a new medical specialty. In 1941, Harry Bakwin (1942), a pediatrician, addressed the issue of hospitalism before the American Pediatric Society, as follows (p.31).

Infants confined in hospitals present a fairly well defined clinical picture. A striking feature is their failure to gain properly, despite the ingestion of diets which in the home are entirely adequate for growth. Infants in hospitals sleep less than infants who are at home, and they rarely smile or babble spontaneously. They are listless, apathetic and look unhappy. The appetite is indifferent, and food is accepted without enthusiasm. The stools tend to be frequent, and, in sharp contrast with the habits of infants cared for in homes, it is unusual for twenty-four hours to pass without an evacuation. Infections of the respiratory tract which last only a day or two in a home often persist for months in a hospital. Return home results in defervescence within a few days and a prompt and striking gain in weight.

Two case illustrations are presented, with figures of before-and after temperature and weight curves, and photographs. The first case is as follows (pp.31-33).

M.K., a girl, was admitted to the hospital on June 18, 1940, at the age of eighteen days, because she had had frequent watery green stools for four days. There was occasional vomiting, but the appetite was good. With treatment the diarrhea subsided promptly. The mother had congenital syphilis and a positive Wassermann reaction. The child had no symptoms of syphilis, and her Wassermann reaction was negative on numerous occasions after the second week of life. She weighed 5 pounds and 6 ounces (2,438 gm) at birth. She gained fairly well at first, but when she was 15 weeks old fever developed and thereafter the gain in weight was slow. At the age of eight months, when she left the hospital, her weight was only 9 pounds (4,082 gm), about one-half the expected weight for infants of her age and sex.

From the age of fifteen weeks until her discharge, when she was eight months old, the temperature was elevated almost daily. Usually the temperature ranged between 102° F and 104° F (39° to 40° C), but on two occasions it rose to 106° F (41.1° C). No definite cause for the fever was ever found, except for a somewhat reddened pharynx and, on one occasion, a stomatitis. Repeated blood cultures, chemical and cytologic examinations and cultures of the urine, roentgenographic examinations of the chest and tuberculin tests gave negative results. The temperature failed to go down in response to sulfanilamide and some of its derivatives. After the child's discharge from the hospital she showed a prompt gain in weight. She was seen six times after she left the hospital, the first time one week after discharge. Each time the temperature was below 100° F (37.8° C). Her weight at the end of 1 year was about 16 pounds (7,257 gm).

Bakwin examined and discounted an explanation of this case in terms of either infection or nutritional deficiency. He presented a second case from New York's Bellevue Hospital, with dramatic before-and-after photographs resembling those of Chapin a quarter of a century earlier (pp.33–34).

A.S., a boy, was the first-born child of healthy parents.

Gestation and birth were normal and the weight at birth was 6 pounds and 14 ounces (3,118 gm). The child was breast fed for only three weeks and then, because of maternal illness, was removed from the breast and given artificial feeding.

He gained well at first and when 6 weeks old weighed 8 pounds and 14 ounces (4,026 gm). Shortly thereafter he had a nasopharyngeal infection accompanied with diarrhea and vomiting. He was admitted to the hospital at the age of eight weeks. The gastrointestinal symptoms disappeared promptly with treatment, but infections followed each other in rapid succession. In spite of fairly large amounts of food, supplemented with accessory food substances and transfusions, the child went downhill rapidly. After eight weeks in the hospital, when he was sixteen weeks old, the infant weighed 6 pounds (2,772 gm), almost a pound less than his weight at birth. He was sick at this time, emaciated, wizened, pale and so weak that it seemed as if he might stop breathing at any moment. His mother, who had been visiting several times a day, seemed to be so deft with him that it was decided to let her take him home. In the hospital the child had been receiving a breast milk feeding, about 65 calories per pound (453 gm) of body weight. The feeding was changed to isocaloric mixture of evaporated milk and cane sugar. The effect of the home environment was well nigh miraculous. The child gained promptly, and he has continued to progress steadily up to the present. Now, at the age of two years, he is a normal, healthy, alert youngster. He weighs 30 pounds (13.86 kg).

The focus of Bakwin's pediatric view of hospitalism was on the phenomenon of physically wasting away or failure to thrive. Retardation of growth in height and weight as a function of the isolation and deprivation that produced hospitalism would continue to be the specialty of pediatricians like Bakwin. Nonetheless, they would be influenced by their colleagues in the newly developing specialty of child psychiatry and psychoanalysis whose focus was on personality pathology as a concomitant of hospitalism. The term hospitalism itself, however, would become replaced by deprivation. Adjectivally qualified, deprivation became also emotional deprivation and maternal deprivation.

4

Maternal Deprivation

David M. Levy, who has already been mentioned, focused on the importance of mothering in infancy and childhood initially by way of psychopathology. He became well known for attributing childhood behavioral disorders to maternal overprotection (Levy, 1931; 1943). The converse, maternal rejection, led him to coin the term, affect hunger (Levy, 1937). He gave case examples in which affect hunger and its psychopathological sequelae were ostensibly contingent on lack of mothering in early infancy by reason of having been institutionalized in an orphanage. Here is one of the examples he cited (1937, p.645).

An unmarried woman, aged forty, adopted a child aged 2 years and 8 months, through private arrangement. The child was the illegitimate son of a woman of high economic and social status. The family history was negative. The child was turned over to an agency very soon after birth, placed in an orphanage from age twelve to twenty-seven months and then transferred to a boarding home, where he remained until the period of adoption. After a year, the adoptive mother gave up the possibility of getting any emotional relationship with the child. She had never been able to get any sign of affection from him. He never accepted her fondling. In the household there was a doting and indulgent grandmother, to whom the child also did not respond. The mother felt she had been taking punishment for a year and could stand it no longer. Besides the lack of emotional response, she complained chiefly of his negativistic behavior. According to tests, the child had superior intelligence, and the physical examination was negative. [By today's criteria this child might be characterized as autistic.]

Lawson G. Lowrey, a child psychiatrist and contemporary of Levy in New York City, adopted Levy's concept of affect hunger in a paper titled "Personality distortion and early institutional care" (1940). In this paper, Lowrey reflected on personality problems manifested by children who had been institutionalized in a home for infants for the first 3 to 3½ years of their lives. Then, in preparation for foster placement, they came to his Study House for evaluation and subsequent followup. Half or more of these children Lowrey rates as having "symptoms of inadequate personality development, chiefly related to an inability to give or receive affection; in other words, inability to relate the self to others—the isolation factor" (p.578). He did not, however, rate the possible morbidities of parenting in the foster home that might have exacerbated, if not provoked the symptoms of inadequate personality development, which he listed as follows (p.579).

Hostile aggressiveness, temper tantrums (often of exceptional violence), e nuresis (often as a regressive phenomenon on placement), speech defects (ranging to near mutism), attention demanding behavior, shyness and sensitiveness, difficulties about food (refusal, fussy, slow eating, refusing meat, voracity), stubbornness and negativism, selfishness, finger sucking and excessive crying. Other, somewhat less frequent problems were: over affectionate and repelling affection, overactivity, seclusiveness, submissiveness, difficulties in school adjustment, sleep disturbances, fears, and soiling.

Masturbation and sex play were reported in six cases. The IQs (N=16) ranged from 52 to 115. [Details of growth and weight were not recorded.]

Some of these symptoms of institutionalism had been recognized independently at the Clinic of Child Development, Yale University School of Medicine, by Arnold Gesell and Catharine Amatruda. Their book, *Developmental Diagnosis* (1941) included a section on "Institutional Syndromes" (pp.283-291). "Environmental impoverishment leads to behavioral impoverishment," they wrote. "It produces palpable reductions of behavior. This is not to say that it produces mental deficiency; but it does produce symptomatic syndromes which are severe enough to make diagnosis difficult and to call for therapeutic intervention" (p.281). These authors gave a very telling description of the impoverishing effects of life in Institution XYZ, "of near average size, moderately well-staffed and equipped, and under medical supervision." They did not, however, pursue the logic of institutional impoverishment all the way to its long-term, deleterious outcome. They wrote instead:

It is not our desire to exaggerate this portrayal of institutional life; but to indicate how the environmental mechanisms operate to bring about the syndromes of retardation. We call them syndromes because they are constituted of more or less characteristic behavior symptoms. Some of the effects may be permanent, but an institutional environment does not create amentia, even when it seriously depresses the D.Q. (Developmental Quotient).

It produces lags, and bogs down both initiative and expressiveness. But fortunately it does not destroy latent maturation. The behavior improves with improvement of environment (p.290). . . . The term institutional is used for descriptive convenience. It should be clearly stated that a faultily managed, over-sanitary family home, or a misguided domineering governess, may create a set of environmental circumstances which have the same psycho-dynamics as an institution, and which will produce the counterpart of an institutional syndrome (p.291).

Affect hunger (Levy), isolation factor (Lowrey) and environmental impoverishment (Gesell and Amatruda) are, all three, names for the phenomenon of failure to thrive that also would, together with its various other names, eventually become subsumed under the generic term, maternal deprivation. Margaret Ribble referred to it as lack of mother love. In her book, *The Rights of Infants: Early Psychological Needs and Their Satisfaction* (1943), she wrote as follows (p.4).

The astonishing discovery was made that babies in the best homes and hospitals, given the most careful physical attention, often drifted into this condition of slow dying, while infants in the poorest homes, with a good mother, often overcame the handicaps of poverty and unhygienic surroundings and became bouncing babies. It was found that the element lacking in the sterilized lives of the babies of the former class, and generously supplied to those that flourished in spite of hit-or-miss environmental conditions, was mother love.

By way of illustration, Ribble gave a "typical life story of a baby who suffered from marasmus . . . that showed in a dramatic way the hunger for mothering experiences and the effect on the child's mental as well as physical functions when this need is not satisfied." It is reproduced here in full (pp.4-7).

Little Bob was born in the maternity hospital where the writer was making studies of infants at the time. He was full-term child and weighed six pounds three ounces at birth. During the two weeks' stay in the hospital the baby was breast fed and there was no apparent difficulty with his body functions. The mother, a professional woman, had been reluctant about breast feeding because she wished to take up her work as soon as possible after the baby was born, but she yielded to the kindly encouragement of the hospital nurses, and the feeding was successful. Both mother and child were thriving when they left the hospital.

On returning home the mother found that her husband had suddenly deserted her—the climax of an unhappy and maladjusted marriage relationship. She discovered soon after that her milk did not agree with the baby. As is frequently the case, the deep emotional reaction had affected her milk secretion. The infant refused the breast and began to vomit. Later he was taken to the hospital and the mother did not call to see him. At the end of the month she wrote that she had been seriously ill and asked the hospital to keep the child until further notice.

In spite of careful medical attention and skillful feeding, this baby remained for two months at practically the same weight. He was in a crowded ward and received very little personal attention. The busy nurses had no time to take him up and work with him as a mother would, by changing his position and making him comfortable at frequent intervals. The habit of finger sucking developed, and gradually the child became what is known as a ruminator, his food coming up and going down with equal ease. At the age of two months he weighed five pounds. The baby at this time was transferred to a small children's hospital, with the idea that this institution might be able to give him more individual care. It became apparent that the mother had abandoned the child altogether.

When seen by the writer, this baby actually looked like a seven months' foetus yet he had also a strange appearance of oldness. His arms and legs were wrinkled and wasted, his head large in proportion to the rest of the body, his chest round and flaring widely at the base over an enormous liver.

His breathing was shallow, he was generally inactive, and his skin was cold and flabby. He took large quantities of milk but did not gain weight since most of it went through him with very little assimilation and with copious discharges of mucus from his intestines. The baby showed at this time the pallor which in our study we have found typical of infants who are not mothered, although careful examination of his blood did not indicate a serious degree of anemia. He was subject to severe sweating, particularly during sleep. A thorough study showed no indication of tuberculosis. The child's abdomen was large and protruding, but this proved to be due to lax intestinal muscles and consequent distended liver, which was actually in proportion to that of the foetus. There was no evidence of organic disease, but growth and development were definitely at a standstill, and it appeared that the child was gradually slipping backward to lower and lower levels of body economy and function.

The routine of treatment of this hospital for babies who are not gaining weight is to give them concentrated nursing care. They are held in the nurses' laps for feeding and allowed at least half an hour to take the bottle. From time to time their position in the crib is changed and when possible the nurse carries them about the ward for a few minutes before or after each feeding. This is the closest possible approach to mothering in a busy infants' ward.

Medical treatment consists of frequent injections of salt solution under the skin to support the weakened circulation in the surface of the body.

With this treatment the child began to improve slowly.

As his physical condition became better, it was possible for our research group to introduce the services of a volunteer "mother" who came to the hospital twice daily in order to give him some of the attention he so greatly needed. What she actually did was to hold him in her lap for a short period before his 10 A.M. and 6 P.M. feedings. She was told that he needed love more than he needed medicine, and she was instructed to stroke the child's head gently and speak or sing softly to him and walk him about. Her daily visits were gradually prolonged until she was spending an hour twice a day, giving the baby his artificial mothering. The result was good. The child remained in the hospital until he was five months of age, at which time he weighed nine pounds. All rumination and diarrhea had stopped, and he had become an alert baby with vigorous muscle activity. His motor coordinations were of course retarded. Although he held up his head well and looked about, focusing his eyes and smiling in response to his familiar nurses, he could not yet grasp his own bottle or turn himself over, as is customary at this age. The finger sucking continued, as is usually the case with babies who have suffered early privation.

In accordance with the new hospital procedure, as soon as the child's life was no longer in danger, he was transferred to a good, supervised foster home in order that he might have still more individual attention. Under this regime, his development proceeded well and gradually he mastered such functions as sitting, creeping, and standing.

His speech was slow in developing, however, and he did not walk until after the second year. The general health of this child is now excellent at the end of his third year; also his "I.Q." is high on standard tests, but his emotional life is deeply damaged. With any change in his routine or with prolonged absence of the foster mother, he goes into a state which is quite similar to depression. He becomes inactive, eats very little, becomes constipated and extremely pale. When his foster mother goes away, he usually reacts with a loss of body tone and alertness, rather than with a definite protest. His emotional relationship to the foster mother is receptive, like that of a young infant, but he makes little response to her mothering activities except to function better when she is there. He has little capacity to express affection, displays no initiative in seeking it, yet fails to thrive without it. This lack of response makes it difficult for the foster mother to show him affection which he so deeply needs. Without the constant friendly explanations of the situation from the visiting nurse, she would probably have given up care of the child.

In addition to exemplifying the principle that the complexities of somatic and behavioral symptoms of maternal deprivation may be persistently difficult to ameliorate, even when substitute mothering is provided, Ribble's case exemplifies also the principle that this syndrome may originate while living at home and not only as a by-product of institutional living. However, it was the institutionalized mass production of the syndrome, as propounded by René Spitz (1946a,b), that had dramatic and lasting impact on child-development theory, in health and pathology.

Spitz, a child psychiatrist and psychoanalyst, used two names for the syndrome, hospitalism, and his own new psychiatric term, anaclitic depression. One source of Spitz's data was an institution he named Foundling Home, in which abandoned infants were reared under conditions of social isolation and insufficient sensory-motor stimulation and contact with other human beings. The partially comparable institution, where conditions for social interaction were more benign, Spitz named Nursery. At the end of two years, the death rate among the original group of ninety-one Foundling Home children, aged up to five years, was reported as 37%, whereas no Nursery children had died.

Spitz's assistant collected data at four month intervals over two years on twenty-one children at Foundling Home who had not died or been relocated. The data pertained to locomotion, eating and dressing skills, toilet training, and speech development. Spitz summed up as follows (1946b, p.115).

> The mental development of these twenty-one children is extraordinarily retarded, compared to that of normal children between the ages of two and four, who move, climb, and babble all day long, and who conform to or struggle against the educational demands of the environment. This retardation, which amounts to a deterioration, is borne out by the weights and heights of these children, as well as their pictures. Normal children, by the end of the second year weigh, on the average, 26½ pounds (12 kg), and the length is 33½ inches (85 cm). At the time of this writing, twelve of the children in Foundling Home range in age between 2.4 and 2.8 years; 4, between 2.8 and 3.2 years; and 5, between 3.2 and 4.1 years. But of all of these children, only three fall into the weight range of a normal two-year-old child, and only two have attained the length of a normal child of that age. All others fall below the normal two-year-level—in one case, as much as 45% in weight and 5 inches (13 cm) in length. In other words, the physical picture of these children impresses the casual observer as that of children half their age. . . . The damage inflicted on the infants in Foundling Home by their being deprived of maternal care, maternal stimulation, and maternal love, as well as by their being completely isolated is irreparable. Our followup confirms this assumption.

The psychological sequelae of the irreparable developmental damage inflicted on the children of Foundling Home constituted for Spitz the syndrome of anaclitic depression. He used the evidence of retarded growth in height and weight as substantive and tangible proof of the morbidity of maternal deprivation, thus adding credibility to the claim that etiology of mental disease, as in anaclitic depression, could be attributed to maternal deprivation. Thenceforth, in child-development and child psychiatric theory, the principle of maternal deprivation would be assigned two roles each detached from the other. One would pertain to the etiology of somatic growth failure. The other would pertain to the etiology of a wide range of emotional disorders, as they came to be called, and of various disorders of conduct and retarded maturation, anaclitic depression included, as well.

As a sequel to the social disruptions of World War II in Britain, the principle of maternal deprivation as a function of institutionalization early in infancy became merged with the principle of separation from the mother, either temporarily to escape bombing, or permanently by reason of her death (Freud and Burlingham, 1944/1973; Bowlby, 1952; Ainsworth, 1962a). Released from its moorings in hospitalism and organic failure to thrive, the new conjoined principle of deprivation/separation took on a somewhat autonomous life of its own. It became utilized as an explanation of numerous psychopathologies and disorders of behavioral development in childhood (see reviews by Glaser and Eisenberg, 1956; Clarke and Clarke, 1960; Casler, 1961; Yarrow, 1962). Whimsically, if not ludicrously, it became utilized also as a nonorganic theory to explain nonorganic failure to thrive organically, a nosological oxymoron if ever there was one.

Deprivation or loss of mothering contingent upon institutionalized living entails a deprivation of sensory and motor stimulation, and of behavioral, linguistic, and social stimulation, as well. The developmental outcomes of these various deprivations show up as age-deficient scores on tests that, in infancy, yield a developmental quotient (DQ) and, from later infancy onward, an intelligence quotient (IQ).

5

Retardation of Intellectual Growth

When the initial warnings of marasmus and hospitalism in institutionalized infants were issued early in the 20th century, failure to thrive mentally was subsumed under failure to thrive physically. The specificity of intellectual failure to thrive could not be parceled out from general mental failure to thrive until after 1916, the year of the publication of the Stanford Binet Scale of Intelligence, the American translation and revision of Alfred Binet's 1905 French original.

One year of Mental Age is the unit of measurement by which intelligence is measured. This unit of measurement is the equivalent of one year of Height Age as the unit of measurement of tallness. Whereas tallness is measured first in centimeters or inches and then translated into Height Age, there is no equivalent of a centimeter or an inch by which to measure intelligence. Therefore, there is no way of knowing whether the rate of intellectual growth is constant, year by year, or whether it fluctuates, being more rapid in some years than others. Thus it is not known, for example, whether there is a growth spurt in intelligence equivalent to the growth spurt in tallness at the time of puberty.

If an individual were to grow in intelligence at exactly the same rate as those whose scores were used to calculate each year's worth of Mental Age on a scale of intelligence, then if that individual were tested on the same scale every year, his/her IQ would remain constant. Serial testing of the same individuals year after year, from infancy to maturity, however, has shown that IQ constancy is not invariably the rule. There are some individuals whose IQ fluctuates, up, down, or both, more so in early childhood than later (see, for example, Dearborn and Rothney, 1941; Cornell and Armstrong, 1955; Bayley, 1949, 1955; Sontag et al., 1958).

In cases in which there is inconstancy in the rate of intellectual growth, with concomitant inconstancy of the IQ, the change in rate of growth may be attributed to either an endogenous or an exogenous determinant or, possibly, some of both. The determinant most favored by the advocates of endogeny is heredity. Paradoxically, however, they use heredity not to explain inconstancies in the rate of intellectual growth, but to shore up the dogma of its constancy, of which the constancy of the IQ is a corollary.

The advocates of exogenous determinants of inconstancy in the rate of intellectual growth, and of concomitant inconstancy of IQ, favored no single determinant, exclusively, as being responsible for either acceleration or retardation of the rate of growth. In the intellectual climate of the early part of the 20th century, however, the opposite of heredity was environment. In the context of intelligence testing, environment was equated with social environment. The effects of social environment on the retardation rather than the acceleration of intellectual growth received priority attention. Gordon (1923), for example, found that among socially deprived canal-boat children in England the older the age group, the lower the average IQ. By age twelve, it had fallen to 60—a finding which tells as much about the irrelevancy of the test questions to canal-boat culture as about the inability of the children to answer them. A finding similar to that of Gordon was obtained by Skeels and Fillmore (1937), in a study of siblings (N=407), aged 1-14 years, from under-privileged families

(N=132) who were transferred from living under conditions of environmental deprivation to the Iowa Child Welfare Research Station. As a group, their IQs were substandard, as compared with a control group. In addition, the IQs of the siblings who were older, and who had, therefore, lived longer in the depriving environment, were lower than the IQs of the younger siblings.

The inference inherent in the data of Skeels and Fillmore and also of Gordon is that the longer the exposure to an environment of intellectual deprivation, the greater the slow down in intellectual growth, and hence the lower the level of IQ. In both studies, the investigative method was that of two matched groups, each serving as a comparison group for the other on the basis of age. Changes in rate of growth are demonstrated with greater confidence, however, if a single group of individuals is followed longitudinally and compared with itself, at two different ages, in a before-and-after research protocol which includes also a contrast or control group.

Skeels, circumventing the formidable fiscal and logistical barriers to long-term outcome research, was able to attribute the long-lasting deleterious effects of early infantile institutionalization to developmental deprivation overall, not to maternal deprivation in particular. His study became possible when the Iowa Board of Control of State Institutions appointed him, already a member of the Iowa Child Welfare Research Station of the State University, to be the Board's first psychologist. Skeels' initial recognition of the developmental effects of deprivation occurred serendipitously in his early days at the state orphanage. He wrote as follows (Skeels, 1966, pp.5–6).

> Two baby girls, neglected by their feebleminded mothers, ignored by their inadequate relatives, malnourished and frail, were legally committed to the orphanage. The youngsters were pitiful little creatures. They were tearful, had runny noses, and sparse, stringy, colorless hair; they were emaciated, undersized, and lacked muscle tone or responsiveness. Sad and inactive, the two spent their days rocking and whining.

The psychological examinations showed developmental levels of six and seven months, respectively, for the two girls, although they were then thirteen and sixteen months old chronologically. This serious delay in mental growth was confirmed by observations of their behavior in the nursery and by reports of the superintendent of nurses, as well as by the pediatrician's examination. There was no evidence of physiological or organic defect, or of birth injury or glandular dysfunction.

The two children were considered unplaceable, and transfer to a school for the mentally retarded was recommended with a high degree of confidence. Accordingly, they were transferred to an institution for the mentally retarded at the next available vacancy, when they were aged fifteen and eighteen months, respectively.

In the meantime, the author's professional responsibilities had been increased to include itinerant psychological services to the two state institutions for the mentally retarded. Six months after the transfer of the two children, he was visiting the wards at an institution for the mentally retarded and noticed two outstanding little girls. They were alert, smiling, running about, responding to the playful attention of adults, and generally behaving and looking like any other toddlers. He scarcely recognized them as the two little girls with the hopeless prognosis, and thereupon tested them again. Although the results indicated that the two were approaching normal mental development for age, the author was skeptical of the validity or permanence of the improvement and no change was instituted in the lives of the children. Twelve months later they were re-examined, and then again when they were forty and forty-three months old. Each examination gave unmistakable evidence of mental development well within the normal range for age.

The two girls had been placed on one of the wards of

older, brighter girls and women, ranging in age from 18 to 50 years and in mental age from 5 to 9 years, where they were the only children of preschool age, except for a few hopeless bed patients with gross physical defects. Two older girls on the ward had each "adopted" one of the two little girls, and other older girls served as adoring aunts. Attendants and nurses showed affection to the two, spending time with them, taking them along on their days off for automobile rides and shopping excursions, and purchasing toys, picture books, and play materials for them in great abundance. The setting seemed to be a homelike one, abundant in affection, rich in wholesome and interesting experiences, and geared to a preschool level of development.

It was recognized that as the children grew older their developmental needs would be less adequately met in the institution for the mentally retarded. Furthermore, they were now normal and the need for care in such an institution no longer existed. Consequently, they were transferred back to the orphanage and shortly thereafter were placed in adoptive homes.

Taking his cue from these two cases, Skeels negotiated with state officials for the placement of another eleven infants from the orphanage as "house guests" in the institution for the older mentally retarded who lavished on them far more individualized attention than they could ever have received from the overworked orphanage staff. In this new environment, each infant was spontaneously "adopted" by one particular older inmate with whom, in today's parlance, the infant became pairbonded.

For the sake of comparison, each "house guest" was age matched with a child who remained living, unpairbonded, in the socially depriving environment of the orphanage to which they had been admitted, in the majority of cases, not as mentally retarded, but illegitimate.

After a period of, on the average, 2½ years, the children of both groups (thirteen "house guests," and twelve not) were retested for intelligence. Overall, the "house guests" manifested catchup growth in intelligence, and hence elevation of IQ, whereas the orphanage children had manifested additional retardation of growth in intelligence, and hence lowering of IQ. That was in 1941. World War II intervened.

In 1961, Skeels embarked on a second followup, and had the remarkable success of obtaining outcome data on all of the thirteen "house guests" and the twelve orphanage inmates. In brief, all of the "house guests" had achieved a position in which society considered them as normal self-supporting citizens, the majority married and with normal children. By contrast, only one of the twelve deprived orphanage children so qualified. One had died at age fifteen, while still institutionalized, five were alive and institutionalized, and the other five had failed to be socially or economically autonomous.

Skeels did not, in his reports, include information on catchup growth in physique. His concern was with catchup growth in intelligence. In this context, he gave information also on the lack of behavioral maturation which was a pathological legacy of the social deprivation of orphanage life. What the orphanage children had lacked, the "house guests" had gained. Of them, Skeels wrote as follows (p.17).

In considering this enriched environment from a dynamic point of view, it must be pointed out that in the case of almost every child, some one adult (older girl or attendant) became particularly attached to him and figuratively "adopted" him. As a consequence, an intense one-to-one adult-child relationship developed, which was supplemented by the less intense but frequent interactions with the other adults in the environment. Each child had some one person with whom he was identified and who was particularly interested in him and his achievements. This highly stimulating emotional impact was observed to be the unique characteristic and one of the main contributions of the experimental setting.

For the protection of human subjects, it is absolutely out of the question to contrive an outcome study in which, by design, children are deprivated of anything that is either known or suspected to be essential to their welfare. Skeels' strategy was to take advantage of a situation that already existed, so that the outcome might be improved. Other psychologists adopted the same strategy.

One of them was William Goldfarb (1945). The children whom he tested and those studied by Lowery (above) had the same history of having been institutionalized in a home for infants from about four months of age until age 2½ to 3½ years. In preparation for foster-home placement, the institutionalized children (N=15) were then given a battery of psychological tests. The same tests were given to a control group (N=15) of children who had been reared not in an institution but a foster home. The test scores of the children with a history of institutionalization were inferior. Their IQs (M±SD) were 68±7 versus 96±29 for the foster-home children. Upon retest seven months later, the scores were respectively, IQ 76±3, and 106±11. Closure of the IQ gap between the two groups, if it were to occur at all, obviously would have required longer than seven months for intellectual catch-up growth to occur in the institutionalized group.

The strategy of taking advantage of an already existing situation was followed by another psychologist, Liselotte Fischer (1952). She used the Cattell Infant Intelligence Scale to obtain a developmental quotient (a Cattell IQ is a de facto DQ) on infants (N=36) institutionalized in a home for unwed mothers while awaiting adoption. They were tested three times: at ages seven and eleven months while still institutionalized, and at age eighteen months, after having lived in the adoptive home for nine months. The mean IQs were, respectively, 77, 86, and 98. The first elevation in IQ prior to adoption was replicated in another group of children (N=25) who were un-available for the third test. The inconsistency of an elevation in IQ prior to as well as after adoption indicates the intrusion of con- taminating variables, incompatible with isolating the effect, if any, of maternal deprivation. Uncontrolled variables have posed grave problems for maternal-deprivation research, as for all investigations based on preexistent research populations or conditions.

Uncontrolled variables proved to be more amenable in Wayne Dennis's (1973) before-and-after adoption study, inaugurated in 1955 in Beirut, Lebanon. This was a study of the effects, especially on intelligence, of an extreme degree of sensory, motor, and social depri- vation experienced by infants, mostly illegitimate, abandoned by their mothers, and cared for in an overcrowded, understaffed foundling home. Dennis named this institution the Crèche.

In Lebanon, at that time, the disgrace of having been born il- legitimately was so great that, until the law was changed in 1956, it was impossible for an illegitimate child to be adopted. Thus, Dennis had a pool of children who had been institutionally reared for many years prior to 1956; and another pool of those who, after 1956, having been accepted for adoption, were released from the institution to be reared as a member of a regular household. In a before-and-after study of intellectual growth, the IQs of the adopted children were tested before they left the institution, and again after an interval of up to ten years. Their IQs on each occasion could be compared with those of a matched group of children who had been permanently institutionalized.

As in any outcome study of IQ, it was logistically impossible for Dennis to hold constant all the variables, for example, age at adoption, and age of followup testing, quality of adoptive home, and so on. Nonetheless, the outcome data indicated, overall, that per- manent residence in an environment of severe institutional deprivation permanently impairs intellectual growth, so that the average IQ is reduced by 50% from 100 to 50. The briefer the period of institutional deprivation in infancy and early childhood, the greater the amount of intellectual catchup growth that is subsequently attained. Complete catchup growth could not be guaranteed, however.

In Dennis's monograph, as in the studies of Fischer, Goldfarb, Skeels and others, the focus was so specifically on the adverse effects of institutional deprivation on retarding the growth of intelligence and lowering the IQ that no attention was paid to the possibility of a concomitant effect on statural growth. In the IQ-testing climate of that earlier era, as still to a considerable extent today, the antithesis of nature and nurture, innate and acquired, held sway. It was to shed light on this antithesis that psychologists investigated the intellectually retarding deprivations—variously named as maternal, social, sensorimotor, or whatever—of institutionalized living. Consideration of hormones and statural growth in relation to intellectual growth would be contingent on advances in pediatrics and pediatric endocrinology with respect to a syndrome of growth failure eventually to be characterized as psychosocial dwarfism.

6

Hormones and Statural Growth

When the world's first textbook of pediatric endocrinology, Lawson Wilkins' *The Diagnosis and Treatment of Endocrine Disorders in Childhood and Adolescence* was published in 1950, the beginning science of pediatric clinical endocrinology was so young that its entire textbook could be written by one author, alone. The endocrinology of statural growth retardation was rudimentary. Congenital lack or deficiency of thyroid hormone was known to be responsible for hypothyroid dwarfism, formerly known as cretinism; it could be prevented by treatment with tablets made from the desiccated thyroid glands of sheep. By contrast, though it was presumed that, in the absence of hypothyroidism, dwarfism might in some cases be attributed to congenital lack or insufficiency of growth hormone from the pituitary gland, no form of hormonal replacement therapy was available. Growth hormone, which is species specific, had not yet been extracted from the human pituitary gland. The technology of its commercial manufacture by genetic engineering would not be realized for another quarter of a century.

Wilkins recognized that hypopituitary dwarfism might be secondary to destruction of the pituitary gland by a tumor or by surgery to remove a tumor. Otherwise, hypopituitarism would be classified as idiopathic failure of the hormonal function of the pituitary gland. There was no test by which to diagnose a specific lack of growth hormone alone. Thus, the diagnosis of idiopathic hypopituitary dwarfism rested on the evidence of at least one other pituitary hormonal deficiency, namely, gonadotropic, adrenocorticotropic, or thyrotropic deficiency.

Persistent failure of the onset of puberty in association with statural dwarfism was recognized as evidence that the pituitary gland was producing neither the gonad-stimulating hormones of puberty, nor growth hormone. Wilkins characterized this type of dwarfism as panhypopituitary dwarfism. Then, in the next sentence, he added a disclaimer: "Pituitary dwarfs," he wrote, "are frequently of normal size at birth and they may continue to grow fairly normally during the first few years of life. This suggests that the growth of very young children may not be dependent upon the growth hormone, but may occur largely as the result of an intrinsic growth tendency of the tissues . . ." (p.123). Alternatively, he could have said that growth hormone deficiency may have its onset not congenitally, but later in infancy or childhood. With the knowledge of hindsight, it is now known that this alternative statement would be applicable to dwarfism not of the idiopathic panhypopituitary type, but of the type, not identified at that earlier time, but now known as a syndrome of hypopituitary dwarfism secondary to child abuse and neglect. Eventually, this syndrome would become variously named psychosocial dwarfism, abuse dwarfism, and in this volume, the Kaspar Hauser syndrome.

The first publication that recognized a syndrome of dwarfism attributable to hypopituitarism, but different from what its authors (Talbot et al., 1947) called the syndrome of "authentic hypopituitarism" was published from the Massachusetts General Hospital under the title of "Dwarfism in healthy children: Its possible relation to emotional, nutritional, and endocrine disturbances." Its authorship was multidisciplinary, representing pediatrics, endocrinology, maternal and child health, psychiatry, psychology, and social work. In their sample of 100 abnormally short children, no etiological diagnosis could be established for 51%, 28 boys and 23 girls. In twenty-one of these cases, all thin as well as short, the outcome of an attempt at nutritional therapy had been failure: "the children could not be interested in the idea of eating more food."

By contrast, with no change in nutritional intake, there was a striking increase in the rate of statural growth in eight patients given a trial treatment with the then newly available anabolic steroid, methyl testosterone. This finding indicated to the authors that, despite no change in appetite, the tissues of the body were capable of accelerated growth in height and weight, provided they were appropriately stimulated with a growth promoting hormone. They had used methyl testosterone as a growth-promoting hormone, insofar as human pituitary growth hormone had not yet been isolated, let alone synthesized and made available commercially. Reasoning by analogy from methyl testosterone to growth hormone, however, the authors ventured the suggestion that "growth in stature is dependent not only on the assimilation and transportation of building materials (proteins, minerals and so forth) to the growing end organs, but also on the presence of the pituitary growth hormone" (p.789).

All twenty-one of the children (Talbot et al., 1947) who had failed to grow, and had lacked appetite, were given a mental health workup. The findings were as follows: no abnormality ascertained, 5%; chronic poverty, 14%; chronic bereavement or loss, 14%; maternal psychopathology, 14%; patient below IQ 70, 19%; child rejected, 34%. One case is briefly mentioned as follows.

This patient was said to have been normal up to the age of four years. At that time his mother died, with the result that for approximately four years he had to shift for himself in the daytime while his father was away at work.

During this period he is reported to have subsisted largely on coffee and doughnuts. When eight years of age he was found by a relative to be small and poorly nourished.

[There were] no early records of his weight. Records of height [though incomplete] show that he had grown very little between the ages of six and nine years. At about the eighth year he was adopted into another home, where he promptly gained much weight. Although he continued to gain in weight from the ninth to the thirteenth year, he failed to accomplish a corresponding increase in stature. Physical examination at the age of thirteen years revealed an apparently healthy, intelligent and well nourished, but abnormally small boy. There were no evidences of sex maturation. Ordinary clinical laboratory tests, as well as roentgenograms of the skull, disclosed nothing of note. The bone age was retarded four years (p.791).

In three of the cases there was a history of psychiatric intervention. The outcome was an improvement of appetite and of rate of growth in height and weight. The authors did not venture a conjecture as to the possibility of a contingent relationship between psychiatric intervention and improvement in rate of growth. Had they done so, they might have ventured yet another conjecture, namely, that the improvement in rate of growth was contingent on an improvement in the secretion of pituitary growth hormone. In 1947 such a conjecture would have been science fictional, for there was no way of measuring the level of growth hormone so as to make a pretreatment-posttreatment comparison. That comparison would not be undertaken until two decades later.

By contrast, a comparative study of rate of growth before and after psychiatric intervention might have been undertaken. Even at that time, postulation of a contingent relationship between psychiatric health and rate of statural growth was, although controversial, not altogether too farfetched. In the very next year Fried and Mayer (1948) published their findings of "Socio-emotional factors accounting for growth failure in children living in an institution." The institution took in dependent and neglected children of different ages "in need of group-living and psychiatric and case-work treatment," usually for "a period not longer than two years." Each medical chart included a Wetzel Grid, a growth chart that Norman C. Wetzel (1948) had standardized some years earlier, on which height and weight were plotted at three-monthly intervals.

On the Grid, some children were seen to manifest a mild slowdown in the rate of growth that otherwise might have passed unnoticed. Recognition of the slowdown would indicate a possible impairment of "social and emotional adjustment" that might otherwise not have been attended to. The authors were led to the following conclusions.

> Socio-emotional disturbance tends to affect physical growth adversely, and growth failure so caused is much more frequent and more extensive than is generally recognized (p.455). . . . As for prognosis and treatment, we have learned that in this institution for dependent and neglected children physical growth failure could not be corrected by relying on physical means alone. Had that been possible, growth failure should not have appeared at all in an environment where efforts to provided shelter, food, and living enabled a good majority of youngsters, similarly experienced, to grow and develop satisfactorily. Additional calories and vitamins with which to pay off "fuel debts" were never of themselves sufficient to induce and to effect recovery until a feeling of security, and simultaneously with that, emotional tranquility, could also be firmly established (p.449).

There are four case illustrations. In all of them the putative source of impaired social and emotional adjustment had been break up of the family by divorce in two cases, and by maternal psychosis in one case, and paternal death in another.

The overall thrust of Fried and Mayer's paper was that good institutional care is compatible with the maintenance of normal growth and socio-emotional adjustment, and with their restoration, if impaired.

Growth retardation and socio-emotional maladjustment attributable to the developmental deprivations of institutionalized life itself, although already in vogue in child psychiatry, was beyond their purview, as was also growth retardation severe enough to produce dwarfing.

The vogue was to attribute environmentally induced retardation of the rate of growth and development to maternal deprivation brought about by institutionalized living. Coleman and Provence (1957) published two cases from the Department of Pediatrics and the Child Study Center at Yale under the title, "Environmental retardation (hospitalism) in infants living in families." In both instances, there was a history of a severely disturbed feeding relationship between mother and child, and the mother was diagnosed as depressed. Her depression disrupted the mother-child bond and its manifest expressions of affection.

Disruption of the mother-child bond characterized also the six cases presented by Patton and Gardner (1962) published under the title of the "Influence of family environment on growth: The syndrome of maternal deprivation." It was followed by a monograph, *Growth Failure in Maternal Deprivation* (1963). Gardner and Patton both had a specialty interest in pediatric endocrinology. Gardner had been one of the first generation trained in Lawson Wilkins' clinic.

Patton and Gardner recognized on behalf of pediatrics and child development the significance of the relationship between maternal deprivation theory and failure to thrive theory. In the Foreword to their monograph, they wrote (p.xi):

This book is based on clinical observations made by the authors during their studies of young children with severe retardation of growth and bone maturation. A significant number of these children, having no detectable endocrine or metabolic disorders, were found to have the physical and behavioral characteristics of "anaclitic depression." Study of the environments in each of these cases revealed severe disturbance of family organization, and deprivation of the normal relationships between parents and children.

Correction of these factors in hospital and foster home produced improvement in growth rates and in emotional and intellectual development. It is proposed here that this syndrome represents a truly "psychosomatic" disorder.

Although it was impossible to reproduce the exactitude of the laboratory, clinical studies indicated that the growth delay was far out of proportion to the caloric deficits. It is thought, then, that this syndrome exemplifies a more direct effect of emotional illness on intermediary metabolism. Neuro-anatomical investigations have shown that the limbic cortex is the "meeting ground" of emotional and metabolic brain functions, and seem to give more substance to our hypothesis.

Patton and Gardner begin their book with a review of relevant experimental animal literature, and include a brief survey of the child-psychiatry literature on maternal deprivation and its sequelae. The primary data consist of the six case reports. In all six cases, the children were living at home and had no history of having been institutionalized. They varied in age from 13 months to 6½ years. All six were developmentally grossly retarded, especially in height and weight, this being the complaint that brought them to medical attention. All had an appalling home-life history characterized by pathologically neglectful or abusive mothering. They did not require pharmacologic intervention nor other pediatric services beyond transfer to a benign living environment, whereupon their growth and development underwent dramatic improvement. In the absence of demonstrable endocrine, metabolic, or genetic disorder, the cases did not fit the criteria for any of the named syndromes of dwarfism, whereas they did fit the criteria for a syndrome of failure to thrive, or growth failure, secondary to maternal deprivation.

Recognition that this form of growth failure represented an as yet unnamed syndrome of dwarfism would be contingent upon the development and application in the early 1960s of Berson and Yalow's extremely accurate radio-immunoassay technique (see Yalow, 1978) into a routine laboratory procedure. By 1963 it was possible to measure pituitary growth hormone with great precision in very small blood samples.

The pituitary gland is located in a saddle-shaped cavity of the sphenoid bone at the base of the skull, deep behind the bridge of the nose. Its immediate neighborhood in the brain is the hypothalamus, a pea-sized regulatory and control center that governs a multitude of vital functions, including the release of growth hormone from the pituitary gland.

The announcement of a new syndrome of "Emotional deprivation and growth retardation simulating idiopathic hypopituitarism" appeared in 1967 in a two-part paper of that name from the Johns Hopkins Pediatric Endocrine Clinic. Part I, the "Clinical evaluation of the syndrome" (Powell et al., 1967a), begins as follows (p.1272).

> During the past six years we have observed and evaluated thirteen children, most of whom initially were believed to have growth failure on the basis of idiopathic hypopituitarism. However, a number of unusual features were noted in the histories that suggested emotional disturbances in the children and abnormal home environments. These were not common to the histories of patients with idiopathic hypopituitarism. When these patients were placed in a convalescent hospital, they demonstrated remarkable growth acceleration without receiving growth hormone or other agents.

Part II, the "Endocrinologic evaluation of the syndrome" contains the trail-blazing information on growth hormone levels. The key piece of information pertained to the six cases in which a growth hormone level was obtained before and after the resumption of growth, that is to say when first admitted for study, and again after a period of residence in a children's recovery center. In these cases, the growth hormone level increased from at or near zero to an adequate level within normal limits in parallel with the resumption of statural growth. This finding did not tie in with other endocrinological test data, all of which were essentially noncontributory. Place of domicile was the only identifiable contributory factor. When they lived at home, the children did not grow and did not secrete growth hormone from their pituitary glands. They did not respond to injections of growth hormone. However, when they lived away from home, even in the hospital or the specially selected children's recovery center, their growth resumed, as did the secretion of growth hormone. The change could be dramatically rapid, a matter of days or two or three weeks, and could occur equally rapidly in reverse if a child returned to the former domicile. The efficacy of change of domicile in initiating resumption of growth ultimately became established as a defining criterion and confirmation of the diagnosis.

The authors concluded in Part II of their report with an etiological conjecture (p.1282).

Although the etiology of the growth failure . . . in these children is at present unsolved, it is very possible that the failure is secondary to the presence or absence of psychic factors. . . . Emotional disturbance may have had an adverse effect upon the release of pituitary tropic hormone via [the hypothalamus] and the central nervous system.

It would subsequently be discovered that the liver produces a growth factor, somatomedin, that works in conjunction with growth hormone. D'Ercole et al. (1977) found that, in the syndrome studied by Powell and coauthors, when the level of growth hormone is diminished, so also is the level of somatomedin. Conversely, when catchup growth begins, the levels of growth hormone and somatomedin both increase.

PART II

KASPAR HAUSER SYNDROME, 1968–1991

7

Deprivation, Abuse, and Neglect

The maternal deprivation syndrome of Patton and Gardner became the emotional deprivation syndrome of Powell et al. In both instances the concept of deprivation had its origins, quite explicitly, in the child psychiatry literature derived from Levy and Lowrey via Spitz and Bowlby, on the pathological effects of maternal deprivation, separation, and loss. In all of this literature, deprivation is defined abstrusely and without substantiative specificity. Thus it is scarcely surprising that, in the Powell et al. papers, there is a lack of substantiative evidence of deprivation that might qualify as emotional. In its place, there are a few sentences about the parents. The thirteen children belonged to eleven pairs of parents. Five pairs were divorced or separated. Marital strife was present in two other pairs. Additional relevant parental data are as follows.

> Four fathers drank excessively, and five were known to be
> having extramarital affairs. The common pattern was to spend
> little time at home, and in no case did the father spend much
> time with the children. All had marked tempers.

Maternal love was more difficult to evaluate. The mothers were interviewed often and provided information about the fathers' behavior but very little about themselves.

However, one mother stated openly that she hated her son; another was an alcoholic and psychotic. In two cases there were suggestions of gross physical maltreatment of siblings.

A sibling of Case 12 was malnourished at four years of age. He reportedly did well in a foster home, when the parents deserted him.

A sibling of Case 2 was treated on several occasions at different hospitals for trauma, which probably was inflicted by the parents (p.1272).

Powell and coauthors recognized, as had Patton and Gardner before them, that abuse and neglect, not just maternal or emotional deprivation, might play an etiological role in some, if not all of the cases of growth failure they had under investigation. Further investigation and followup of the parent-child relationship in the cases diagnosed by Powell et al. was reported by Drash, Greenberg, and Money (1968, p.576) as follows.

The parental attitude toward these children was typically one of rejection. Nine of the fourteen children were rejected by one or both parents. In at least two cases there was evidence of the "battered child" syndrome. One child had deep scars about the head which were reportedly the result of parental beatings. In two other cases the child was isolated from the family by being locked in a room or left in a crib for long periods at a time.

Longitudinal followup of several affected children and their parents led Money, Annecillo, and Werlwas (1976) to formulate a statement about the behavioral characteristics of the families in the growth retarding environment, as follows (pp.250-51; see also Chapter 18).

Evidence for somatic and psychic trauma ranges widely. It includes identifying the child as different from siblings or peers; rejection of the child from family activities; enforced isolation; questionably authentic accidents and signs of excessive physical trauma including bruises, scars, broken bones, and infected lesions; restriction of food and water; insufficient warmth in winter or cooling in summer; and punishment at night while asleep. The validity of parental reporting is doubtful and requires corroboration from independent sources, which is not easy to obtain.

Proof of suspected abuse in the domicile of origin is often extremely difficult to establish because abused children deny, euphemize, and adamantly cover up their plight. The adults in charge, much in the manner of Munchausen's syndrome, are mendacious and deceitful, and are experts at hoodwinking professionals, playing off one against the other. Uncovering the correct biography of suspected abuse is facilitated by the use of auxiliary informants; home visits; precision interviewing of the parents for hour-by-hour, daily, and weekly happenings; and by long-term study until the child loosens up and talks. We are currently investigating these matters further by undertaking an extensive investigation of two families.

Like the case of Kaspar Hauser himself, there are some instances of abuse dwarfism that reach epic proportions. Some come to trial and are authenticated in the court record, and made public in the media, as exemplified in the following (Money, 1977, pp.508-510).

He had first come to public attention at the age of 2½ months, when he was hospitalized with fever and malnutrition. During his childhood, neighbors and relatives sporadically complained of his maltreatment, but no effective action was taken, and he was not seen again in the hospital until he was sixteen years old. At that time he was brought to the hospital as a sequel to legal intervention initiated by the complaint of an older half sister. This sister, aware of the history of child abuse, had recently married and was at last in a position of personal safety from which to take action on her brother's behalf. Four years earlier, acting on a relative's complaint, the police had found the boy nailed up naked, in a closet, with his own excrement. They took pictures and warned the parents, but did nothing further. At the age of fourteen, the boy had never attended school. Despite their repeated resistance, the parents finally were forced to release him to the Division of Special Education for a day of testing. The history of abuse was recorded, but no effective measures were undertaken on his behalf. He returned home, where he suffered another 1½ years of brutality and confinement. When he was finally liberated, he went to live with a relative for six weeks prior to hospitalization, and then was placed in a recovery center and eventually in a church-sponsored institutional community for the handicapped and retarded.

By the time he was rescued at age sixteen, there was some plausibility in the parents' claim that he was mentally retarded, a freak, and an animal, but only because they had, in effect, engineered it so. They required, for example, that if he were allowed any food at the time the rest of the family were at the meal table, he would like an animal be restricted to scraps from the others' plates, fed to him only if he were on all fours on the floor. They prevented him, as when they locked him in the closet, from having access to the bathroom and the toilet, so that he had no option but to soil himself, for which he was whipped. They gave him no chance to play and develop motor coordination and skills. They restricted his chance to hear language and use it; his speech was so defective and his vocabulary so impoverished that at age sixteen, when he was freed, he could scarcely be understood when he tried to communicate.

Occasionally he had been allowed the stimulation of looking at the television, but even this recreation was an ordeal, for his parents obliged him to stand motionless in a corner of the room. If he was seen moving, he was required to stand on his head for up to two hours. There were some occasions when he was removed from the house and taken with the family to the shore. While the other children played and swam, he was forced to sit in the blazing sun, forbidden to move to a shady place. If an adult relative took pity on him and defied his stepmother's order not to feed him or give him fluids, she threatened that person with physical assault with a knife. Any attempt at intervention on the boy's behalf met with such a threat.

Approximately once a week, he was tied to the newel post of the staircase in order to receive a beating with a stick, bat, or board. All of his siblings were required to beat him in turn. Otherwise their mother would beat them for disobedience. At the time of his rescue, the boy had permanent scars on his scalp as a result of his beatings.

He was marked by dog bites as a result of having had the family's German shepherd set on him. Roentgenographically it was shown that his right elbow had been fractured and had healed without having been set. The boy said, and a relative confirmed, that it was his stepmother who had broken his elbow. She then refused to take him to a doctor.

As far as can be inferred in retrospect, the boy did not sleep regularly or soundly during the years of abuse, for his parents contrived to prevent proper sleep. They did so by confining him in too small a place to permit an ordinary, full-length sleeping position. He had no mattress, only bare boards. At different periods of his life his sleeping place was a wooden box, a locked closet, an unventilated attic in midsummer when the outside temperature was over 32° C (90° F), and an outside dog kennel when the frosts of early winter had arrived. Usually he had no blankets and, even though shivering, might be required to shed his usual dirty, ragged clothes and spend the night naked. A few months before his rescue, the boy demolished the lock of his prison closet. As punishment, his parents handcuffed him to the post of their bed and at night required him to sleep naked on the bare floor. As he told the story, recalling it with utmost reluctance when he was nineteen, they also padlocked the bedroom door at night and dragged their bed across it. The father pinned the padlock key to his undershorts in which he slept. Starving and thirsty, the boy used the night not to sleep but to free himself to forage for food and water, hiding whatever he could on an outside window ledge, or in a secret hole in the ceiling of his prison-closet. He got free by using a bobby pin, which he kept hidden in the crack between two floor boards, to open his handcuffs. While his father slept, he then unpinned the key to the padlock on the door, and moved the bed enough to be able to open the door and go to the kitchen in search of food, collecting scraps from the garbage if nothing else was available. Before he broke the lock on his closet, he had no way of getting food and water at night, and so had to make the best of daytime opportunities to take food surreptitiously and hide it.

Not only hunger and thirst, but also fear of punishment, by day or night, interfered with his ability to sleep. When he was locked away, he was not always able to distinguish day from night. Except by sounds, he could not predict the safe times when, with the rest of the household sleeping, he might sleep too. For self-preservation, he needed to be constantly vigilant.

At chronological age 16 years 0 months, the height was 129.5 cm (51 inches), which represents a height age of 8 years, and weight was 27.5 kg (61 pounds), a weight age of 7 years 11 months. The bone age was recorded as 11½ years.

During the first six weeks of rescue there was a 4.5 kg (10 pound) gain in weight. Catchup growth in height was slower in onset, and ended at the short and slender extreme of low average.

Although it had been carried in the media, the foregoing case was considered by one referee as too lurid for reporting in the pediatric literature on growth failure. The venerable tradition of the sanctity of motherhood, and the contemporary nostalgia to return to the mythical ideal of the traditional family (of the 1950s!) conspire still today against public recognition of parental child abuse and neglect, unless the abuse is sexual.

Nonetheless, there is recognition in the professional literature of the relationship between abuse and neglect, on the one hand, and growth retardation, on the other. Barbero and Shaheen (1967) mentioned the connection and gave one case example in a survey of failure to thrive. Silver and Finkelstein (1967) "had findings suggestive of physical neglect and/or abuse" in three of five children whom they diagnosed as cases of "deprivation dwarfism," and as representing "one segment of the battered child syndrome." Evans et al. (1972) recognized maternal abuse and neglect in eleven of a clinical sample of forty-five cases of "failure to thrive" admitted to a children's hospital. Chesney and Brusilow (1980) reported the case of a twenty-one month old girl with growth failure and extreme hypernatremia (i.e. salt poisoning from an excessive concentration of sodium in the blood stream) attributable to water deprivation as a component of child abuse. Silverton (1982) published details of five cases of abuse referred from a pediatric endocrine clinic to pediatric social service. Skuse (1984a,b) reviewed seven published cases of extreme deprivation and abuse, and added two new cases (sisters) of his own.

Methodologically reversing gears so as to commence with a population of parentally abused children yields confirmatory findings of growth failure. King and Taitz (1985) found that height and weight were significantly below the norms for age in 95 abused children.

Catchup growth was significantly more prevalent (p<0.001) in those placed in long-term foster care than in those who were not (N=7; 11%). After the cohort had been enlarged from 95 to 260 abused children (Taitz and King, 1988a,b) the correlation between abuse and growth retardation continued to hold up, and to extend also to general developmental and language retardation. Among severely growth retarded children placed in a foster home, 10 out of 11 demonstrated significant catchup growth, whereas only 4 out of 28 who remained in the abusive home of origin did so.

8

Nutritional Deprivation

As long ago as 1940, Mulinos and Pomerantz investigated the effect of nutritional deficiency on the pituitary and other glands and organs in the rat. They found that the pituitary showed histological evidence of atrophy as a sequel to acute, but not chronic starvation; but they could not partial out secondary effects of impaired pituitary function on other bodily functions. Their investigation is of historic importance, however, in pointing to a conjunction between nutrition and pituitary hormones.

Nutritional disturbance and its possible relationship to hypopituitarism was one of the issues addressed by Talbot and coauthors in their 1947 paper. They wrote as follows.

It is known that malnutrition secondary to famine or to anorexia nervosa is accompanied by a tendency to amenorrhea, aspermatogenesis, retarded sexual maturation and the like.

These changes in all probability signify that the organism tends to adapt itself to nutritional privation by becoming relatively hypopituitary (p.791). . . . Nutritional studies revealed that although the intake of protein was probably adequate for growth, the total caloric intake appeared to be undesirably low. In the majority of cases this predominantly caloric malnutrition appeared to be related to anorexia secondary to emotional disturbances. In three cases correction of emotional difficulties resulted in an improvement in appetite that was followed, in turn, by a rapid gain in weight and an appreciable increase in the rates of growth and maturation (p.792).

Patton and Gardner (1963, p.43) noted that disturbance of gastrointestinal function in their sample of patients included vomiting, diarrhea, and constipation. Thus, gastrointestinal malfunction might account for nutritional deficit, rather than the other way round. They allowed that, whereas in some cases the child was deprived of adequate nutrients, in others deficient nutrition appeared not to be the limiting factor. Additional factors which they considered were as follows (1962, p.961).

A reduction in appetite and feeding behavior might result from the lethargy and depression which these children often have. Another possibility is that intestinal motility and rates of absorption might be altered so as to prevent complete assimilation of ingested nutrients. The observations of Engel and Reichsman (1956) have shown a close association between gastric secretion and emotional status. There is also the possibility that emotional disturbances might have a direct effect on intermediary metabolism so as to interfere with anabolic processes. It is well known that the production and release of several anterior pituitary hormones are influenced by hypothalamic centers, which are, in turn, recipients of pathways from higher neural centers, particularly the limbic cortex and amygdaloid nuclei. It is of more than passing interest, then, that the limbic cortex is also thought to be the locus of emotional feeling and behavior.

Patton and Gardner (1963, p.42) did not ignore the possibility of "an actual failure, deliberate or otherwise, by the parents to provide adequate calories, proteins, or other essential nutrients," to which they added the proviso that "the degree to which this occurs [as it had done in three of their cases] is difficult to ascertain or control."

Patton and Gardner left unresolved the issue of whether nutritional insufficiency would be attributed to a breakdown of supply, on the part of the parents, or of demand, on the part of the child. As seen by the parents in the distorting mirror of child abuse, the child was held responsible. Through their distorted reporting, the pediatrician also might hold the child responsible for feeding difficulties. Silver and Finkelstein (1967), for example, in their report on deprivation dwarfism, classified voracious appetite, together with short stature and delayed skeletal maturation, as pathognomonic of the syndrome. They wrote as follows (pp.320-21).

Feeding difficulties occurred in four of the five children who were said to have been fussy and irritable, with excessive crying and failure to be satisfied with feedings.

Two of the mothers reported that their children "vomited" in infancy, but careful questioning suggested that the infants simply allowed milk or other fluids to run out of their mouths. In three of the five infants, appetite and food intake were said to be markedly increased. In two of them bowel movements were said to be loose and frequent, but not watery. In one, the stools were described as being foul smelling. Four of the five tended to sleep very little as infants and were frequently awake at night. As they grew older, they reportedly prowled about at night, often in search of food.

When the children were first seen by us, all of them were described as being constantly hungry, with the terms "voracious" and "ravenous" being used in three instances to describe their appetite. A detailed review of the dietary intake with the parents, other relatives, neighbors, and personnel from various social agencies indicated that the actual intake of food was large and often unorthodox. It was said that they would "eat anything, even garbage." There were no reports of pica. Two of the mothers stated that the children stole and hid food in their rooms. In no instance was economic privation a factor in limiting the food available to the children, and none of them appeared to have suffered from nutritional inadequacy. They were not obese despite their excessive intake of food.

Powell et al. (1967a) paralleled Silver and Finkelstein in accepting the reports of parents at face value. They (pp.1272–73) wrote about the children's bizarre water and food intake and feeding practices as symptoms of emotional disturbance, not as ways in which patients circumvented fluid and nutritional deprivation, as follows.

A bizarre type of polydipsia and polyphagia was present in all. Water was drunk from the toilet bowl, glasses filled with dish water, puddles filled with rain water, old beer cans filled with stagnant water and the hot-water faucet.

Water was requested frequently during the night. Case 11 had been locked in her room to prevent her from repeatedly getting up for water.

According to the history the patients often ate two or three times as much as siblings at the same dinner table.

Examples of aberration included eating a whole jar of mustard or mayonaise, a package of lunch meat, a whole loaf of bread, corn flour from a box and seven eggs at one sitting. Two ate food from the cat's dish. Food was frequently stolen. Case 8 stole food from neighbors and a nearby grocery store but never from home. Case 13 hid food in various places throughout the house. Eating from garbage cans was characteristic. Many gorged themselves. Their "stomach would swell," and they vomited frequently. Case 13 had abdominal swelling after gorging but no vomiting.

Several children got up at night. This was often to obtain food or water, but a frequent characteristic was to find children "roaming the house" or "standing looking out the window." Case 11 frequently ran out into the street during the night.

Insofar as bizarrerie of eating and drinking was not recognized as a direct sequela of abusive deprivation of water and food, it was, by implication, attributed to an amorphous and insubstantial deprivation characterized as maternal or emotional. Whitten et al. (1969) took exception to the vagueness of the concept of maternal deprivation and "instituted a study to test the validity of the assumption that the growth failure in the 'maternal deprivation syndrome' is due to psychological factors." Overall, undersized infants (N=16) with the syndrome gained weight provided the nutritional supply and intake was increased either in the hospital (N=13) or in the home (N=3) to which meals were supplied and nutritional intake recorded by a home visitor. When the hospital environment simulated maternal and social deprivation, except for adequate nutrition, eleven children gained weight, but two did not. The failure of these two to eat and gain weight persisted even under nondeprivational conditions, and so could not be explained on the basis of nutritional deprivation alone. Both had a history of abusive force feeding. Otherwise physical abuse and neglect were ascertained in only two other cases. However, many mothers were said to be under grave social stress and to be psychologically malfunctional. If they were not mendacious about nutritionally depriving their children, then, according to the claims they made of how the children devoured food, their perception was, if not delusional, then grossly distorted. Despite the evidence of weight gain during the test period, the long-term outcome, if the child remained at home, was dismal. The authors made a distinction between deficient and distorted mothering, either of which might have led to the mother's failure to feed her infant adequately.

In another study (Krieger, 1974), designed to test the relationship between growth failure and nutritional deficiency, ten children above age three years with a diagnosis of "psychosocial deprivation syndrome," were selected on the basis of a reported history of voracious appetite and garbage eating, linear growth failure, retarded bone age, and assorted behavioral abnormalities. Summarizing, Krieger wrote (p.127):

> Weight recovery occurred regularly in the hospital and in three cases in the home, provided food was not restricted.
> Diagnosis was difficult because ravenous appetites and abnormal stools suggested malabsorption in seven cases; however, histories, absorption tests, and weight recovery which occurred despite temporary persistence of abnormal stools indicated that malabsorption was not the primary cause of malnutrition. The child's deviant behavior and abnormal stools were used by the mother to rationalize frustration and food restriction. Intensive psychotherapy of the mother is necessary.

The special feature of this study, as compared with an earlier metabolic and hormonal study by Krieger and Mellinger (1971) is that more information was obtained about maternal child abuse, as "questioning was done in a less direct manner and, by assuming at the outset that the mother needed help, resentment toward the child and the therapeutic intervention was apparently avoided." Hence the following indirect evidence of starvation (p.131):

> Remarks indicated in all but one case that food had been restricted at home although the appetite and intake were described as excessive. Typical remarks were as follows: "If I let him eat as much as he wants he would get sick," "get bloated," or "vomit;" "If I let him overeat he'll get loose stools." Two mothers considered it "unhealthy" if their (malnourished) child would eat "too much!" Overeating occurred frequently on visits, picnics, and holiday dinners, and the mothers did

not hesitate to attribute this to the presence of third persons who would prevent the mother from interfering. As they elaborated they appeared to be protective. In the light of their child's malnutrition, the self-righteousness of some was incongruous. Thus, one mother was instructed after a first admission to offer double food portions to the boy. Yet, when we saw him two and a half years later he weighed less than at discharge.

She explained that it would not be "fair" to the other children to "spoil him" and let him "have more than they get." Three mothers did not deem it inappropriate to complain about a malnourished child raiding the refrigerator or taking food from the table "while no one was looking." Conversations with two mothers indicated selective restriction of this one child by the family. All members were trained to keep snack foods out of the reach of the patient although older siblings were allowed to help themselves. "If they get themselves a snack I'll let her have a little too, so she won't feel bad," was the remark made by one mother.

An unusual daily routine and irregular meal times made food deprivation possible in some cases. Three mothers did not rise and feed breakfast until 10:00 or 11:00 A.M., and they put the children to bed early in the evening. Husbands were unable to gain insight into the feeding situation because they were obviously weak, or they were absent or asleep during most of the waking hours because of double employment and unusual working hours.

Krieger leaves no doubt that restriction of nutriment is an effective form of child abuse. Whether or not growth deficiency in the deprivation syndrome can be attributed exclusively to nutritional deficiency is challenged, however, in those cases in which growth failure continues despite adequate nutrition (see Saenger's case, Chapter 13). In addition, nutritional deficiency alone does not explain the manifestation of growth failure as miniaturization, or dwarfism, instead of cachexia and death from starvation.

9

Sleep Deprivation

Sleep deprivation, often in conjunction with torture, is a tactic of secret police abuse. It appears also in the repertory of parental child abuse (see Chapter 7). Disordered sleep has been mentioned in passing in publications on deprivation and growth retardation (Powell et al., 1967a; Drash et al., 1968; Capitanio and Kirkpatrick, 1969).

Wolff and Money (1973) made a systematic study of the "Relationship between sleep and growth in patients with reversible somatotropin deficiency (psychosocial dwarfism)," of which the rationale was explicated as follows (pp.25-26).

There is a relationship between the sleeping brain and the release of growth hormone from the pituitary gland.

Takahashi et al. (1968), Honda et al. (1969), and Sassin et al. (1969) observed in their sleep EEG (electroencephalogram) studies that marked elevated secretion of plasma human growth hormone (HGH) is consistently related to slow wave, synchronized sleep stages (EEG stages 3 and 4). This finding pertains to normal healthy adult subjects, comparable sleep EEG studies in children having not yet been reported. However, total HGH secretion during the night, irrespective of EEG sleep stages, was shown by Hunter and Rigal (1965) to be many times greater than that for the same subjects during the day. Their subjects were children, aged 8 to 15 years, free of known growth disorder or other endocrinopathy.

Honda and coworkers (1969) conclude "that nocturnal sleep is a potent stimulator for the secretion of growth hormone, and that the secretion pattern of HGH is closely correlated with the depth and course of sleep. HGH secretion reaches its peak always soon after the sleeper passes the EEG stages 3 and 4, regardless of the hour he went to sleep. Inability to go to sleep and insomnia during the night may have an adverse effect on HGH release (H. P. Roffwarg, personal communication). Hypothetically, it is possible that patients with reversible somatotropin deficiency might, during periods when they sleep poorly, have a subnormal proportion of EEG stages 3 and 4. They might therefore also be deprived of considerable amounts of growth hormone, which deprivation in turn might be one reason for subnormal growth rates. The crucial sleep EEG studies to test this hypothesis remain to be done.

The findings, in synopsis, were as follows (p.18).

In a partly retrospective, partly followup study, twenty seven patients aged 1 year 10 months to 16 years 2 months with reversible somatotropin deficiency, showed a relationship between the rate of statural growth and sleep, graded as good, poor, or mixed. During periods of good sleep the overall growth rate averaged 1.04 cm per month, and during periods of poor sleep it averaged 0.34 cm per month (t=8.46, df=32, P<0.001). Presumably, good growth, good sleep, and optimal nocturnal somatotropin release intercorrelate in this syndrome of dwarfism, but the data with regard to nocturnal somato-tropin release remain to be demonstrated empirically.

Figures 9.1 and 9.2 illustrate two examples of the relationship between sleep, domicile, and growth in height.

The first study that included measurement of growth hormone and of EEG sleep stages in a case of "emotional deprivation and short stature" was authored by Powell et al. (1973). The patient, a girl, was 9.3 years old, with a height age of 3.3 years, weight age of 2.5 years, and bone age of 3.5 years. No anomalies were observed in the EEG sleep stages, but on the first sleep test nights (hospital days 5 and 6 of the first admission) there was no significant output of growth hormone during sleep, whereas six weeks later, on followup testing, there was. It is possible that a prior EEG sleep stage anomaly had rectified itself by day five of the hospitalization.

In a British study, Howse et al. (1977) compared four syndromes of short stature and found a correspondence between diagnosis and level of growth hormone (GH) in the blood stream during Stage III-IV sleep. In short children with short parents (N=14) and dwarfed children with growth retardation of intrauterine onset (N=3) the findings were within normal limits. By contrast, in children diagnosed with hypopituitarism (N=12) and in children diagnosed with psychosocial GH deficiency, the mean level of growth hormone while asleep was more than 2 SD (standard deviations) below the mean for short-statured controls. The study did not measure changes in the psychosocial GH deficient children after the onset of catchup growth.

Before-and-after data were, however, obtained in a French study authored by Guilhaume et al. (1982) of the "Relationship between sleep Stage IV deficit and reversible HGH deficiency in psychosocial dwarfism," in which four patients, aged one to three years, and ten normal controls were compared. At the time of the study, the pituitary gland had not yet recovered its ability to secrete HGH (human growth hormone) in response to a challenge test with ornithine. The EEG sleep wave test showed a deficit of Stage IV sleep, the stage when

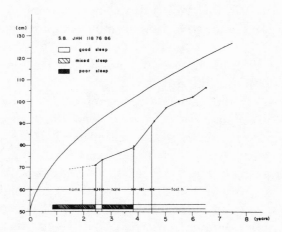

Fig. 9.1. Growth chart of patient S.B. Vertical lines indicate at which time the patient was transferred from one domicile to another. Intervals between vertical lines indicate length of time the patient lived in the respective domicile. The dotted line before the first hospital referral and accurately recorded height measurement represents an estimate of the growth rate between the age of 1 year, the usual age of onset of growth retardation, and the age when the dwarfed stature was first measured. Home=home of origin; JHH=The Johns Hopkins Hospital; HH=Happy Hills Hospital; fost.h.=foster home.

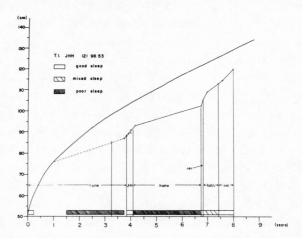

Fig. 9.2. Growth chart of patient T.I. Home=home of origin; JHH=The Johns Hopkins Hospital; HH=Happy Hills Hospital; fost.h.=foster home; inst.=residential institution (see also legend to Fig. 9.1).

the level of growth hormone secreted is highest. The authors summarized their findings as follows (p.299).

Polygraphic sleep recordings were done in four children with psychosocial dwarfism. The first recordings, performed within the first days after hospitalization, exhibited a gross deficit of stage IV sleep and a decrease of the durations of slow wave sleep episodes (SWS stages III and IV). The second recordings were performed after several weeks (3-15) in the new environment, during the growth recovery period. A clear improvement of sleep quality was observed, namely an increase of stage IV amounts. In two of the four patients, HGH release was studied by means of the ornithine test. A low response was found in the first (two) days of hospitalization whereas a normal response was observed during the recovery period suggesting a partial and reversible HGH deficiency. A simultaneous recovery of both stage IV sleep and the growth rate was observed in the four patients. These data suggest that sleep disturbances are strongly linked to growth failure in psychosocial dwarfism.

Going to sleep in an unfamiliar bed, as in a sleep laboratory, may itself disturb one's sleep rhythms for a couple of nights. With the technological advance of portable EEG apparatus, it became logistically feasible for Taylor and Brook (1986) to do EEG sleep wave and eye movement recordings in a child's own house. They studied 33 healthy boys and girls, and 30 short-statured children, among whom were 13 with a diagnosis of psychosocial dwarfism, severe in 5 cases, and less so in 8 cases. They found that the five children with the severe degree of psychosocial dwarfism had significantly less stage IV sleep ($p < 0.05$) and spent more time awake than did the healthy controls. All thirteen of the psychosocial dwarfed children had a significant increase ($p < 0.01$) in the percentage of rapid eye movement sleep, the stage associated with dreaming, restlessness, and being nearly awake. The five in the severe group had strikingly more rapid eye movements, and a higher nightly proportion of rapid eye movement sleep stages than did the others.

As in the case of nutrition, the finding of a correlation between impaired sleep and impaired growth does not justify jumping to a simple conclusion about cause and effect. Both impairments may be the sequelae of a common determining factor. Moreover, they may not be the only sequelae, and there may be a concatenation of multiple determinants. Another such candidate is grooming (haptic or tactile) deprivation.

10

Grooming Deprivation

In a perspicacious and wide-range review of maternal deprivation, Casler (1961) covers the literature on sensory stimulation of the skin and haptic (tactile) deprivation (pp.15), in other words, deprivation of grooming. Casler refers to Ashley Montagu (1953) as follows.

> Montagu, after reminding us that the skin and the nervous system are derived from the same blastocystic ectodermal layer, makes the suggestion that tactile stimulation during infancy, and especially during the first months of nursing, is extremely important for the subsequent development of the person, [and that those] who have recorded insufficient tactile stimulation in infancy frequently [may be] susceptible to disorders of the gastrointestinal and respiratory tracts, and possibly the genitourinary tract.

Casler (p.16) refers also to the work of the Prussian physiologist, Orbelli, quoted in Bowlby (1954, p.81) as follows.

Orbelli suggested that there are sympathetic connections from the skin to the various organ systems, such as the gastrointestinal tract, and to striped muscles, so that patting, cuddling, soothing the body by caresses, et cetera, may operate to bring release of muscular tensions and of smooth muscles.

According to Bakwin and Bakwin (1960, p.418), also quoted by Casler (p.39):

With free manipulation, cuddling and vocal stimulation, the behavior [of emotionally deprived babies] brightens in a matter of days. The appetite improves, motility increases, listlessness disappears, and weight gain proceeds apace.

Far-sighted for his time, Casler, quoting Bovard, also recognized a possible connection between skin stimulation and growth hormone. Bovard (1958) in a review of "The effects of early handling on the viability of the albino rat" reached the conclusion (p.264-5) that early handling of rats had been found in a number of studies to increase their weight and skeletal length, as a result of better food assimilation rather than of greater consumption. He quoted McClelland (1956) as having demonstrated that stroking a rat in a restraining box with an artist's brush had exactly the same effect in inducing weight gain as did handling by the experimenter for the same length of time. Bovard summarized his review as follows (p.267-68).

The central proposition of this paper is, therefore, that effects of early handling on viability of the albino rat are mediated by a permanent alteration in the balance of hypothalamic activity, in favor of the anterior region.

This alteration results in increased growth hormone output under normal conditions, and increased activity of the pituitary-adrenal cortex and sympathetico-adrenal medulla systems under both normal and stress conditions. In turn, this alteration in hypothalamic balance is itself the result of a change in amygdaloid complex activity, arising from the sensory input from early handling.

The common denominator of the inexact term, handling, is presumably some form of sensory stimulation. McClelland, with more precision, specified the stimulation as stroking with an artist's brush, which is a method of grooming. Grooming is what mother rats do to their babies when, with strong strokes of the tongue, they lick their skin. Deprived of tongue grooming by the mother, newborn rats are unable to urinate or defecate. In addition, they are unable to grow.

In a step-by-step series of experiments, Schanberg and various associates (Schanberg and Kuhn, 1985) have been able to demonstrate that, when rat pups are deprived of maternal licking (herein renamed as maternal tongue grooming), one highly specific outcome is a depleted level of growth hormone circulating in the blood stream. This depletion, they discovered, is accompanied by a deficiency in the brain, liver, heart, and kidneys of ornithine decarboxylase (ODC), an enzyme that acts as a powerful catalyst in the regulation of cell growth. For as long as grooming deprivation persists, so also does ODC deficiency, so that tissue growth fails, and it continues to do so even if, by injection, the blood level of growth hormone is restored to normal.

If the rat mothers were anesthetized with urethane, their milk supply was not affected, so that the pups were fed but not groomed. ODC and growth hormone were again depleted as a function of grooming deprivation, despite adequate nutrition. By contrast, if by being placed with a nipple-ligated mother, the pups were deprived of nutrition but not grooming, then the ODC and growth hormone effect on cell growth in vital organs was not impaired.

The negative effect of tongue-grooming deficiency was demonstrated to be reversible by the quite simple method of vigorously stroking the pups on the back and head with a moistened artist's paint brush, applying brush strokes that mimicked the maternal licking pattern. The growth hormone level in the blood stream, the ODC activity in the brain, and the other vital organs then recovered.

With the newborn rat as an experimental model, attention was then turned to the effect of grooming on preterm human infants (Field et al., 1986; Schanberg and Field, 1987). The babies (N=20) were housed in "premie" incubators. Their grooming consisted of a combination of stroking the body (as in massage) and of moving the limbs for fifteen minute periods three times a day for ten days. The control group (N=20) were routinely cared for, with no grooming added. Nutritional intake was the same for both groups. The outcome was that the groomed babies averaged 47% greater weight gain daily, were more active and alert, scored higher developmental ratings on the Brazelton scale, and went home from the hospital six days sooner than did the nongroomed babies.

Schanberg and Field recognized that the experimental rat model, having proved applicable to preterm infants, might serve also as an experimental model for older infants and juveniles with a diagnosis of psychosocial dwarfism. Among the multiple manifestations deprivation, neglect, and abuse that concatenate in this syndrome, it may well be, especially in the earliest years, that grooming deprivation is responsible for the onset of growth stagnation. By affecting the growth of the brain as well as of other organs, grooming deprivation may also initiate failure of mental growth. ODC and growth hormone, however, are only two of the brain's myriad chemistries that have already been discovered to affect growth. Another is beta-endorphin.

11

Pain Agnosia

Beta-endorphin is one of the brain's natural chemistries. It is an opioid peptide which means that it belongs to the same class of chemical substances as does opium, and its derivatives, morphine and heroin.

Like growth hormone, beta-endorphin has been shown to have an effect on the cell-growth catalyst, ODC (ornithine decarboxylase), and hence on growth (Bartolome et al., 1986). When injected subcutaneously, beta-endorphin increased ODC cell growth activity in heart and liver tissue. By contrast, when injected directly into brain fluid at the base of the skull, the effect of beta-endorphin was to decrease ODC activity not only in the peripheral organs, but also in the tissues of the brain itself. This suppressant effect could be canceled by an injection of naltrexone, a potent and long-lasting antagonist of opioids like beta-endorphin.

Bartolome and coauthors theorized that beta-endorphin, like grooming deprivation, inhibits growth by first inhibiting the release of growth promoting substances from the brain. They found indirect support for this idea from an experiment by Kehoe and Blass (1986) which suggested that endogenous opioid release might mediate in-

93

creased pain tolerance in ten-day-old rats subjected to isolation stress by being separated from the dam. Thus one may conjecture a possible connection between grooming deprivation and, by way of the release of beta-endorphin in the brain, a pain-killing or analgesic effect (see also Spaziante et al., 1990).

This inference of a beta-endorphin connection between lack of growth and lack of pain helps to make sense of the observations published by Money et al. (1972) under the title of "Pain agnosia and self-injury in the syndrome of reversible somatotropin deficiency (psychosocial dwarfism)."

In this publication, the sample comprised a census of all 32 children in the clinic at that time (9 girls, 23 boys; 25 white, 7 black) who had been given a diagnosis of psychosocial dwarfism. At the time of admission 24 (75%) of the children showed signs of single or multiple injuries that typically are characterized as painful: bruises, scars, bone fractures, and unhealed skin lesions. According to all sources of evidence available, so called accidents and parentally inflicted injuries coexisted with self-injuries and with those of undecided origin. The varieties of self-harming behavior (with number of instances in parentheses) were as follows: head banging (7); hair twisting and plucking (6); nail-biting and tearing nailbed skin (5); falling and bumping into corners, walls, windows, doors, and posts (10); temper tantrums with self-banging and self-biting (9); eating indigestible substances, swallowing hard objects, and ingesting pills and medicines (5); not protecting with hands when falling (2); and other self-inflicted injuries as from swallowing uncooled food (7).

Evidence for lack of pain response (pain agnosia) was negative in only 2 cases, uncertain in 16 and positive in 14. The noxious stimuli to which pain response was not in evidence were corporal punishment; alleged accidents, including for example a fractured clavicle; self-inflicted traumas; infections or inflammatory illnesses; injections and blood taking; minor surgery; and dental treatment. The parents or guardians of eleven children alleged that the children never complained about anything, never cried or shed tears when punished, and generally did not react or object when being hurt or ignored. In one case, a girl of eight had her fingers sharply bitten by her foster mother who had become exasperated by the child's indifference to punishment and her persistence in salvaging chewing gum from the street so as to chew it herself.

Evidence of pain agnosia faded and pain response returned after the children's transfer from the home of abuse to the hospital, and from there to a nonabusive environment. During the same period, catchup growth had its onset. The chi-square test of the before-and-after comparison was statistically significant (N=14; chi square=21.4; p<.001). By contrast, when eventually 21 of the children were returned to the home of origin, there was, in 10 cases, a relapse into pain agnosia, together with documented signs of bodily injury, abuse, and self-harming behavior. Three of these ten children when rescued for a second time recovered from pain agnosia and became pain responsive again.

In addition to being situationally determined and reversible, pain agnosia may also be genetically determined and irreversible (see Money et al., 1972). The reversible type has been experimentally studied as analgesia in response to stress (Kelly, 1986). In human beings, reversible pain agnosia is not unique to the syndrome of child-abuse (psychosocial) dwarfism. It occurs also, together with elevated brain opioid (metencephalin) release, in patients who are habitual self-mutilators (Coid et al., 1983). Insofar as opioids, in general, induce euphoria as well as pain agnosia, brain opioids point towards an explanation for the reiteration of self-mutilation, and also for what can best be characterized in the syndrome of dwarfism contingent on child abuse as addiction to abuse.

12

Addiction to Abuse

Animal trainers know that it is possible to obtain obedience and fidelity not only by the positive reinforcement of reward, but also by the negative reinforcement of punishment for disobedience and infidelity. Common sense says that obedience and fidelity are the outcome of either attraction to the reward, or avoidance of the punishment. It runs counter to common sense to say that a bond may become established between obedient fidelity as the response, on the one hand, and either reward or punishment as the stimulus, on the other. Common sense is not always correct. The beaten dog does repeat the behavior that earned a beating and returns to its master for a repeat performance. The released prisoner, habituated to life in prison, becomes a recidivist and is reincarcerated. The patient with the self-induced symptoms and injuries of Munchausen's syndrome relapses into self-induction of the same symptoms and injuries, over and over again.

Likewise, the abused, neglected, and dwarfed child becomes addicted to abuse. One of the self-justifications used by abusing parents is that their child instigates abuse. Having been rescued, the child may contrive situations that taunt and provoke unforewarned and untrained foster parents to retaliate with abusive disciplinary action and punishment, or else to give up, and have the child returned to a less than satisfactory institutional environment. Money et al. (1985) presented two examples, one female, one male (see Chapter 7) as follows (p.36–37).

In both cases, the children's addiction to abuse became evident soon after they had been rescued and were living for a period in a children's recovery center, and for a period with a foster family. It is typical in the syndrome of abuse dwarfism that, following rescue from the home of abuse, the child goes through a phase of noisy hyperactivity. This phase persists for several months, and possibly for as long as two years. It is marked by disputatiousness and noncompliance which exasperates other people and provokes their retaliation. At first glance, it may seem that the naughtiness and disobedience of this early postrescue phase is no different than that encountered in children without the same history of severe abuse. A closer search, however, reveals a difference.

Thus, in the case of the girl, her foster mother told of how the child had asked why she hadn't been paddled as her foster sister had been. "I guess she thought I didn't love her, if I didn't paddle her, the way her mother used to beat her," the foster mother conjectured. This foster mother was unable to cope with the challenge of rehabilitating an abused child, and requested that the girl be placed elsewhere. The new placement was in a home for the retarded, not an ideal placement for a family-deprived child, since it replicated the deprivation of parent-child bonding to which the child had so long been subjected.

In the case of the boy, the first foster parents encountered a similar problem. They also were unable to meet the challenge of rehabilitating him in their home, as they had hoped to be able to do. His next placement was in the children's recovery center. There he was said to provoke fights with other children. Though he yearned to be accepted by his relatives, they neglected him. On one occasion he became upset and protested that people were mean to him. That evening the staff found him outside, under a pavilion, cold and crying. He said he wanted to die. After an emergency session with his therapist, he went to sleep.

The next morning he continued with wanting to die. He went to a storage room to get some personal belongings, but instead wrapped around his neck a belt and a wire coat hanger. They were removed by the two staff members who found him. Next day, considered still to be a suicide risk, he was put in an unfurnished room. There he swung from overhead pipes, and banged his head against the wall.

The staff considered the aforesaid behavior as psychotic and had the boy transferred to a state mental hospital. With the knowledge of hindsight, another interpretation is possible, namely, that the boy was homesick for the only family life that he knew, in which the only child-to-parent bond familiar to him was that of victim to victimizer.

The boy was eventually located in a church-sponsored institution for the chronically mentally retarded, not an ideal environment to foster intellectual and social catch-up growth in the syndrome of abuse dwarfism. With the passage of years, he was able to live away from the institution, but only with the help of a disability pension. He continued to attract abusive attacks on himself by at times tangling with members of an organized street gang, and at other times antagonizing the police with minor misdemeanors childishly unsuited to his adult age. He needed a protector and did, in fact, meet people who took on that role.

When aversion turns to addiction, there is a polar reversal of negative and positive. The negative of tragedy is switched over to the positive of triumph over tragedy. Agony becomes ecstasy. The religious zealot, suspended from a wooden frame by fleshhooks through his shoulder muscles experiences not pain, but its metamorphosis into religious ecstasy. The paraphilic masochist, in the same position, experiences sexuoerotical ecstasy. These are exemplifications of the principle of opponent-process, experimentally investigated and named by the psychologist Richard Solomon (1980). In abuse dwarfism, when addiction to abuse is manifest, opponent process is at work. Speculatively, opponent process may be linked to release within the brain of the brain's own opioids. They transform the pain of an abusive act into a euphoric rush, or high. It is a transformation that forges a bond of appeasement between the abused and the abuser.

13

Affiliative Bonding

The principle of appeasement bonding between the abused and the abuser was put to use in former times in the abusive practices of "nigger-breaking" farms from which recalcitrant teenaged slaves emerged broken-in, like horses broken-in to the harness, or else dead. The same principle is applied today in the training of young recruits into torture police.

The bond of appeasement that in some cases develops between captor and captive, terrorist and hostage, has become known as the Stockholm syndrome. The name derives from a bank robbery in the city of Stockholm in which a young Swedish woman, captured and held hostage, became bonded to one of her captors. After she was released, her attachment to him continued with an intensity sufficient to warrant breaking up with her erstwhile lover. She remained bonded, or in bondage, to her former captor while he served a prison sentence. A more recent example is that of the American newspaper heiress, Patty Hearst, kidnapped and held captive by the Symbionese Liberation Army on February 4, 1974.

A comment on appeasement bonding in the syndrome of abuse dwarfism (Money, 1977, p.510; see also chapter 7) is as follows.

It was difficult for him to talk about the rigors of his life, and he was explicit in saying that he did not want to be reminded of the past by talking about it. With the passage of time, [freed from the Catch-22 of reprisals if he did talk, and continued abuse if he didn't], he was able to supply more details of what had actually happened to him.

In this respect, this patient was typical of abused children. Usually they are so tight-lipped that it seems as though there must be some complicity between abuser and abused. The cover-up continues for quite some time after removal to a safe environment, so that it is not simply a precaution against immediate reprisals. Perhaps the only way to comprehend it is to recognize that the abused child is an involuntary martyr and that martyrdom becomes a deeply imbedded trait in his personality, imperative to survival.

For him abuse is as inevitable a part of life as ice is an inevitable part of life for an Eskimo. It is pointless for an Eskimo to complain about ice, snow, and subzero weather, for they constitute the only environment he knows.

Likewise, it is pointless for an abused child to complain about his forms of abuse, because they constitute the only environment he knows. Here, perhaps lies a key to the appealing and appeasing ways of many children with the syndrome of abuse dwarfism. Like the kicked and beaten cur that repeatedly returns to the farmer begging for affection and kindness, abused children relentlessly try to meet their abusers' demands as if trying finally to win love and appreciation. It was only by a slow process of disillusionment that the patient finally gave up trying to contact his relatives in order to establish some sort of family membership for himself. They all failed him, as did society at large by not succeeding in providing him with the surrogate, foster family he so greatly needed.

Pairbonding in infancy is phylogenetically ordained for both the infant and the parents. In all mammals, without bonding between the newborn and its mother there is no suckling, no nourishment, and no survival. Infant and parent communicate through the medium of body language in establishing a pairbond. Body-language signaling goes back and forth, from stimulus to response to stimulus to response, and so on, reciprocally.

In the absence of reciprocality, pairbond signaling may be lacking in both parent and child, or more likely, the lack may be one-sided. On the basis of the truism that anything in human development that can go wrong will sooner or later produce an example of itself gone wrong, it may be assumed that the pairbond signaling of either the parent or the child may be subject to impairment. Mothers with a post-partum depression, for example, relate poorly to their newborn babies, and in some instances are panic stricken by a fixation on the possibility of killing the baby. The infants and young children of severely depressed mothers are at increased risk for "failure to thrive" (see, for example, Evans et al., 1972).

One of the cases published by Elmer (1960) illustrates the adverse effect of a depressed and noncoping mother on her baby son's growth. She had not wanted her fifth pregnancy, as her husband had deserted her. She could not safely request her public assistance worker for more money for the coming child, as the Department of Welfare and the Housing Authority penalized illegitimately pregnant women. Between the ages of three and seven months, the baby had gained only 8 ounces (0.23 kg) and weighed 11 pounds 7 ounces (5.2 kg). He was described as a somber, withdrawn, unhappy infant who appeared somewhat drowsy and did not sit up well. He sucked not on his thumb but his entire hand, with his unusually long fingers far back in the throat, thus precipitating frequent vomiting. A new nursing plan was devised, as follows (p.723).

The nursing personnel would embark on a conscious, planned program of special, individualized attention to the infant, with all the carrying, cuddling, and playing normally accorded to infants by their mothers. Insofar as possible, the same nurse was to feed the child. The resulting changes were startling. Within two weeks of the initiation of the new regimen, he became much more friendly and alert. He smiled readily. There was some decrease in the amount and frequency of vomiting, and he showed a weight gain of 14 ounces (0.42 kg) during these two weeks.

The case management plan provided the mother with improved support from the social agency and the child with a three-month respite in a foster home where the rate of catchup growth was 1 pound 2 ounces (0.52 kg) per month. He returned home and continued to develop satisfactorily during a 2½ year followup period.

There are some babies, for example those with a diagnosis of infantile autism, who do not pairbond well, but their growth in height and weight is unremarkable. By contrast, in children with severe growth failure attributable to deprivation, neglect, and abuse, the evidence is, as it was in Elmer's case, that the phylogenetic basis of pairbonding is intact in the child, whereas in the mother it is impaired (see Money and Needleman, 1976; Herrenkohl and Herrenkohl, 1979; Abramson, 1991).

The child may be characterized as starving for grooming, and, unless listless and excessively debilitated from neglect and abuse, actively inviting affiliative bondedness. Younger children, still living at home, show unrelenting persistence in meeting their abusive parents more than half-way in a plea for affiliative cuddling and hugging. Taken at face value, the parent-child relationship may look idyllic, while totally belying the scene of abuse and neglect behind the facade as effectively as if the abused were in complicity with the abuser. The same as-if complicity applies also to older, formerly abused children. Rescued and living away from the home of abuse, they show unrelenting persistence in fixating on a fantasy of regaining paradise if only they would be given just one more chance to return home and appease their parents.

Affiliative restitution, unattainable at home, may be otherwise achieved. One way is that of promiscuous, puppy-like friendliness in becoming affectionate and cuddly with newcomers and strangers. Among older children with a history of abuse dwarfism, puppy-like attachment to an older person may be manifested quite explicitly in the body language of sexuoerotical flirtatiousness and seductiveness, reinforced by explicit verbal declarations. The approach may be insistently unrelenting (see Chapter 21, S67Pf; W65Lf; S67Tf). For someone such as a young doctor unrehearsed in how to respond, it becomes embarrassing and difficult to deal with, so as not to appear cruelly rejecting. This is a difficulty not unlike that encountered in cases of erotomania, also known as Clérambault-Kandinsky syndrome (Jordan and Howe, 1980).

At a younger age, another way of achieving affiliative restitution is to become attached solely and exclusively to one person, over whom is exercised a sort of affiliative tyranny, analogous to the tyranny of love. There is a meticulously well documented example of such exclusivity which is unique in the case literature (Saenger et al., 1977).

This case demonstrates a period of deceleration of catchup growth in a boy of seven during the period when his special nurse, with whom he had established a strong affiliative bond, was on vacation. Upon first admission to the hospital, his medical chart had recorded a history of full-term pregnancy and a normal birth weight of 3000 grams; a height age of 12 months at chronological age of 2 years (more than 3.5 standard deviations below the mean); and of standing as late as age 3 years and of not walking until age 5 years. At chronological age 6 years 10 months, the height age was 17 months and the weight age 16 months. The abdomen was protuberant, the extremities slender, and the expression sad looking. Food and water intake was ravenous for only the first three weeks of a seven-month hospital stay, after which the intake of calories gradually decreased.

Sleep disturbance was not observed. He became larger in size, active, outgoing, and apparently happy. The parents visited only three times during the seven months.

There was no change in dietary intake in the periods before, during, or after the separation from his favorite nurse, so that nutritional deficit alone could not explain the deceleration of catchup growth contingent on the nurse's absence.

The authors' summary (p.1) includes data on blood levels of somatomedin, the growth factor formed in the liver that mediates the effect of growth hormone, as well as growth hormone itself. Despite the technical detail, it is too informative to omit.

The diagnosis of psychosocial dwarfism (PSD) was made in a 7 year old boy upon admission to the hospital. In the period following admission, he grew at a slightly accelerated rate of 0.6 cm in 24 days (extrapolated growth rate 9.1 cm/yr); his caloric intake was 1663 calories/day (147 cal/kg/day), stimulable growth hormone was 5.9 ng/ml and somatomedin activity was in the hypopituitary range (0.24, 0.05 U/ml).

In the following period of marked catch-up growth of 8.6 cm in 102 days (extrapolated growth rate 30.8 cm/yr), his caloric intake decreased significantly to 1514 cal/day (106 cal/kg/day, $0.005 < p < 0.01$), stimulable growth hormone in this period was 13.6 ng/ml and somatomedin activity normalized (0.98 U/ml).

While under continued observation, with separation from his favorite nurse his growth velocity dropped significantly to the rate immediately following admission, but there was no change in his stimulable growth hormone or in somatomedin activity. With the return of his favorite nurse, he resumed his previous rapid catch-up growth with no change in caloric intake (p=not significant), growth hormone level, or somatomedin activity. Upon transient return to his depriving home, his growth rate decreased to 1.4 cm in 70 days (extrapolated growth rate 7.2 cm/yr): growth hormone remained in the normal range. Somatomedin activity was in the low normal range (0.57 U/ml) and rose to high normal activity (1.31 U/ml) as rapid catch-up growth resumed after he had been readmitted.

We conclude from these data that: 1) serum somatomedin in longstanding untreated psychosocial dwarfism (PSD) may be in the hypopituitary range; 2) markedly fluctuating growth rates during recovery in this patient with PSD were not due to changes in caloric nutrition, growth hormone release or somatomedin activity, but to an as yet unidentified factor affecting growth during emotional stress.

14

Diagnosis and Nomenclature

It requires special funding to keep a dwarfed child suspected of having been parentally deprived, neglected, or abused in a hospital for a seven-month period, as in the foregoing case of Saenger and coauthors. Although so long a period of time was not needed to confirm the diagnosis, it was needed to monitor the environment in which recovery was taking place and to keep exact measurements of the velocity of catchup growth and of its nutritional and hormonal correlates.

With respect to hormonal measurements, the unattainable ideal would be for the baseline levels to be established under the conditions of living in the home environment. With each day of delay in obtaining measurements after transfer to the hospital environment, the greater the possibility of an elevation of plasma growth hormone levels. Thus, laboratory tests alone cannot be relied upon to confirm suspected diagnosis. The ultimate confirmation is, as in the case of Saenger et al., an increase in growth velocity and normalization of hormone levels in the bloodstream as a sequel to change of domicile and, perhaps, a concomitant increase in nutritional intake and in amount of grooming.

Before the diagnosis can be confirmed it must, of course, be suspected. The first suspicious evidence is that the infant or young child is deficient in size for age. The commonly used criterion is that the height age and weight age are both below the third percentile, relative to chronological age, and that bone age is correspondingly grossly deficient. The weight age may match the height age, so that the child does not look emaciated. The belly may be protuberant.

Disclosure of neglect and abuse cannot be routinely expected from those parents (or guardians) who, in the very act of disclosure, would also be incriminating themselves. Some avoid self-incrimination by incriminating the child against whom they lay a list of complaints so as to justify their imposition of excessive discipline and punishment by way of beating, solitary confinement, food and fluid deprivation, sleep deprivation, unprotected exposure to filth or extreme temperatures, and other tortures. Such parents have alibis for the evidence of the child's bodily injuries by complaining about the child's clumsiness and accident proneness.

Another way of avoiding self-incrimination is by becoming inaccessible, avoiding confrontation, and threatening litigation. In some such cases, it may prove possible for a case worker or a pastor to establish rapport with the parents and to be entrusted with otherwise suppressed information. In other cases, a neighbor, relative, or friend may be able to supply missing evidence, despite wariness of reprisals, and the murkiness of the law regarding the responsibility of informants. The ideal is not to alienate the parents, but to rescue them from their pathological dilemma, as well as to rescue the child. Access to information regarding abuse or neglect may be the only way of confirming the diagnosis in cases in which growth failure is far less extreme than in those cases which qualify as dwarfism.

The problems inherent in ascertaining and defining abuse, neglect, and deprivation, may be held responsible historically for the plurality of names that have created much confusion in the literature on this syndrome of growth failure. The name used by Powell et al. (1967a), syndrome of emotional deprivation and growth retardation simulating idiopathic hypopituitarism, was too wordy to survive. Green (1986) compiled a list of alternative synonyms that subsequently appeared.

> . . . deprivation dwarfism (Silver and Finkelstein, 1967), deprivation syndrome dwarfism (Drash, Greenberg, and Money, 1968), psychosocial dwarfism (Reinhart and Drash, 1969), reversible somatotropin deficiency (Money, Wolff, and Annecillo, 1972), psychosocial deprivation dwarfism (Krieger, 1974), reversible hyposomatotropinism (Money and Annecillo, 1976), abuse dwarfism (Money, 1977), nonorganic failure to thrive (Hufton and Oates, 1977), psychosocial short stature (Tanner, 1973; Meyer-Bahlburg, 1985), and psychosomatic dwarfism (Ferholt et al., 1985).

From among these alternatives the one that has gained most currency is psychosocial dwarfism. Despite its irrational ambiguity, nonorganic failure to thrive has offered some competition, but it is not specific to dwarfism of statural growth.

Kaspar Hauser syndrome, the eponymic term, cuts through the tangle of too many names for the condition, and the false implication of etiological certainty that they convey. In addition, it is simple and easy to use. Kaspar Hauser is a symbol of the abusive neglect and deprivation that have typified case reports of the syndrome for over a century.

15

Delayed Onset of Puberty

Variations in nomenclature notwithstanding, the literature on growth failure as related to deprivation, neglect, and abuse has pertained almost exclusively to infancy and the early to middle years of childhood, prior to the age of the expected onset of puberty. The statistical norm for the age of onset of puberty is 11 to 13 years for girls, and 12 to 14 years for boys.

It was the case already mentioned in chapter 7 that first drew attention to the fact that prolonged growth delay would include pubertal delay (Money and Wolff, 1974). The authors summarized the case as follows (p.121ff).

> Three years ago we had the opportunity to see a sixteen year-old boy whose case warranted the triple diagnosis of battered child syndrome, reversible hyposomatotropic dwarfism, and delayed puberty. He had the physique of an 8½-year-old boy, with a bone age of 11½. Since infancy, he had been imprisoned at home, often locked for hours in a closet, and otherwise severely traumatized somatically and psychically by his par-

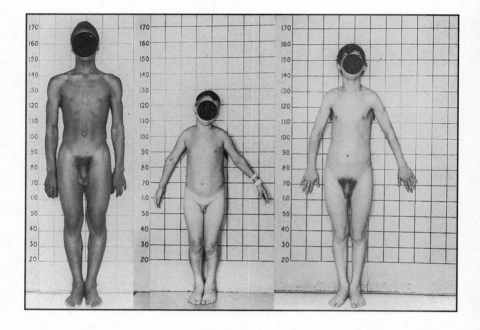

Fig. 15.1. Left, youth aged 16 years, with normal growth history. Center, patient with history of growth inhibition, aged 16 years 1 month, one month after release from the growth-inhibiting environment. Right, the same patient at age 18 years 11 months, showing the effects of catchup growth and pubertal maturation after 2 years 10 months in growth-promoting environments.

ents. There were no clinical signs of puberty. Ten months later, the height had increased from 51 to 55 inches (130 to 140 cm), and the weight from 70 to 79 pounds (32 to 36 kg). The first growth of a few pubic hairs was in evidence. The scrotal skin had darkened and the testes, described formerly as almost atrophied, had become easily palpable. The shaft of the penis had increased 1 cm in length.

At the time of the most recent interview, the boy was one month short of his nineteenth birthday (Fig.15.1). He had the appearance of being two to three years postpubertal and could have passed as a fifteen year old. His height was 62¼ inches (158 cm) and his weight 100 pounds (45 kg). The height age was 13½ and the bone age 15½ years. He had well-developed pubic and axillary hair and a thin moustache, but did not yet need to shave. He was appealing and friendly in manner, with none of the hyperkinesis and hypomanic tendency formerly evident.

This boy's case fitted very well into two long-term psychohormonal studies, one on the types and psychology of retarded puberty, and one on the psychology of so-called psychosocial dwarfism (better defined operationally as reversible hyposomatotropic dwarfism). He was kept in follow-up, despite the limitations of a long-distance foster placement. Along with other children being followed with a diagnosis of reversible hyposomatotropic dwarfism—some of whom had, and some whom had not been transferred from the home where they did not grow to one where catch-up growth began—this boy raised the issue of a possible relationship between an adverse living environment, on the one hand, and delayed puberty associated with statural growth retardation, on the other.

Including this one case, there were in the clinic sample (N=32) ten boys and two girls who had reached or advanced beyond the expected age of puberty, and who already had pubic hair rated at Tanner Stage 2 (Tanner, 1962, 1969). Before the onset of puberty, eight of the twelve had been transferred from the growth-retarding domicile to a growth-promoting domicile up to and beyond the onset of puberty. The other four had remained at, or been returned to the original domicile. The findings demonstrated that the longer the period spent in the growth delaying domicile, the later the onset of puberty. There were three boys who had lived until beyond age sixteen in the growth delaying domicile, and in all three the onset of puberty was delayed until the seventeenth year of age.

These examples of prolonged growth delay extending so as to

include delay in the onset of puberty implicate the suppression not only of growth hormone release from the pituitary, but also of gonadotropin release. When the gonad stimulating gonadotropins, LH (luteinizing hormone) and FSH (follicle stimulating hormone) are not released on schedule, then the testicles and the ovaries are not stimulated to release the hormones of puberty—testosterone to masculinize, and estrogen and progesterone to feminize. This chain of releasing events begins with releasing hormone secreted from brain cells in the hypothalamus, close by the pituitary. The releasing hormone for gonadotropin is LHRH (luteinizing hormone releasing hormone), also known as GNRH (gonadotropin releasing hormone). These hormones are testimony to the intricacy of the relationship of the brain, through hormones, to growth in size, and to pubertal maturation.

Money and Wolff speculated that their findings might have relevance for other cases of "constitutional delay of puberty and adolescence" which may, in fact, be an unnamed syndrome of retarded onset of puberty that may represent a late-onset variant of the syndrome of reversible hyposomatotropinism, without extreme dwarfism of stature.

Preliminary evidence to support this speculation was found by Lewis, Money, and Bobrow (1977) in a followup survey and classification of 150 cases of delay or failure of the onset of puberty in males. In a group of twelve cases that had been diagnosed, by default, as constitutional delay of growth and adolescence, there were five that were, at age fifteen, prepubertal in development; no taller than five feet (152 cm); retarded in bone age by at least two years; and, in four of the five cases, symptomatic for psychopathology. Enmeshment of the boy in family psychopathology, although not systematically investigated, was evident to a major degree in one case. All five received brief treatment with either testosterone or chorionic gonadotropin to circumvent further delay in the onset of puberty, and all five eventually achieved complete virilization.

These cases are, perhaps, not unlike the case published by Magner et al. (1984). This is a case of late onset of growth hormone failure (hyposomatotropinism) in synchrony with late onset of puberty following a potentially traumatizing experience described as follows (p.738).

In April 1967, his stepfather grew angry when the patient, aged twelve years, three months, and an older brother did not return home until very late. Although he generally had a warm and loving relationship with his stepfather, the patient admits that in anger he wished for his stepfather's death, and verbalized this to his brother. The very next day the stepfather fell from a church steeple and required a long hospitalization during which the patient was not allowed visitation privileges. One day, a "notice of death" arrived by mail when the patient was home alone—he was profoundly shocked and hid the notice from the family. The next day it was learned that the notice had been sent in error (the stepfather ultimately recovered fully). However, the patient remained extremely upset, refused food, and caused himself to vomit. His weight, initially about 75 pounds (34 kg), fell progressively for several months, possibly to below 50 pounds (23 kg).

Proximity in time does not, per se, signify cause and effect. Thus it cannot be assumed that the traumatic experience per se, precipitated the syndrome that ensued, rather than that the trauma became a flag with which the onset of the syndrome became retrospectively marked. The symptoms were prolonged anorexia and suicidal threats requiring residential psychiatric hospitalization; deficient gain in height, weight, and bone age; and delayed onset of puberty. Between ages 17 and 21, the patient was admitted to the National Institute of Health for six study periods. At age 17 years 8 months, pubic hair and genital development were rated at Tanner Stage 2 of puberty (Tanner Stage 4 is early postpubertal). The medical photograph shows the overall appearance of the body as that of a juvenile on the threshold of puberty. For the next two years the progress of puberty was stalled.

The very low basal level of growth hormone was minimally responsive to the arginine-insulin challenge test, and remained so until age 19 years 4 months when injections of growth hormone were commenced and continued until age 20 years 7 months. Under this treatment the level of pituitary gonadotropin (LH) increased, and the level of testosterone from the testes became postpubertal. After cessation of growth hormone injections, height and weight improved, hormonal measurements were maintained at the postpubertal level, and the body became increasingly virilized. It was fully virilized at the time of followup at age twenty-seven; the height was 171 cm (67 inches) and the weight 63.6 kg (140 pounds). Nothing more was said of sexual function than that it was normal. The former symptoms of psychopathology appeared to have been resolved.

16

Social Age and Psychopathology

Infants and children reared in institutions and placed in foster homes provided, in the symptoms of their own behavioral pathology, the raw data for the theory that attributed these very symptoms to the deprivations of institutional life—more amorphously to maternal deprivation, and more amorphously still to emotional deprivation (see Chapter 4).

The terms, maternal deprivation, emotional deprivation, and just plain deprivation were destined to become appropriated by pediatric endocrinology and applied to the explanation of the hitherto unexplained syndrome of reversible dwarfism (see Chapter 6). With their original amorphousness retained, they were used no longer to explain the genesis of behavioral disorder, but the genesis of growth failure. Then, in a remarkable reversal that put the cart before the horse, behavioral symptomology of the syndrome subtly changed in significance from being a direct outcome of deprivation, to being a source of parental annoyance and aggravation that induced deprivation. Parentally reported bizarre behavioral symptoms became pathognomonic and more or less a sine qua non of the diagnosis.

Patton and Gardner (1963, p.20) wrote of developmental retardation in five of their six cases, thus.

None was walking alone. Only the thirty-six month old child was talking, and he only with a few unintelligible single words. All were lethargic, apathetic and withdrawn in their behavior. Exaggerated rhythmic body movements were frequently seen. The six and one-half year old boy was extremely shy, unable to form good relationships with his peers, and had enuresis and encopresis.

Silver and Finkelstein (1967, pp.320-21) wrote of fussiness and irritability in infancy, excessive crying and failure to be satisfied with feedings. Later the appetite was voracious and ravenous. The children would eat anything, even garbage. Two stole and hid food in their rooms. With siblings and peers, they were either very passive and withdrawn, or aggressive to the point of cruelty. Two were enuretic. One was characterized as borderline psychotic.

Powell et al. (1967a, p.1272) listed thirteen behavioral aberrations: polydipsia; drinking from toilet bowl; polyphagia; stealing food; eating from garbage can; gorging and vomiting; getting up at night; playing alone; shyness; retarded speech; temper tantrums; suggestive steatorrhea; and encopresis. Commenting on this list, the authors wrote as follows (pp.1273).

In spite of large families, most of the patients did not join in games and tended to sit and watch the others. Two children are known to have bitten their arms on occasion and drawn blood. Retarded speech was present in 11. This consisted of delayed, immature and indistinct speech. Eight of 13 walked after fifteen months of age. . . . Many of the symptoms, including the aberrations of food and water intake, began before two years of age.

Evaluated with the knowledge of hindsight, and against the criterion of parental abuse and neglect, the foregoing behavioral aberrations may need to be somewhat discounted, since the primary informants were the parents themselves. Nonetheless, they are not arbitrarily bizarre, but have their own coherency as responses to abuse. Some cohere together as behavioral responses and bodily reactions to abusive deprivation of food and water, and also of toilet facilities. Other pertain to sleep deprivation. Still others pertain to overall retardation in behavioral and social age.

Behavioral age is an all inclusive entity that includes academic, social, recreational, vocational, sartorial, sexuoerotical, and mental age. Mental age, from which the IQ is calculated, is measured on standardized tests of intelligence. Academic age is gauged on the basis of school grade level attained on a standardized achievement test. The fashion industry has age-graded clothing styles, but does not have standardized norms. Other components of behavioral age similarly lack standardized norms. There are age norms for checklist ratings of social skills, including self-reliance, but they are too simple for the older, more sophisticated age levels.

The concept of social age presupposes that a child will have been exposed to socializing experiences, which is not the case when parental child abuse includes social deprivation and isolation. In the case of Joanne Gray (see Chapter 18), the child at the age of four years weighed only thirteen pounds (5.9 kg) and had the height of a baby no more than a year old. She could not stand on her bird-like legs. She had not begun to talk, but she comprehended and responded to some words. For four years, she had been reared in a crib in a closed room, and excluded from contact with siblings. When first transferred from her home to the hospital, whereas she was in general unresponsive to strangers who befriended her, there were some few people whom she would approach in a strongly affiliative way, signaling to be picked up and cuddled.

Social aloofness is not uncommon in children with the abuse dwarfism syndrome. Ferholt et al. (1985) in a study of ten children aged 3 to 16 years, equated it with a primary diagnosis of childhood depression combined with narcissistic personality disorder; and speculated that "the very slow rate of linear growth could be understood as a neuroendocrine concomitant of a severe depressive disorder in a person who is still growing."

Social aloofness, however, is not synonymous with depression insofar as it is counterbalanced by affiliative responses and friendliness toward trusted people. On the same criterion, it is not synonymous with the self-isolation of infantile and childhood autism. The most appropriate term with which to name it is social aloofness or distancing. After rescue from the domicile of abuse, it gives way progressively to friendliness and affiliative bonding, with occasional noncommunicative relapses.

For as long as two years following rescue, friendliness and affiliative bonding may merge into a hyperkinetic rush of excessive activity and garrulity. Many adults find it insufferable. It may lead to antagonisms and outbursts of temper which in turn provoke retaliation and insidious resumption of the cycle of abuse. Forewarned care givers are able to intervene so as to stop the cycle, and eventually the period of hyperkinesis passes.

The amount of catchup growth in social and motoric developmental age that is required in order to be fully caught up is presumably independent of brain size and microscopic neuroanatomy, according to a study, the only one of its kind, by Perry and Freedman (1973). These authors autopsied the brain of a boy who had died at age twenty-three months, with a diagnosis of "massive neonatal environmental deprivation." He had the size of a one-year-old baby, and a history of motoric development of a baby still younger. The authors concluded (p.261):

> One cannot fail to be impressed by the absence of a demonstrable correlation between structure and function, or, in this case, absence of function. Within the limits imposed by the histological techniques, it has not been possible to demonstrate

tissue changes which could be associated with the profound emotional and behavioral retardation shown by our subject. Neither the dendritic pattern nor the thickness and lamination of the cortex could be distinguished from those of the brains of our two controls. Although his brain weighed less than those of the controls (1000 gm as opposed to 1280 gm and 1200 gm), its weight was identical with that given as average for his age (1064 gm). In the presence of a clinical syndrome which includes at age twenty-three months the inability to sit without support, failure of the completion of the evolution of crawling, only tentative evidence of the inception of hand to mouth coordination, nearly total absence of voluntarily initiated motor activity and only minimal evidence of interest in the environment, all that can be said with certainty about the subject's brain is that it may be somewhat small for his age.

Brain findings notwithstanding, in the living patients the level of social age finally achieved during the period of catchup growth appears to correlate more or less inversely with the number of years of deprivation and abuse.

In some cases the outcome, academically and vocationally, is highly satisfactory, although there may be a residual vulnerability with respect to affiliatively intimate relationships. In less successful cases, the outcome is one of insufficient autonomous independence in the affairs of daily living, and a reliance, not unlike the reliance of a pet on its master, on someone who will be on hand when help or rescue is needed. The sexuoerotical outcome is varied (see Chapter 21), and may bring the grown-up patient into conflict with the law. There is no known evidence of an increased prevalence of a major psychiatric diagnosis in adulthood.

The state of the art being as it is, there are no tests or techniques for measuring the levels of catchup growth in social age, with or without psychopathology, relative to duration of abuse and duration of rescue. It is necessary to rely instead on overall estimates of deficiency or severity, which is better than nothing, but scientifically not very satisfying. By contrast, there is the intelligence test with which to measure the level of catchup growth in intelligence, calculated as the before-and after difference in IQ.

17

IQ and Intellectual Catchup Growth

Chapter 4 tells the story of the gradual recognition that reduced velocity of intellectual growth, with concomitant shrinkage of IQ, might be a concomitant of sensory and cognitional deprivation—and conversely that catchup growth and improved IQ might be a concomitant of the cessation of deprivation. This story unfolded prior to the recognition that reduced velocity of intellectual growth might take place concurrently with reduced velocity of statural growth, and that acceleration in the velocity of catchup growth in each might also take place concurrently. Money et al. (1983a,b) were able to investigate this issue of catchup growth in intelligence and its relationship to catchup growth in stature in two papers based on IQ followup data from their clinic population of children with a diagnosis of abuse (psychosocial) dwarfism. Their data read as follows.

Patients and Procedures

The sample comprised a group of 34 patients—15 females and 19 males (27 whites and 7 blacks)—with a diagnosis of

125

abuse dwarfism, which was confirmed in the endocrine examination, laboratory tests, and followup. Except for four patients at around the fourth percentile, all were below the third percentile in stature. Some were far below the first percentile. For example, one patient at age 4½ years had a height age of 11 months, and another patient at age 16 had a height age of 8 years. These two, like all the other patients, had a history of child abuse documented in their medical and social service records.

All the patients were seen and evaluated in both the Psychohormonal Research Unit and the Pediatric Endocrine Clinic at The Johns Hopkins Hospital during the period 1958–1975. They were the 34 among 50 who met the criteria of having at least one followup IQ testing for before-and-after comparison. There were four sets of siblings (two pairs of sisters, one pair of brothers, and one trio of brothers) in the total group (N=34) of patients. The presence of siblings does not introduce a statistical artifact into the present findings, as the basic statistical design is not that of a frequency distribution but of a before-and-after study, with each patient as his/her own control.

The first IQ was obtained while the children were at the stage of being abused (N=29) or, though having been ostensibly rescued, were in actuality rated as only equivocally rescued (N=5). The second or followup IQ was obtained while they were at the stage of living in an environment of rescue (N=23) or, because rescue had been ineffectual, in a less than ideal environment in which abuse persisted (N=2) or was equivocal (N=9). Some patients had more than one followup IQ and more than one change of environment.

Table I presents the patients' duration of followup in clinics at The Johns Hopkins Hospital, together with the duration of followup for IQ.

Table I. Duration of Follow-up at the Johns Hopkins Hospital
and Duration of IQ Follow-up (N=34)

	JHH follow-up, first to last visit (yr, month)			IQ follow-up, first to last test (yr, month)		
	range	mean	S.D.	range	mean	S.D.
Age first seen	2, 4 to 16, 1	5, 11	3, 2	2, 4 to 14, 5	6, 5	2, 9
Age last seen	5, 9 to 24, 1	14, 3	5, 2	3, 6 to 24, 1	14, 1	5, 2
Duration of follow-up	>2 to 20, 3	8, 5	5, 4	>4 to 15, 10	7, 8	4, 6

Each patient was referred to the Psychohormonal Research Unit on one of three tracks: through the judicial system, including social services and police personnel (11 patients); through someone not acting under either judicial or medical authority (3 patients); and through medical personnel, usually physicians (20 patients).

The data on domiciles and families, in addition to abuse, pertain to socioeconomic status; location, type, and quality of domiciles; age, ethnic background, and religion of parents of birth; ordinal sibling position; and composition of household. These data, except for abuse itself, revealed no characteristics or trends of potential etiological significance to the syndrome.

Each patient has a consolidated case history on file in the Psychohormonal Research Unit. These histories contain information collected sequentially from various clinics and social agencies as well as information obtained from within the Unit itself.

Most of the intelligence testing for this study was conducted by members of the Psychohormonal Research Unit.

Tests conducted in the Unit were always double checked for errors in scoring and computation. Other tests scores were obtained from professionals associated with the Department of Social Services and various residential facilities. The tests used were the Cattell, Stanford-Binet, and most often, the Wechsler scales of intelligence (WISC; WAIS).

The case history data were organized into three sections: somatic data obtained primarily by physicians, social data obtained primarily by social services personnel and behavioral data obtained primarily by members of the Psychohormonal Research Unit. The latter section contains interviews with professional personnel, for example, case workers associated with the patients, as well as with the parents and the patients themselves. The interviews followed a systematic schedule of inquiry designed for the syndrome of abuse dwarfism. The sequence of inquiry was from open-ended to forced choice.

Relevant information was abstracted and reduced for each patient in chronological order of IQ testing and history of abuse and rescue. So as to avoid spurious accuracy, abuse was rated as either ascertained or not ascertained. If the former, the rating was either present, equivocal or absent. Abuse was rated as present only if the evidence was incontrovertible. Otherwise abuse was rated as equivocal, unless it was incontrovertibly absent. This procedure was followed so as not to bias the data in the direction of an excessive prevalence of abuse. In other words we preferred to err against rather than for our hypothesis regarding abuse and IQ. One example of information on which abuse ratings were based is the account of a patient who, 10 years after rescue, stated that both parents used to beat him and lock him in a closet. By contrast, absence of abuse characterized the rehabilitation program at Mount Washington Pediatric Hospital, well known for its excellence in rehabilitating abused dwarfs.

Whenever uncertainty existed about a rating, the jury-consensus method was used. This method requires the judgement of one or more additional investigators trained and experienced in the application of rating criteria to the type of data under study.

The baseline or starting position for the patients' IQ data is the time at which they were first ascertained in and rescued from the environment of abuse. All thirty-four patients were rescued from environments for which evidence of abuse existed. After their initial rescue, three patients, two of whom were sisters, were placed in foster home environments which proved to be abusive; two patients who were brothers returned to their original home which qualified as an abusing environment. IQs obtained on these five patients provided the only repeat IQs of patients who remained in abusing environments. The remaining twenty-nine patients were rescued from abuse and placed in environments of rescue (N=20) or environments equivocal for rescue (N=9).

In order to have comparable units of growth in both height and intelligence, both were reduced to a ratio of which the denominator was chronological age. Thus, the familiar derivation of IQ by dividing Mental Age by Chronological Age (IQ=MA/CA x 100) was paralleled by the derivation of HQ (Height Quotient) by dividing Height Age by Chronological Age (HQ=HA/CA x 100). The norms used for Height Age determination were those in the growth tables of Data from the National Health Survey of the National Center for Health Statistics (Hamill et al., 1977).

In two cases, one height measurement was missing so that N=32. In Tables VII-X, N=32 for some comparisons as some patients were multitested and so contributed more than one set of data to the findings.

Table II. Baseline of Abuse to Final Follow-up after Consistent Rescue (N=23)‡

	Baseline abuse IQ	Age at rescue (yr, month)	Final IQ in rescue	Age (yr, month)	Time in rescue (yr, month)	IQ change
B68D	50	4, 3	48	4, 7	0, 4	– 2
C67D	62	7, 7	77	7, 11	0, 4	+15
M71R	83	3, 2	105	3, 6	0, 4	+22
S58R	57	7, 4	77	9, 9	2, 5	+20
W58V	42	6, 11	56	9, 8	2, 9	+14
M69S	83	4, 0	118	7, 3	3, 3	+35
H63R	101	4, 3	89	7, 8	3, 5	–12
T72TB	80	2, 4	107	5, 9	3, 5	+27
T72TA	80	2, 4	104	5, 9	3, 5	+24
S67P	43	8, 10	63	13, 3	4, 5	+20
N61S	74	12, 3	91	17, 1	4, 10	+17
R60M	56	12, 8	73	17, 7	4, 11	+17
R62V	55	10, 0	73	14, 11	4, 11	+18
H54G	80	7, 10	80	12, 10	5, 0	0
S67T	62	7, 0	93	12, 3	5, 3	+31
H54RB	80	17, 5	90	23, 7	6, 2	+10
H55RN	68	15, 1	96	22, 9	7, 8	+28
B64S	81	5, 8	99	13, 8	8, 0	+18
T63S	57	5, 5	112	13, 8	8, 3	+55
I63T	79	6, 8	93	15, 2	8, 6	+14
K53J	51	15, 7	87	24, 1	8, 6	+36
D64M	61	4, 1	133	12, 11	8, 10	+72
B63S	36	3, 10	115	16, 4	12, 6	+79
Mean	66	7, 7	90	12, 8	5, 1	24
S.D.	16	4, 4	21	5, 11	3, 1	21

‡Variations in the time intervals between the IQ assessments and in the number of retests per person were the consequence of the usual hospital exigencies of scheduling, appointments missed, travel distances, and being lost to follow-up.

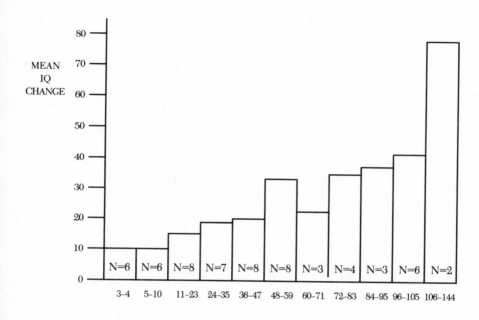

FOLLOW-UP INTERVAL IN MONTHS

Fig. 17.1. IQ change at different intervals of follow-up after rescue (N=23, with 16 tested in follow-up more than once).

Findings

IQ Change (Elevation) in Consistent Rescue

Table II lists the patients (N=23) with an abuse/rescue history and a before/after IQ. In Fig.17.1, the data, including interim IQs, are displayed graphically. The overall finding is one of a 24±21 (Mean±S.D.) points of IQ elevation with statistical significance, tested for correlated samples, at the level of $p<.001$ (z=5.5).

In order to take account of variability in age, baseline IQ level, and duration of rescue, a multiple regression analysis was applied. It revealed that these differences together account for 60% of the variance in IQ elevation ($r=0.779$, $p<0.005$). Time in rescue accounts for most of the variance (z beta=4.47) as compared with baseline IQ level (z beta=3.02), with baseline age acting as a moderator variable with a negative beta weight (z beta=–2.59). The moderating role of age means that the younger the age at the time of rescue, the greater the amount of IQ elevation during a comparable period of time after rescue.

Overall, the regression analysis supports the hypothesis that post-rescue growth of intelligence is not sudden, but progressive over time.

Younger vs Older Age Groups

In order to test further the age hypothesis, namely, that the younger the age at the time of rescue, the greater the amount of intellectual catchup growth and IQ elevation, two age-divergent subsets of patients were assembled (Table III). The table shows a mean elevation of IQ in each subset (33 and 16, respectively) which, when combined, attained a high degree of significance ($F=27.18$, $p<0.001$). Though this significance applies regardless of age of rescue, it is also evident that the younger the age at rescue, the greater the gain in IQ. Analysis of variance showed that the difference between the two subsets reached significance at the level of $p<0.1$ ($F=3.46$), which in view of the small size of the sample is quite substantial. In addition, the effect of age at the time of testing reached significance at the level of $p<0.05$ ($F=5.39$), reflecting rather convincingly the fact that the younger patients had, in general, higher IQ.

Because they were younger, one may infer, they had suffered less IQ impairment prior to being rescued and therefore were able to benefit more from catchup growth.

Table III. Post-Abuse Elevation of IQ Relative to Age at Time of Rescue

N	Age at rescue (yr, month) Range	Age at rescue (yr, month) Mean	Rescue (yr, month) Mean	Baseline IQ $\bar{x}$ & S.D.	Follow-up IQ $\bar{x}$ & S.D.	IQ Elevation $\bar{x}$ & S.D.
7	2, 4 to 5, 5	3, 9	3, 11	71±21	104±11	33±24
7	5, 8 to 15, 7	10, 3	4, 1	63±15	78±16	16± 7

IQ Change in Patients with More Than One Followup

IQ Sixteen of the twenty-three patients had more than one post-rescue IQ determination. The progressive elevation of IQ from one test to the next is graphically evident in Fig.17.1.

Another strategy by which to investigate the phenomenon of progressive IQ increase takes advantage of the fact that eight patients were tested as juveniles, again at around puberty, and again post-pubertally; and under different conditions of abuse and rescue (Table IV).

Table IV. Progressive Change of Mean IQ: Juvenile to Peripubertal to Postpubertal Years (N=8)

N	Environmental sequence	Juvenile $\bar{x}$ IQ	Juvenile Range	Peripubertal $\bar{x}$ IQ	Peripubertal Range	Postpubertal $\bar{x}$ IQ	Postpubertal Range
2	Abuse/abuse/abuse	98	87–109	82	75–90	76	75– 77
3	Abuse/abuse/rescue	73	72– 74	76	68–80	92	90– 96
3	Abuse/rescue/rescue	55	36– 79	85	72–93	98	87–115

Because of the small numbers, Table IV is for visual inspection only. The trend is quite consistent, namely that IQ increases after change from an environment of abuse to one of rescue.

The two patients for whom rescue was not effected progressively deteriorated in IQ. The other six who were rescued
continued to show IQ improvement postpubertally. They
ranged in age from 15 to 24 years (median 17) when last treated.

IQ Change in Equivocal vs Abuse or Rescue Environments

Some patients spent at least one period of their lives in
conditions that qualified as equivocal, that is as definitively
neither abusive nor nonabusive, or an alternation of both. If
they were IQ tested at the onset and conclusion of this period,
regardless of how many other tests they had had, then they
qualified for inclusion in Table V. Table V shows a consistent
trend confirming IQ impairment in an environment of abuse
and IQ elevation after change to an environment of rescue.
The new finding of this table is that after removal from the

Table V. Change in IQ Relative to Abuse, Equivocal, and Rescue Environments*

Row	Environmental sequence	N	Mean test—test interval (yr, month)	$\bar{x}$ IQ Baseline	$\bar{x}$ IQ Follow-up	$\bar{x}$ IQ Diff.
1	Abuse/abuse	5	8,0	83±16	75± 4	–8±15
2	Abuse/equivocal	6	4, 11	61± 9	78± 7	17± 8
3	Abuse/rescue	16	4, 11	67±17	92±16	24±18
4	Equivocal/equivocal	8	4, 6	75±12	82±13	7±10
5	Rescue/rescue	12	4, 2	77±17	96±19	19±13

*N=34, but 13 patients qualified for inclusion in two different sequences because
of multiple changes of domicile over widely spaced periods of their lives.

Analysis of variance:
Rows 1, 2, 3: trials ($F=12.52$, $p < 0.01$)
         interaction ($F=3.43$, $p < 0.05$)
Rows 1, 4, 5: trials ($F=6.12$, $p < 0.01$)
         interaction ($F=3.55$, $p < 0.05$)

environment of abuse, even when the change was rated as equivocal and not as full rescue, IQ deterioration ceased or showed a minor degree of elevation.

Statistical evaluation of Table V required two analyses of variance—one comparing the three environmental sequences that began with abuse, and the other comparing the three sequences in which the second condition was unchanged from the first. In both analyses, the main effect for trials was significant at the level of $p < 0.01$ (F=12.52 and 6.12, respectively), despite the deviant effect of the abuse/abuse group. Correspondingly, in both analyses the interaction effect between IQ change and change from one environment to the other was significant at the level of $p < 0.05$ (F=3.43 and 3.55, respectively).

A post hoc test of simple main effects using a pooled error term showed that the interactions were largely the result of the dramatic improvements showed by the abuse/rescue and rescue/rescue groups. These data yet again confirm the impairment or deterioration of intellectual growth in association with abuse environments and improvements of intellectual growth in rescue, even when rescue is equivocal.

Progressive IQ Elevation, Multiple Testing (N=1)

The IQ change of greatest magnitude, from 36 to 120 (Table VI), was registered between the ages of 3 years 8 months and 13 years 11 months in a girl who had experienced major abuse up to the age of first testing.

Correlation of IQ and HQ Increments

Table VII represents a straightforward before-and-after strategy, namely a correlation of the difference between the pairs of IQs and the pairs of HQs (one obtained before followup, the other after), regardless of the intervening growth velocity. The duration of followup varied from around four months

Table VI. Progressive IQ Increase (N=1)

Age (yr. month)	Full IQ	Verbal IQ	Performance IQ	Test
3, 10	36	—	—	S—B, L
5, 1	73	—	—	S—B, L
6, 8	81	74	93	WISC
8, 8	91	92	90	WISC
10, 1	91	89	94	WISC
12, 3	110	120	97	WISC
13, 11	120	126	110	WISC

Table VII. Means and Correlation of Increments of
IQ and HQ Accrued During Follow-up (N=32)

Follow-up Status	IQ(M±SD)	HQ(M±SD)
Before Rescue	69±17	55±17
After Rescue	88±18	82±11
Difference	19±22	27±18
	r(Diff.)=0.42; $p < 0.01$	

(2 cases) to thirteen years (1 case) with a median of five years, three months. The longer the followup, the more likely a variation in growth rate because of, for example, the intervention of the pubertal growth spurt, or the effects of multiple changes in domicile.

Because of such sources of variation, the strength of the correlation between rates of intellectual and statural catchup growth, as reflected in the quotients, is all the more noteworthy.

Correlation of IQ and HQ Increments and Domiciliary History

Table VIII presents a breakdown of the findings in Table VII, so that the size of N in each subsection is smaller than

Table VIII. Means and Correlation of Increments of IQ and HQ
Accrued During Follow-up: Three Domiciliary Histories

Domicilliary History	Follow-up Status	IQ(*M±SD*)	HQ(*M±SD*)
Abuse/Rescue (N=21)	Before	66±17	48±15
	After	89±22	79±17
	Difference	23±23	30±15
		r(Diff.)=0.37; *p* <0.05	
Abuse/Abuse (N=3)	Before	89±19	63±22
	After	82± 8	74± 8
	Difference	–8±14	12±18
		r(Diff.)=0.86; *p* not sig.	
Abuse/?Rescue (N=6)	Before	64±11	50±16
	After	78± 7	83±12
	Difference	14±11	33±12
		r(Diff.)=0.31; *p* not sig.	

N=32. Some cases are represented in Table VIII more than once by reason of the fact that they were IQ tested more than twice, and changed living environment more than once. The three possible changes were from abuse to rescue; rescue back to abuse; and abuse to questionable rescue. The smaller sample size under the abuse/rescue condition (N=21) as compared with Table VII (N=32) probably accounts for the lesser significance (p<0.05) of the correlation between improvement in IQ and HQ.

Nonetheless, Table VIII is consistent with Table VII, even despite the small subsamples in the abuse/abuse and abuse/rescue categories. In addition it indicates that the strongest correlation between IQ and HQ improvement occurs when rescue is consistent in an unequivocally good environment.

Table IX. Means and Correlation of Increments of IQ and HQ Accrued
During Follow-up from Early to Late Prepubertal Age (N=28)

Follow-up Status	IQ(M±SD)	HQ(M±SD)
Early Prepuberty	68±18	55±18
Late Prepuberty	85±20	80±11
Difference	16±21	25±19
	r(Diff.)=0.45; p <0.01	

Correlation of IQ and HQ Increments from Early to Late Puberty

Table IX was constructed to test for a possible confounding effect of the rapid rate of statural growth known as the growth spurt of puberty. All followup IQs and HQs (N=28) in Table IX were obtained in late childhood, prior to the onset of puberty. The initial IQs and HQs had been obtained during the early juvenile years. The correlation between IQ and HQ elevation holds up at the p<0.01 level, thus ruling out the pubertal growth spurt as an interfering artifact in the correlations of Table VII and VIII.

Correlation of IQ and HQ Increments from Prepuberty to Early Postpuberty

Table X was designed with a view to pursuing still further the possible effect of the pubertal growth spurt.

In this table, the two sets of measurements were taken, one just before the onset of puberty and the other in early, postpubertal adolescence, respectively. The findings show that correlation between the increments of catchup growth in mental age and height age (IQ and HQ), is maintained during puberty, though in so small a sample (N=5), it is weak and does not reach significance.

Table X. Means and Correlation of Increments of IQ and HQ Accrued
During the Period from Prepuberty to Early Postpuberty (N=5)

Follow-up Status	IQ(M±SD)	HQ(M±SD)
Prepuberty	88±15	80±19
Early Postpuberty	97±14	86±16
Difference	9±9	6±10
	r(Diff.)=0.26; p not sig.	

The foregoing ten tables and the statistical technicalities that go with them may seem to disguise rather than simplify their underlying message which is: under conditions of abusive deprivation and neglect, when the velocity of growth in size slows down, so also does the velocity of intellectual growth. In addition, the magnitude of catchup intellectual growth (and thus the number of IQ points regained) is contingent on the promptness of rescue from the abusing domicile to a nonabusing one. The tables and statistics are imperative, however, in order to countermand the misapplication of statistics by others who support the dogma that IQ is innately preordained, in toto, by familial or racial inheritance. The syndrome of abuse dwarfism demonstrates, once and for all time, that the velocity of intellectual growth is not innately preordained, but is subject to the same postnatal forces of retardation as is statural growth. The syndrome demonstrates also that catchup growth may never be sufficient to restore either stature or intellect to what they would otherwise have been. In the terminology of the now outmoded polarization of nature versus nurture, this means that IQ may be permanently lowered by nurture.

Explaining the mystery of how hormones and other brain chemistries may change the velocity of intellectual growth congruently with growth in stature remains still to be solved. Change in the velocity of sociobehavioral growth is part of the same mystery.

18

Parental Collusion

The data on affiliative bonding examined in Chapter 13 indicated that in cases of bonding deprivation, it was on the mother's side of the bond, not the baby's that a flaw exists. Bonding failure may possibly predicate the onset of abusive neglect, but it does not by itself alone predicate the onset of abusive brutality. Nor does it predicate in the father a role either of indifference to neglect and abuse, or of collusional participation in neglect and abuse.

Collusional participation of one parent with the other in the abuse and neglect of a child represents a manifestation of shared irrationality known by its French psychiatric name, folie à deux (madness of two): one person of the pair has a fixated irrational belief or a delusion which is assimilated by the partner. Money and Werlwas (1976) investigated this phenomenon under the title of "Folie à deux in the parents of psychosocial dwarfs: Two cases." The findings are here reproduced unabridged.

The Sample

The two families of this study were selected from forty documented cases of the syndrome, not at random, but because of their diversity. They were similar and different as follows: 1) each family resides within commuting distance of the hospital; 2) there exists sufficient evidence in both case histories to warrant further research into family dynamics, in that one family history clearly indicates psychopathology, whereas the other gives an overt appearance of stability with covert indications that surface appearances may be deceiving; 3) one patient is female, one male; 4) the girl spent eight months away from home, the boy eight years; and 5) the girl is a child, the boy an adolescent.

The two children have been seen repeatedly by members of the pediatric endocrine clinic and its psychohormonal research unit from 1965 (Patient H.K.) and 1973 (Patient J.G.) until the present. They were both referred primarily because of growth failure. Family members were included in interviews when they accompanied the child to a scheduled hospital appointment; of if they agreed to, or requested, individual interviews.

No known systematic bias exists with respect to selection of these two cases from among the other patients (N=38) with the same diagnosis. Probably the process which brings about referral of reversible dwarfism from the community at large is subject to bias, though to an unknown degree. The morbidity and mortality of the syndrome are unknown. Affected individuals may, or may not, survive without receiving professional attention.

Procedures

Original and followup taped and transcribed interviews and notes were obtained from patients, parents, guardians, social workers, and nurses.

The interviews always began with open-ended inquiry prior to factual and true-false questioning. Direct observation of child and parental behavior in the hospital and during home visits provided additional information, as did school reports.

To provide contemporary followup and to fill any gaps in historical data, the two sets of parents of origin in this study were interviewed in their homes for approximately six (Patient J.G.) and eight (Patient H.K.) hours, respectively. The parents consented to use of their information, including tape-recorded portions, as data for a written report concerning families of children with the same diagnosis as that of their own growth-retarded child.

Proper names, including initials, used in this study for patients and family members are pseudonymous.

Background Data: The Kirk Family

The parents of seventeen-year-old Herbert Kirk married twenty years ago. This is the first marriage for the mother and the second for the father. They have always belonged to the blue-collar, lower-white middle class socioeconomically.

They have four living sons. The husband is seven years older than the wife.

Two successive miscarriages preceded their second child's birth. This child, Herbert, with a history of reversible hypo-somatotropinism, was the product of an unexpected twin birth. The twin who died at four days of age reputedly had cystic fibrosis. The parents' suspicion that Herbert had cystic fibrosis, because of his odor as a neonate, was not corroborated by medical records.

Herbert had six major hospital admissions during his first six years of life. Reasons for referral varied.

Referrals were either initiated by physicians for further

studies or initiated by the parents when they were dissatisfied with prior treatments or test results.

When first measured in the pediatric endocrine clinic at age 6 11/12 years, Herbert had the height of less than a three-year-old. Accelerated growth occurred during subsequent hospitalizations and five foster home placements. At present he has average height for age seventeen years.

A son of the father's first marriage lived with Mr. and Mrs. Kirk for the first two years of their marriage. At approximately age three he was admitted to a state hospital for severe mental retardation. At his present age of twenty-two, he resides at this same hospital. Mr. Kirk dubiously suspected his first wife of having dropped this son in early infancy, ostensibly causing brain injury and retardation. The reason Mr. Kirk gave for his suspicion was that the first wife "refused" to take the baby to a physician at any time following the birth, which occurred at home. When asked why he didn't take the child to a physician himself, Mr. Kirk said that his first wife made the decisions and his role was "just going along with her like blowin' with the wind." A similar attitude characterizes his relationship with his second wife.

According to Mr. Kirk, he and his second wife made the following agreements concerning the retarded son: immediately after their marriage they agreed to assume full caretaking responsibility for their son; one year after the marriage, they agreed to hospitalize the son, who ostensibly became difficult for the second Mrs. Kirk to manage; before and after state hospitalization, they agreed to prevent, by legal means, the son's mother-of-birth from visiting him; during the past few years, they agreed never to visit, plan to visit, or make contact with the son at all, and not to sign permission for release of his records.

Mr. Kirk's siblings of origin are three brothers, one of whom is younger than he. After his father's death when Mr. Kirk was seventeen years old, he helped his mother raise his younger brother. He recalled never "raising a hand" to the younger brother because discipline was his mother's job.

His mother and brothers do not, at present, live within easy visiting distance.

By self-report, Mr. Kirk has been unemployed for the past twelve years owing to a "heart condition and nerves." Hospital records include suggestions by a cardiologist and two psychiatrists that Mr. Kirk return to work. As a former union laborer, he now receives unemployment disability payments sufficient to support his family. He spends his time building intricate wooden models, for example, of locomotives, and performing light housekeeping chores.

Mrs. Kirk is the second of four siblings and has two living brothers. She had an allegedly mentally retarded younger sister who died at age nineteen at a state hospital, the day following the birth of Herbert and his deceased twin. Because her mother worked, Mrs. Kirk as a young girl had caretaking responsibility for the sister until her admission to the state hospital three weeks before her death. Mrs. Kirk adamantly refused to release the medical records of her sister. Nothing is known concerning the etiology of her mental retardation, or indeed of the authenticity of its diagnosis.

Mrs. Kirk has always lived within easy visiting distance of her parents and brothers. She has, during the past two years, attempted to work as a shop clerk from time to time. Family illness was, by her report, the reason for her inability to work steadily. Mrs. Kirk said that she "took care of" the following members of her immediate family when they were ill: her sister, her husband's son; her second child, Herbert; her husband, who 12 years ago was briefly hospitalized for psychiatric reasons, and has recurring attacks of "nerves;" her aging parents; and her fourth son, 10-year-old Luther.

Luther was designated by his parents as a surrogate, or

substitute patient, after Herbert left the Kirk family to live with foster parents. His behavior, according to the parents, was similar to what Herbert's behavior had been while he was living with them (see Findings).

Within the past year, Mr. and Mrs. Kirk, and two of their four sons moved, from their long-term residence in an apartment in the home of Mrs. Kirk's parents into a three bedroom house of their own. The reasons for the move, according to Mrs. Kirk, were to prevent her mother's interfering with the firm discipline used by Mrs. Kirk in her attempt to control Luther's behavior, and to be closer to Herbert, insofar as he had arranged to have himself adopted by his foster parents. Meantime, Luther was living at a residential school for emotionally handicapped children. Approximately two months after Luther's residential placement, Mr. Kirk became ill again, according to his wife.

During recent husband-wife interviews in the Kirks' home, Mrs. Kirk was observed clearly to dominate the conversation while Mr. Kirk repeatedly nodded his head in agreement. Mr. Kirk did state that he loves his wife and sees her as a wonderful woman who can manage almost anything. This statement was repeated by Mr. Kirk at a later date during an individual interview.

Background Data: The Gray Family

The parents of Joanne Gray were married 11 years ago. This is the only marriage for both parents, whose age difference is four years, the husband being older.

Occupationally, the father has been able to upgrade his family's socioeconomic status so that it is now trades, managerial, black middle class.

The parents have six children, five boys and one girl. The fifth child in birth order, Joanne, age seven, is diagnosed as having reversible hyposomatotropic dwarfism.

The third child in birth order, ten-year-old Matthew, was the designated surrogate patient in this family; he exhibited symptoms similar to his sister's, such as growth failure and behavioral impairments. Matthew's diagnosis was not confirmed owing to his parent's failure to bring him to the hospital for outpatient appointments. His impairments of growth and behavior accelerated during the time when Joanne's growth and behavior improved.

Home visits were conducted between two and three years after Joanne's diagnosis and treatment. During these visits, neither Joanne nor Matthew was observed to exhibit the behavioral characteristics typical of reversible hyposomatotropinism. However, the sixth child, age 5, was by sibling and parental report different from the others.

His behavior, as observed by two interviewers, was hyperactive and included hitting, kicking and punching siblings; jumping, tumbling and running during a quiet recording session; and dumping the contents of a large drawer on the floor.

During this same home visit, Mr. Gray reported that no problems presently exist with respect to any of the children. Mrs. Gray agreed with him. Together they seemed oblivious to their sixth child's hyperactivity. They ignored it, much in the same way as they had ignored Joanne's and Matthew's former physical and behavioral impairments.

By Mrs. Gray's report and Mr. Gray's agreement, Joanne's birth was different from the births of the other five children in that Joanne "was taken from" the mother.

According to hospital records, delivery, at about the expected due date, was accomplished by Caesarian section 1½ hours after admission. The diagnosis was placenta praevia. The newborn was normal and weighed six pounds two ounces.

On the surface, the family appears to give no evidence of psychopathology: the home, in a well-kept residential area, is itself well-kept but not scrupulously clean; the father is successful at work; the mother tried working but prefers to be home with her children; neither parent has received psychiatric treatment; both parents speak positively about all their children; the father talks of pleasurable family outings, both past and planned; both parents keep in contact with their own families of origin; and both parents have high ambitions for their children's success.

Mrs. Gray is the second child in a family of 13 and the oldest living girl. Her parents are both living. In her family of origin, she had caretaking responsibility of a retarded sibling. As observed in the clinic and at home, she appeared to be impaired in spontaneity and to experience some degree of constraint in emotional expression and responsiveness, though placid and pleasant. She was described by school personnel as cooperative and congenial. By contrast, a psychologist described her as quasi-catatonic.

Mr. Gray is personable, outgoing, and verbal. In interviews with hospital professionals he supplied the most information concerning the development of the children. He is third in a family of four. He has an older sister and brother and a younger sister. Since the death of Mr. Gray's mother six years ago, his father lives alone and visits the family frequently.

During eight months in a recovery center, nearly three years ago, Joanne exhibited a remarkable reversal of growth and behavioral impairments. When first seen at age 4 3/12, she had the weight of a four-month-old, the height of a one year-old and the bone age of a fifteen-month-old. While in the recovery center, she gained over 12 pounds (5.4 kg) and grew 6 inches (15.3 cm) in eight months. The growth rate was 10 inches (25.4 cm) a year and demonstrated the catchup growth spurt by which the diagnosis of reversible dwarfism was confirmed. After returning to the home of origin, her growth rate decreased to approximately 3 inches (7.6 cm) a year, a rate within the normal limits of yearly growth, but not sufficient for adequate catchup growth.

The parents did not agree to having their daughter discharged from the recovery center to a foster home, but did consent to having her stay with an aunt who lived near them and who had always shown a special degree of understanding of the child. Then they unilaterally decided to keep their daughter at home, without informing their doctors or other case workers of their action.

Both Mr. and Mrs. Gray presented to friends, relatives and professionals an image of their family life as intact and harmonious. There were, however, obvious discrepancies with this image which are included in the following sections.

Examples of Abuse: Two Families

For the purposes of this paper, abuse is defined as documented noxious motor and/or vocal behavior of parents and guardians toward a child such that it injures or impairs the child's somatic, behavioral and mental growth, to such a degree that an impartial jury of peers in consultation with experts would call the child abused. Medical reports of the initial referrals of both Herbert Kirk and Joanne Gray to the hospital document impairments of growth and behavior.

The existence of parental abuse was not recorded in the medical history at the time of the children's initial visits. It required followup interviews with both the Kirk and Gray families to ascertain the following forms of abuse: corporal punishment, and deprivation of food, sleep, social contact, and sensory stimulation.

Mrs. Kirk, in the presence of her husband, admitted that she had used the following disciplinary techniques with Herbert: whipping; locking him in a closet; tying him to his bed and also a chair; restricting food and drink by constant watchfulness; and restricting social play.

The following disciplinary actions which occurred in his home-of-origin were reported by Herbert to his present adopted mother: he was locked in a closet for several days without food; he was tied to his bed; he was given only mushy cereal to eat while siblings ate fresh cereal; he did not get enough to eat, whereas his siblings had plenty; often he was tied to a chair; and he had been made to lie naked on the floor next to his mother's bed while his mother stepped on him.

In the Gray family, the father disclosed that he regularly used his belt to discipline his daughter for soiling herself. He self-righteously used her age, four years, as his criterion for bowel control, ignoring the fact that she weighed only thirteen pounds. The mother disclosed that she restricted Joanne's food and drink because of bad eating habits. She kept the child isolated in her crib away from other family members for most of the time she was awake, claiming she was happier when left alone. The child had a deep scar across the bridge of her nose, possibly from being trapped between the rungs of the crib.

Findings

The parents in each of the two families maintained their role as child abusers in such a way that amounted, within their contriving, to psychopathological collusion. This was true whether the abuse was corporal or psychic.

Sometimes each parent reiterated the pathological idea of the other. Sometimes each endorsed the pathology of the other by way of silent consent instead of critical intervention. Their collusion was manifested in such a way that it was difficult for professional observers to differentiate beliefs from rationalizations, or idées fixes from quasi-delusions.

Collusion: The Kirk Family

Discipline

When both parents together were interviewed at home, the interviewer noted that the father agreed verbally and by head nodding that his wife's descriptions of past punitive actions with Herbert were necessary "for the good of the family." They gave the following examples of Herbert's behavior, each time failing to mention why he may have done it: he constantly frustrated his mother and would not allow her to have any peace of mind; he deliberately provoked other family members; he roamed the house at night whenever he could get away with it; he had to be watched constantly because he would eat anything he could get his hands on; he made strange repetitious whining and moaning noises and talked and sang to himself; he picked bedding and clothing to pieces and tried to hide the resulting lint; he drank water from the toilet bowl; and he sat in one position, without responding, once for as long as forty-seven minutes.

Subsequent investigations revealed that the parents, knowingly or unknowingly, instigated the behavior they deplored. For example, the child's bizarre eating and drinking habits and roaming at night appeared, in retrospect, as a response to being hungry and thirsty. His alleged provocation of family members was probably a response to documented physical abuse from siblings as well as parents. His perseverative sounds and activities were a response to discipline and to long periods of isolation.

Consistently in all their interviews over the years, both parents maintained that Herbert had created "a wall" between his mother and himself since birth. They cited this wall as the main reason for their use of harsh discipline.

Both of them believed that the wall prevented Mrs. Kirk

from communicating with Herbert in the same way she communicated with her other children.

It was the opinion of all the professionals concerned with the case that the mother was the primary initiator of abuse and the father, the secondary consenter.

Placements

Mr. and Mrs. Kirk's collusion was unbroken when Herbert was away from their home in the hospital or a foster home.

According to medical records, during each placement they pled for their child's return to the home. The last time he was returned home they became frustrated with his behavior, threatened to send him away, and again requested his removal from their home.

Interviews with present and past foster parents included the following examples of the Kirk parents' behavior during Herbert's placements: they would plead with him to visit them and then mistreat him with verbal and physical abuse; they would, for long periods of time, make no effort to contact him or return his phone calls; they seemed unable to treat the child as a human being; they would repeatedly break promises; they once responded to a phone call from Herbert, who said he'd be a little late for his expected Christmas visit to their home with, "Don't bother to come at all."

When Herbert at age nineteen had himself legally adopted by his foster parents, both Mr. and Mrs. Kirk agreed that it was a shame. Mrs. Kirk said that one of the reasons (see Background Data) she wanted her family to move from their former residence was to be closer to Herbert. The adoptive mother said that she viewed the move as another attempt by Herbert's family to interfere with his progress.

She cited that prior to the adoption, Herbert ceased his former practice of phoning the Kirks and/or requesting to visit them.

Because of his adoptive father's change of job, Herbert and his adoptive family recently moved out of state. The patient maintains contact with the psychohormonal research unit. He is doing well.

The Surrogate (Substitute) Patient

In the Kirk family, the patient's younger brother, Luther, has consistently been the surrogate, although his statural growth has not been retarded. His two admissions to a children's psychiatric ward were for treatment of school phobia and other behavioral symptoms. The first admission coincided with Herbert's legal adoption by his foster family.

Luther's problems were described by Mrs. Kirk, with Mr. Kirk in agreement, in the following manner: "Yes, he's picked up some of Herbert's ways because Luther always watched everything he did. And true, he picked up his 'oohing' bit" (tic-like moans) "and his throwing a fit if he can't have his way. He knows, because he used to watch Herbert and all, and he has taken up at the same place Herbert left off. And I tell him to stop that. I'll tell him, I'll tell him too, 'You're acting just like Herbert.' " The parents described other undesirable behavior that Luther had copied from Herbert, classifiable as social distancing; temper tantrums; problems of eating, sleeping, playing; and pain agnosia. An example of pain agnosia, as well as abuse, was evidenced when Mrs. Kirk described Luther's standing outside in the cold in his bare feet and not feeling the cold. She reported that since Luther doesn't feel anything, she pulled him up the steps by the hair ("for that he feels") to get him out of the cold.

The Kirk parents did not allow Luther to join the Boy Scouts, as formerly they had prohibited Herbert from doing. The two other siblings were active in scouting. Luther, in the presence of an interviewer and both parents, said he wanted to join the Scouts. The mother, with the father verbally supporting her, said that Luther could not join because he would come running home on the first camping trip. As if they together followed the same script, both parents gave their son several reasons why he would come running home.

Luther presently lives in a residential institution. In the absence of both Luther and Herbert, Mr. Kirk is the member of the family who has developed psychiatric symptoms which, according to his wife, require her to stay home and care for him.

Collusion: The Gray Family

Discipline

Mr. Gray accepted his wife's absurd dietary ideas. During a home interview he actually verbalized agreement with her stated reasons for restricting Joanne's nutrition. Mrs. Gray said that Joanne had bad eating and drinking habits, which included gulping food and drink, eating too fast, eating garbage, chewing and swallowing poorly, and intermittently refusing to eat. These habits ostensibly cause the daughter to have a bloated stomach, to wheeze, and to be susceptible to germs. According to the mother, food restriction was a method of discipline to correct bad habits as well as to prevent physical illness.

Collusion with respect to discipline was further evidenced by Mrs. Gray's denial of any knowledge that her husband used his belt to beat the thirteen-pound child. Mr. Gray had reported spanking his daughter, "maybe two or three times a week" for soiling her diapers. Mrs. Gray, in a separate interview, said, "I will spank her if she's really wrong but he won't spank her."

Joanne's isolation from family activities involved further parental collusion in defining the daughter's isolation from her brothers not as deprivation or punishment but as a form of protection. According to Mrs. Gray, the other children were not permitted to go upstairs near Joanne's crib because she caught colds and germs easily.

Mr. Gray agreed with his wife's statement that Joanne "was always the type to stay to herself. She didn't want to be around nobody." The parents said that, rather than being with the other children, Joanne preferred being quiet most of the time; playing with her hands; staring; just sitting; and mumbling to herself.

Placements

During Joanne's eight-month placement in the recovery center, her parents visited regularly. Mrs. Gray's actions during those visits were described by a hospital clinician as "removed and distant." She would, for example, sit and do needlework while watching Joanne play rather than attempt to talk or play with the child directly. Though Mr. Gray did play with Joanne during these visits, he did not attempt to involve his wife in closer contact with her daughter.

During her stay at the recovery center, Joanne learned to walk, to control elimination, and to speak in three-word sentences. She grew rapidly in height and weight (see Background Data).

After their child's discharge from the recovery center, the parents missed the next three scheduled appointments at the pediatric endocrine clinic. The father brought the child for a check-up only after the family was informed that protective services would be notified if the patient missed further appointments.

The parents cited their prayers as an explanation for her

growth during the recovery placement. Acknowledged with head-nodding by her husband, Mrs. Gray said, "All I know is we prayed every night, and by her being out there, our praying, and the different climate she was surrounded by, I think it really caused her to start growing and walking and doing all the things she was supposed to be doing." Mr. Gray gave his description of the recovery center as: "You know, that's the place where all the children go, out there, and they let them run wild and let them do anything they want to do." Mrs. Gray nodded in approval of his statement.

The Surrogate (Substitute) Patient

In addition to Joanne, Matthew, who is two years older than his sister, has exhibited symptoms of lack of statural and behavioral maturation. As if on a see-saw, one child's health has been balanced by the other's illness.

Prior to Joanne's birth, Matthew was the growth retarded member of the family. At age 1½ he was hospitalized and diagnosed as failure to thrive. He allegedly ceased to have growth and behavior problems near the time of Joanne's first hospitalization at age two, when she was diagnosed as failure to thrive. The parents did not keep clinic appointments for Matthew during the three years that Joanne was the obvious, nongrowing, nonmaturing patient in the family. Matthew returned for a medical check-up at a comprehensive clinic at the time of Joanne's return home from the recovery center. Mrs. Gray reported that Matthew overate, gulped his food, and had "milk poisoning" which caused his stomach to bloat. She forbade him to eat any food at school except what she gave him. When he returned from school, she lifted his shirt to see if his abdomen was bloated. If so, that was her proof that he had illicitly eaten milk-containing food at school.

The family pediatrician suggested residential placement

for Matthew, but the parents refused. Again they did not keep scheduled appointments. When the family was threatened by protective services for missed appointments, both Joanne and Matthew improved in growth and behavior.

At present, the Gray parents have been keeping appointments at a comprehensive clinic for Joanne and Matthew. During a recent home visit the parents spoke with pride of their two children who formerly "were shy and didn't grow."

None of the Gray children appears shy or dwarfed at present. Their sixth child, however, a boy age 5, is regarded by parents and siblings as the "trouble causer."

He shows classic signs of the hyperactive child. His activity rarely is shared with that of his siblings, and he is recognized in the family as being odd.

In each of these two cases, it was the mother who began the folie à deux and the father who became the collusional partner. This sequence is not a fortuitous coincidence, for it appears to apply routinely in the syndrome of abuse dwarfism. Maternal abuse is a pathology of motherhood, whereas paternal abuse is a pathology of collusion when the outcome in the child is abuse dwarfism. Typically, only one child in a family, or only one at a time, is the collusional victim.

In the clinical literature on dwarfism or on failure to thrive attributed to maternal deprivation, the focus has been more on deprivation than on the psychopathology of the depriving mother. Leonard et al. (1966) found multiple problems in all thirteen of the families of their study and, among the mothers, several who were immobilized by anxiety and depression. "Each can be said to be failing to thrive as a mother," they wrote, "and to be herself in need of nurturing to promote her capacity and ability to nurture her baby." Fischhoff et al. (1971) made a psychiatric assessment of the sixteen mothers in their study, and diagnosed two as psychoneurotic and fourteen as character disordered. There was, at the time, no name for the psychopathology that would in 1976 become known as Munchausen's syndrome by proxy.

19

Munchausen's Syndrome by Proxy

In discussing the finding of their paper on collusion (Chapter 18), Money and Werlwas in 1976 coined the term, Munchausen's syndrome by proxy and utilized it for the first time with reference to the abuse-induced and neglect-induced symptoms of the syndrome of abuse dwarfism. They wrote as follows (p.360).

> In its classic form, Munchausen's syndrome is a condition in which the etiology of symptoms appears completely hidden whereas, in fact, the symptoms are self-induced. There is a close parallel with the symptoms observed in abuse dwarfism except that the symptoms are parent-produced in the child instead of self-induced. Whereas in Munchausen's syndrome the patient gives a false medical history, in abuse dwarfism the parents give the false history while the child remains silent. That is to say, one has a case of Munchausen's syndrome by proxy.

Medical impostoring was eponymously and somewhat facetiously named Munchausen's syndrome in 1951 by Richard Asher. The name is derived from Rudolf E. Raspe's account of *Baron Munchausen's Narrative of His Marvellous Travels and Campaigns in Russia,* first published in London in 1785. The book was progressively enlarged in many subsequent editions, so that Hieronymous Karl Friedrich von Munchausen became in literature, even more than in life, a symbol of mendacious exaggeration and imposture. A diagnosis of Munchausen's syndrome or Munchausen's syndrome by proxy is given to those patients whose illness is an imposture.

In pediatrics, the presenting complaints of Munchausen's syndrome by proxy are more varied than failure to grow, or failure to thrive. The following is a near fatal example from a report by Southall et al. (1987), summarized in Money (1989, p.16).

A twenty month old boy, the third child of a twenty-two year old mother, had been admitted because of series of sudden and unexplained attacks of suffocation. Four more attacks in the hospital were diagnostically without explanation, so the boy was linked to diagnostic monitors and put in a special observation room. The next attack occurred when the special nurse briefly left the boy alone with his mother.

The child was resuscitated and tested. The results raised suspicions. The mother refused to have her constant vigil relieved by a replacement. To prevent the child's sudden death, a consultative committee decided to coopt the security police, and hidden video cameras were installed in the child's hospital room.

For sixteen hours the cameras recorded nothing untoward in the mother's bedside behavior. Then, after moving her chair away and lowering the railing of the baby's bed, she placed a tee shirt close to the baby's face. Five minutes later, she stuffed the shirt into the baby's mouth and nose, and held his head down forcibly. The baby struggled violently until the nursing staff, having been alerted, intervened.

The published report indicated that the mother admitted that this was not the only occasion that she had suffocated her baby. She was sentenced to three years on probation, with psychiatric treatment recommended. The only information of potential explanatory value was the mother's own history of having herself been an abused child.

This case is only one of dozens that have appeared in the pediatric literature since 1976, the year in which the term, Munchausen's syndrome by proxy, was coined and applied diagnostically to parental child abusers, so that their behavior became classified not only as criminological, but also as medical and pathological.

In the official taxonomy of psychiatric syndromes, there is no category that properly accommodates Munchausen's syndrome either plain or by proxy. It does not meet the criteria of conduct disorder, antisocial personality disorder, or borderline personality disorder. Nor does it meet the criteria of schizophrenia, or mood disorder, nor of dissociative disorder which is its closest fit. Munchausen's syndrome is a disorder in its own right, and Munchausen's by proxy is a variant. Its severity and morbidity may be so intense as to justify in some instances a diagnosis of Munchausen psychosis, with or without a proxy. It is an extremely insidious psychosis, in that it is capable of masquerading behind a mask of sanity and enlisting the collusion of others, including physicians, nurses, social workers, and psychologists.

Most physicians and other health care providers are so dedicated to the alleviation of suffering and disease that they are naively unprepared to encounter medical impostoring by those who are equally dedicated to experiencing martyrdom, suffering, and disease. Such providers fall readily into the role of being enlisted and manipulated into collusion with the medical impostor. Not infrequently, the medical impostor has had some medical education, or has engaged in intensive self-training. A good impostor has the equivalent of a degree in impostoring his/her particular medical specialty, so that even an expert is duped—unless he asks for official certification and authenticity. It is all too easy to take for granted that such exist, for professionals are not trained as sleuths. In the case of Munchausen's syndrome by proxy, it is all too easy for pediatric supervisors also to take for granted that the virtual invasion of the Munchausen mother into the ranks of the ward personnel signifies the utmost in maternal altruism and self-sacrifice. Thus they miss the clues of her role as an impostor who is inducing her child's symptoms. To suspect such dedication seems equivalent to committing sacrilege at the shrine of motherhood.

The very act of suspicion implies that one has been professionally duped, and to have been duped by criminal wrong doing enrages most medical people. Even to have been duped into not recognizing Munchausen psychosis is destructive of professional self-esteem, particularly insofar as the outcome is an entirely erroneous diagnosis, and injurious forms of treatment, in pediatrics, for the child. Under such a circumstance, it is difficult to maintain professional impartiality and nonjudgmentalism, both of which are imperative to the scientific understanding, control, and above all prevention of maternal Munchausen psychosis, and the protection of the child from abuse and abusive neglect.

20

The Paleodigms of Sacrifice

When baby monkeys annoy their mothers, they are likely to get rebuffed with a slap or a bite. Thus, in terms of phylogenetic heritage, the possibility that a mother might injure her young has extremely ancient evolutionary origins. Responding to an annoyance with a swift slap or bite is not, however, the same as being a consistently abusive and neglectful mother. The type of consistent and prolonged abuse and neglect associated with the syndrome of abuse dwarfism may be regarded as phylogenetically derived, but it has roots also in the less remote past of human paleohistory. More precisely it has its roots in the paleodigms (Money, 1989) of paleohistory.

The newly coined, newly defined term, paleodigm, came into being to fill a conceptual void and provide a name for the irrational absurdity of what it is that a mother is doing when she becomes a cruel tyrant who presides over the systematic sacrifice and possible death of her child. Paleodigm is defined and explained as follows (Money, 1989, p.15).

Paleodigm: an ancient example or model of a concept, explanation, instruction, idea or notion, preserved in the folk wisdom of mottos, maxims, proverbs, superstitions, incantations, rhymes, songs, fables, myths, parables, revered writings, sacred books, dramas, and visual emblems [from Greek, *paleo,* ancient + *deigma,* example, from *deiknynai,* to show]. Paleodigmatics is the organized body of knowledge and theory of paleodigms.

Folk wisdom penetrates the idiom of our everyday language. We assimilate its paleodigmatic meanings, make them our own, and then, though failing to recognize what we are doing, may put them to our own use.

Take for example, the paleodigm of a child being sacrificed by a parent. It is found in the Biblical story of Abraham sacrificing Isaac, in which the sacrifice is discontinued before being consummated in death. It is found also in the very basis of the Christian religion (John 3:16), insofar as God the father so loved the world that he gave his only begotten son to die on the cross, so that sinners might believe and not perish, but have everlasting life. It is symbolized in the crosses that Christians carry on gold chains, even around their necks.

The paleodigm of salvation by sacrifice is of ancient, almost certainly pre-Biblical origin. Geographically, it is widely diffused. In Greek mythology it appeared as the story of Andromeda, daughter of the Ethiopian king, Cepheus, and Cassiopea. She was rescued by Perseus from the rock where she had been chained as a sacrifice to the sea monster from whom the people sought deliverance.

Some of the modern day stand-ins for Abraham and Cepheus and Cassiopea do progressively sacrifice their child and ultimately terminate its life. Other are suspected or confronted before the sacrifice is completed, and while the child is still alive. They are then uncannily resourceful at camouflaging what they are doing, and explaining away the evidence, no matter how convincingly it implicates them.

That is why they themselves are said to have Munchausen's syndrome by proxy, when the history of sacrifice, not yet completed, is finally authenticated.

The manifestations of sacrificial abuse that are encountered in the syndrome of abuse dwarfism fall into five categories, namely, violent brutality, torture, coercion, and constraint; exposure to extremes of temperature, silence, darkness, and dampness; solitary confinement; deprivation of nourishment, fluid, hygiene, physical exercise, sensory stimulation, and learning; and insulting and accusatory threatening, screaming, shouting, and yelling.

Sacrifice, according to its paleodigm, does not typically include sexual coercion or brutality. Correspondingly sexual abuse, although present in a small proportion of cases, is not a prominent feature of sacrificial abuse in the syndrome of abuse dwarfism. When there is a history of sexual abuse, it may have occurred, if not in the home of abuse, then in the foster home in which the child was relocated.

Paleodigmatically, sacrifice is performed as an atonement for sin. The sin to be atoned for is that of the person offering up the sacrifice. In the syndrome of abuse dwarfism, this person is, if not invariably, then almost invariably the mother. Her sin may, however, be not only unspoken, but an unspeakable monster in her life, held at bay by reiteration of the acts of sacrifice. One cannot simply ask a mother why she is sacrificing her child, and expect a lucid answer. The answer must be decoded and pieced together from information that augments whatever fragmentary data the mother, herself, is able to disclose explicitly.

An example of such piecing together pertains to the case of the boy presented in Chapter 7. It was formulated as follows (Money, 1989, pp.17-18).

I first deciphered the quasi-religious principle of sacrifice camouflaged in Munchausen's syndrome by proxy in connection with the case of the boy of sixteen who had the physique age, mental age, and social age of a child of eight.

The story of abuse could be told by the boy himself and confirmed by relatives, but they could not explain why it had happened. The information from which an explanation could be deduced was gradually produced by relatives, over a period of months. The parents themselves were in prison. They also had no reasonable explanation. As pieced together, the biography of a child abuser belonged chiefly to the mother, with the father being one of mostly passive collusion.

The mother was, in fact, his stepmother. His natal mother and her paramour, his father of conception, had died in an auto crash when he was a baby. He was around three years old when his deceased mother's husband, his legal father, remarried. The new wife had had four children of her own. The oldest, a daughter, had been born out of wedlock when the mother was a teenager. The next three were children of her first marriage. These three, but not the oldest daughter, were given up for adoption after the marriage failed. At that time the mother had been clinically diagnosed as depressed, but she did not pursue treatment.

In middle teenage, this woman's personality had reputedly undergone a rapid change. From a well-behaved religious girl, she had become a rebellious delinquent. The change followed hospitalization for third-degree burns suffered when her robe had caught fire, apparently accidentally. While she was in the hospital, her grandmother, devoutly religious, prepared her for final absolution in anticipation of the last rites, by disclosing to her the secret of her birth. Her natal father was not the same man as the father of her siblings, she being their half-sister. She herself had been born out of wedlock. Her grandmother's husband, the man she knew as grandfather, was actually her natal father. Knowing this incest secret traumatized and reshaped her life.

At the time she remarried, she was well thought of in the neighborhood, and had no reputation for cruelty or abusiveness toward children. She quit working to become a full-time homemaker. Her husband needed her not only as a wife, but also as a mother to his four children. He was a hard-working wage earner who could not run his household as a single parent. He had no reputation as a child abuser in his former marriage.

Of the four children, it was the youngest, the three year old boy, who became the sacrificial lamb. Like his stepmother, he also had been born out of wedlock. It was his destiny to become a stand-in for herself, an atonement to redeem her from the original sin of incest in which she had been conceived, and with which she was forever tainted.

Intellectually, of course, she did not make this connection, nor did her husband. The enormity of the deprivation and cruelty she meted out on the child was beyond her own explanation, as well as her husband's. Self-righteously, she justified herself as being generous toward the boy by keeping him at home instead of putting him away in an institution for the hopelessly retarded.

A priori, there is no reason why the ratio of fathers to mothers who sacrifice a child for atonement of sin should not be 1:1 instead of 0:1 or thereabouts. So great is the disparity that one must assume that mother-child bonding, without which a suckling infant dies, is different from that of father-child bonding and, in addition, is more vulnerable to pathology. The pathology of child sacrifice in the syndrome of abuse dwarfism is primarily a pathology of mothering. That formulation, however, fails to account for the secondary, collusional pathology of fathering which remains for the most part an unexplained mystery.

The collusional bond between the two parents is a strong one, so strong that it gives to the marriages the appearance of being ideally conventional and, for the most part, unthreatened by separation or divorce. The husband appears to be more conforming to the dictates of the wife than vice versa.

The possibility that the strength of the collusional bond might be related to a peculiarity of sexual compatibility, as is the case in some marriages, was investigated in three cases by undertaking home visits and talking with both partners, each separately (Money and Werlwas, 1982). Cooperation was minimal, as for example, in repeatedly failing to be at home to keep an appointment.

Information disclosed about sexuoerotical arousal, practices, and frequency was guarded. Couples depicted themselves as conventional, without giving clues as to whether their sex lives were more prudish than kinky (paraphilic) or vice versa.

On the topic of the sex education of their children, these parents depicted themselves as conventional and inactive. There were discrepancies, however. One mother, for instance (see Chapter 18, Kirk Family) at a later date, had the top floor of her house reconstructed as a private apartment in which she installed the oldest teenaged son and his teenaged girlfriend. This arrangement replicated the tyranny with which her own mother had held sway over her. It also had the darkly ominous potential of providing a successor to her sister, her stepson, and two of her own younger sons, in the role of sacrificial abuse.

The convergence of child abuse and sadomasochistic sexuoeroticality is illustrated in the following example of parental collusion, ascertained and reported by a neighbor of the family who had trained as a case worker. It is reproduced from Money and Werlwas (1982, pp.62-63).

I observed Marshall's inability to sit down, and decided to investigate. I found a number of bruises and welts on his behind, lower legs, and his back. He said that his mother got angry at his father, so his father had beaten him up and then left him alone with his younger brother, Clive, to watch a late movie. The father and mother then went to bed. Later, Clive opened up and said they got hit three or four times a week, but only when his father was home at night, not when he did the midnight shift.

I visited the home and became friendly with the parents. It was obvious they had social problems. They had no friends. So I began doing things—volley ball, shopping—with them; and Victor opened up to me. He talked a lot about his experiences as a green beret in Vietnam. I talked about the problems of children. I had better rapport with him than her. She was still threatened by my presence. He was not. I realized it when he said something about having sexual problems with her and that she didn't enjoy having sex with him any more. He said, "It seems as though the only time I ever have sex with her is after I spank the kids."

He was a very active male sexually, and seemed to want and get sex often. He was up front with me about how easily he got women.

The first instance I actually observed was on one of the weekends I stayed over. Marshall wanted to go to a dance for junior teens at the church. His father said no.

I urged him to give in and let the boy go with his friends.

The mother was listening, angry at something. I went outside to warn the child, "When your father says come home by eleven, you come home by eleven, and don't be a jerk, if you don't want to get a beating."

So the child did not come home on time, and in addition he left his coat at the dance. The father beat the kid pretty badly, and then was rewarded later on that night with sex. I heard them doing it.

Another incident happened with Clive. His mother found a cigarette butt in the bathroom. The next thing I hear was her calling Victor upstairs, and it amazed me how he seemed to know, just by the way she called him. He picked up his police belt which he had worn earlier and gave the boy a beating. They had sex again that night. Earlier in the day he had been told, no sex. So when she found the cigarette butt, he capitalized on it. Next morning, he and I took the boys away camping. He and I were in the front of the van, and I said you must have had a good fuck last night, you almost knocked the walls down; and he said, "Sure did." In the seven days we were away, he never once took a strap to the boys.

The girl, the youngest, got hit only once that I know of. His wife went crazy, and threw glasses at him in the kitchen, because he hit the girl. If anyone would hit the girl, she would do it, she said, not him.

Maureen herself had been an abused child. She had been made a ward of the state at age 10. She lived with her parents and four sisters, but all decisions about punishments or denials were made by a probation officer. At 17 she married Victor and left home. Then her youngest sister was abused.

Her story about the boys' beatings was that she realized that Victor was very cruel to the children and she didn't know how to stop it. She thought that if she gave him sex, he would be less cruel to the children, but she really didn't enjoy having sex with him. But the way it actually went was that he got sex only when he did beat the kids. He told me some things about Vietnam, about torturing and killing people, whole families, to get confessions about the Viet Cong and about sexually exploiting early teenaged girls.

Eventually, with judicious maneuvering, both parents were obliged to take up psychotherapy, and to be under surveillance to prevent further child-beating. Their initial resistance yielded to approval. They reported change and an improved sense of well-being, and the mother in particular was enthusiastic about the benefits of therapy.

21

Lovemaps

A lovemap is analogous to a native language. It exists synchronously in the brain and the mind as a functioning entity. It is formally defined as a developmental representation or template depicting the idealized lover, the idealized love affair, and the idealized program of sexuo-erotical activity with that lover, projected in imagery and ideation, or in actual performance (Money, 1986, 1988).

Lovemaps are classifiable as normophilic, hypophilic, hyperphilic, or paraphilic. Normophilic might be defined as conforming to the statistical norm, except that no statistics have ever been collected. By default, therefore, normophilic means conforming to an ideological norm. What is ideal in sex, and hence ideal in the lovemap, varies historically and transculturally; and for the most part is imposed by those with more power on those with less. Thus there are no absolute dividing lines between normophilic and hypophilic (unsufficient) or hyperphilic (excessive) sexuoeroticality, nor between normophilic and paraphilic (altered) sexuoeroticality.

Paraphilic sexuoeroticality is known on the street as kinky or deviant sex, and in psychoanalysis and the criminal justice system

171

as perverted. The formal definition of paraphilia is as follows (Money, 1988, p.216).

> **Paraphilia:** a condition occurring in men and women of being compulsively responsive to and obligatively dependent on an unusual and personally or socially unacceptable stimulus or scene, which may be experienced perceptually or ideationally and imagistically, as in fantasy or dream, and which is prerequisite to initiation and maintenance of sexuoerotical arousal and the facilitation or attainment of orgasm (from Greek, *para-*, altered, + *philia*, love).

Growth and development of the lovemap is quantitively estimated as years of sexuoerotical age. Even though the criterion standards for each year of age have not yet been established, extremes of precocity or immaturity are recognizable. Sexuoerotical age is a component of social age, and it may or may not be concordant with the other components. Likewise, it may or may not be concordant with statural age (height age, weight age, and bone age), nor with intellectual age.

The societal ban on juvenile and adolescent sexological research is responsible for the data on lovemap development in children, with or without a history of abuse and neglect, being fortuitous rather than systematic. Money et al. (1990) published a study, the only one of its kind on "Paraphilic and other sexological anomalies as a sequel to the syndrome of child-abuse (psychosocial) dwarfism." It is a report of a followup of sixteen children into young adulthood, ranging in age from 18 to 30 years. From among fifty cases first referred in childhood, these sixteen qualified for inclusion in the young adult study on the criteria of not having been lost to followup, and of being located within commuting distance of the hospital. Thus there was no bias toward the inclusion of sexuoerotical anomalies. The sixteen patients were evaluated on the criteria of heterosexual, bisexual, and homosexual; and on the criteria of normophilic, hypo-

Table I. Statistical Characteristics of the 16 Patients

Code & Sex	d.o.b.	Ethnic	Age First Seen	Age Last Seen	Age Rescue	Age Puberty	Marital	Children
B63Sf	09/63	W	02-04	23	03-10	N	S	0
D64Mm	12/64	W	05-04	23	04-01	N	S	0
G60Wm	01/60	W	03-09	27	03-09	E	S	0
H54Rm	12/54	W	03-04	27	17-05	L	M	1f
H55Rm	11/55	W	03-11	22	10-00	L	S	1m
I63Tm	01/63	W	03-09	24	06-08	E	2M	2f
K53Jm	06/53	W	16-01	30	16-00	L	S	0
M64Km	05/64	W	05-07	24	05-11	L	M	0
P62Mm	10/62	W	06-10	24	02-10	N	S	0
R53Am	12/53	W	11-06	18	11-06	N	S	0
S67Pf	08/67	W	09-00	20	08-10	E	S	0
S58Rm	09/58	W	06-11	24	07-04	N	M	2m
S68Jf	01/68	W	15-02	20	09-00	E	S	1f
S67Tf	06/67	W	03-05	21	07-00	N	S	0
W65Lf	07/65	W	03-10	20	01-10	E	M	2f
W58Vf	09/58	B	04-01	22	06-11	N	S	1*

Legend:

W; B = White; Black
E; N; L = Early; Normal; Late
S; M = Single; Married
f; m = female; male
* = Early abortion

philic, hyperphilic, and paraphilic. Table I lists various statistics that characterize the sample.

Ratings were based on the content of sexuoerotical imagery, ideation and practice. The findings included: no cases of homosexual orientation, one (Case I63Tm) of bisexual orientation (coexistent with a rating for paraphilia) and fifteen cases of heterosexual orientation. In the philia categories, the numbers of cases were: normophilia, 5; hypophilia, 5; hyperphilia, 1; and paraphilia, 5. In each case, the categorization was augmented with supporting data. They are here reproduced in extenso.

Normophilic Rating (N=5)

In 2 of the 5 instances of a normophilic rating (D64Mm and S58Rm) there had been a prolonged postpubertal phase in which the rating had been hypophilic before it became normophilic. There was no correspondinging postpubertal hypophilic phase associated with ratings of hyperphilia or paraphilia.

Of the 5 normophilic ratings, 3 might not have held up, had there been a more recently available update in their respective histories. The other 2 normophilic ratings were based on recent and detailed interviews. In both cases, the period of continuous abuse had been interrupted by age 7, after which each boy had been, for the most part, reared in a benign, nonabusing environment.

In the case of S58Rm, there had been no known untoward sexual incidents in childhood, and sexual learning had been monitored by PRU staff members. At age 27, he returned with his wife. They gave an unblemished account of family life with two young sons, and of a sex life that satisfied them. Three years later, however, while divorce was still pending, he returned with his new lady friend. She talked about her future plans as a musician, and as a dominatrix engaged in training her husband-to-be as a slave in sexual games of bondage and discipline. Although he was reverting quite clearly to the role of self-arranged victim and martyr, the extent to which sexuoerotic masochism would be included was not yet clear. In the meantime, therefore, he was rated as normophilic.

In the case of M64Km, there was one report of an untoward sexual incident in late prepuberty, namely "actual sex play" with sisters and a stepsister which so inflamed the stepfather that the boy was put again in foster care. At age 24, it was literally and dramatically a case of love at first sight when he and his wife first saw each other. He spoke of their sex life with exuberant hyperbole. It includes magnificent copulatory reconciliations as the culmination of outrageous feuding that neither of them can forestall. The present rating of normophilic may or may not be sustained.

Data retrieved from the juvenile sexual history in cases with other than normophilic ratings are given in the sections on hypophilic, hyperphilic, and paraphilic ratings that follow. Each section opens with a general statement. Then follow the synopses of cases. Each synopsis begins with the taxonomic classification of the lovemap that the case exemplifies, is followed by developmental data pertaining to the sexological history, and concludes with a conceptual formulation. Each case has the same identifying code symbol as in Table I.

Hypophilic rating (N=5)

Patients in this category met the criterion of being handicapped in sexuoerotic, lover-lover pairbonding. Only 3 of the 5 had experienced sexual intercourse. All 3 were women. All 3 had experienced an insufficiency of genital response, and had found intercourse unpleasurable. The 2 who were inexperienced in intercourse were men. One of them was forthright about being inexperienced. The other had had very little, if any experience.

B63Sf

Lovemap: Hypophilic; apathetically inert with respect to age-matched pairbonding; genitalia dysfunctional in coitus, and devoid of pleasurable feeling.

Developmental Data: Rescued from extreme neglect and injurious abuse at age 3:10, the patient was adopted into very good parenting by a paternal uncle and his wife. She eventually became disengaged from the pairbond with her natal mother, but not from the pairbond with her natal father who treated her with callous indifference after he remarried at age 30. All her life, males of that same age have fascinated her—to the exculsion of males of her own age.

Throughout childhood, masturbation was an index of inner distress, for example when her father failed to remember her at Christmas, or on her birthday. It was done absent-mindedly. The foster mother did very well in enabling the girl to establish masturbation as a private practice. She also did excellently in mother-daughter sex education.

As a child, the patient subsequently disclosed, she had dreaded physical examinations. Examination of the genitalia had at the time been for her the equivalent of sex abuse—the probing, and so many people looking. The sequel in the high-school years was that, if a boy asked her for a date, she forewarned him, "I don't put out." She effectively insulated herself from being dated twice. Skin contact with a boy was a turnoff, she said. In her twenties, her rule still was "absolutely nothing below the belt." She had tried intercourse only twice, each time with a different partner at age 18, and found no pleasure in it. At age 21, her self-rating on romantic development was that "it is a little belated."

Formulation: From the time of rescue onward, the child was able to break away from the pairbond with her pathologically child-abusing natal mother, but not from being bonded with her natal father. He was not a child abuser, but a self-preoccupied narcissist, too egocentric to be bothered with the daughter he had abandoned. Had it not been for the exemplary role of the aunt and uncle who became the permanent adoptive parents, the child may well have developed to be not simply "a little belated," in her sexuerotic development, but possibly to be more severely afflicted, perhaps paraphilically as a gerontophile in search of a father-lover.

S67Pf

Lovemap: Hypophilic since prepuberty; yearning for paternal love became fused with flirtatious infatuation with older males; phobic response to tacticle contact, except for hugging; phobic of vaginal penetration; genital intercourse, construed as reenactment of incest-rape enforced in childhood, is dysfunctional and unpleasurable.

Developmental Data: Reluctantly, at age 20, this patient authenticated from "flashbacks for a lot of things" the documented facts of her first 8 years: "Sexually abused, raped, locked in a closet for seven years with nothing in it, it's scary," she said. "No food and no education, beaten, and burned with cigarette lighters and on the stove top. My hands and feet have got scars." The record shows that the genitals also were burned. Her left leg had been forcibly broken and left to heal with the bone not set, so that surgical correction was necessary after she had been rescued.

The child had been conceived illegitimately. The mother had initiated abuse from birth onward, and was joined by her second husband, the child's stepfather. He was the one responsible for sexual abuse. The patient did not give details of what actually happened: "I don't feel like getting upset," she said.

It is typical for the syndrome of child abuse that the patient has a paradise-fantasy of a reconstituted nonabusing family while being concurrently addicted to abuse so as to provoke more of it. This patient did not, from the time of rescue at age 8, maneuver to get a maternal replacement, but she did become extravangantly flirtatious toward older men with an infatuated attachment that endured in one known instance for twelve years and beyond. By the time she was 18, she was gullibly attracted to delinquent older males who exploited her savings and became abusive when she fended them off from attempts at sexual intercourse which she defined as sexual abuse and rape. After her fiancé of two years got drunk at his brother's wedding and forced her to have intercourse, she broke with him permanently.

Although the patient's chronological age was 20 at this time, catchup growth in social and mental age was to a level no higher than that of age 15. The degree of social savoir faire was predominantly naive, with a veneer of sophistication here and there. Thus she was a young lady sophisticated about exposure to AIDS and about taking the pill, but naive about boyfriends and courtship sex. She identified her biggest sexual turn-on as "a romantic candlelight dinner." Her limited experience of sexual intercourse with her fiancé had been genitally dysfunctional and unpleasurable. She did not know the meaning of orgasm, sexual climax, or coming; and claimed not to have masturbated either before or after puberty at age 12.

Formulation: From birth until age 8, the mother's relationship to the child had been one of inflicting torture and suffering. The stepfather's relationship was similar, except that it may have been punctuated with more benign episodes of hugging and genital stimulation. After rescue at age 8, the child's disengagement from the pathological relationship with her bad mother did not lead to a search for a substitute good mother. The disengagement from the bad stepfather, by contrast, did lead to a search for a good father who would not only be paternal but also a romantic lover. Romantic affection and hugging above the belt became dissociated from carnal knowledge below the belt, and they have remained so until young adulthood. The combination of flirtatiousness and phobia of vaginal penetration exposes the patient to the risk of a reenactment of the sexual coercion and abuse experienced in childlhood.

W58Vf

Lovemap: Hypophilic; copulation perfunctory, genitally dysfunctional (vaginospasm), anorgasmic, and devoid of pleasurable feeling.

Developmental Data: When first evaluated at age 7, the child had the size and developmental status of a 3-year-old. She lived in a children's recovery center for 3 years. Despite progressive catchup growth and maturation, she remained consistently disadvantaged in conversational comprehension and expression. At age 12 she was able to say that babies came from "inside the mothers," and that "they have to operate" to get them out. Neither parent gave sexual or other information about the child at home, as they both worked to support their eleven children, among whom the patient was sixth. In addition, the mother drank to excess.

By age 22, the patient was still unable to function independently, was receiving vocational rehabilitation assistance and was seeing a psychiatrist regarding mother-daughter conflict. She said she had had sexual intercourse for the first time at age 20 or 21, and had an abortion on her 22nd birthday. "I had my reason," she said. "People have bad nerves and they hit the child, and bruise them and stuff. I can't be doing all that."

There were two boys with whom she'd had intercourse. "I was just seeing how they were going to treat me, just testing them," she explained. "I didn't feel anything. I didn't tell him that. I told him I did. But I didn't. . . . I don't like it, really. . . . My muscles tighten up. The doctor told me when he put his fingers up there and checking up there [with a speculum] that, if I didn't relax, the thing would have pinched the hell out of me." Her final verdict on having a sex life was: "The way things have been going the past couple of years, it ain't for nothing."

Formulation: Though the IQ elevated to 80 by age 22, at age 7 it had been 42. Thus there were many years when the patient could not give information about her juvenile sexual history, and there was no information from other sources. Thus, the relationship of hypophilia to the history of abuse dwarfism in this case remains unascertained.

K53Jm

Lovemap: Hypophilic; indifferent to romantic and erotic overtures; boyishly inept and awkward as an adult companion; listless disregard for genital stimulation and orgasm.

Developmental Data: Conceived and born out of wedlock, this patient, orphaned at age 3 months, was actually the stepson of the deceased natal mother's surviving husband and his second wife, who became the boy's stepmother when he was 3 years old. He became

the victim of her reign of unsurpassed terror, torture, and deprivation until he was rescued at age 16 (Money, 1977; Money and Wolff,
1974; Money, Annecillo and Hutchson, 1985).

At age 16, he had the dimensions and overall developmental status of an 8-year-old. There was an additional deficit in conversational understanding and expression, and in pronunciation. Sexological information was a hit-and-miss blend of fact and fancy, much
of it retrieved from informal conversations that the boy had with
a male case worker at the recovery center where his rehabilitation
began. He knew that "babies come from a lady," because an aide
at the center was pregnant and had told him, but he did not know
how the baby got out, or in. However, through the keyhole of his
closet-prison at home, he had seen "my mother and my father jumping up and down on the bed. . . the man gets on the lady. . . . I
seen my father's penis, and my mother suck it. That's all." He told
that, on one occasion, his mother had told him to come and watch
her and his father having intercourse, and also to fondle her breasts.
He told also that his mother made him have sex with the dog, a
German shepherd, and got down on his knees to demonstrate. He
and other boys in the center would exchange their knowledge of
curse words. The case worker "caught him in the shower playing
with hisself one time. . . . and sometimes in bed I catch him in the
act, and sometimes in the bed, doing it to the bed, like he would
be asleep. . . . I don't know where he picked up the word, but he
said he had a wet dream." It would have been a non-ejaculatory
dream, even though he was aged 16:6, for the first sign that catchup growth had advanced to the onset of puberty was the appearance of five black pubic hairs which he first noticed at age 16:11.
He noticed also morning erections but not, he said, an inclination
to masturbate.

After age 16:11, return for follow-up was at intervals of 2 years
and longer, as the charity responsible for his care relocated him at
a far distant institution, out of state. At age 21:4 he was released
from a group home to live independently in the community, in his

own apartment. Somatically, the degree of catchup growth and maturation had been adequate, whereas mental and social catchup growth and maturation were not at a level compatible with autonomus existence. However, like the others with a history of the syndrome of abuse dwarfism, this patient was rescued by what, in the language of ethology, would be called the signaling system of appeasement and filial appeal for a response of parental loyalty, nurturance, and protection. Being a male, this patient evoked the response most often from women, whereas the response from men was more often intolerance and repudiation.

There were two women whose protective loyalty extended over a period of years. Each accompanied the patient on different occasions when he had follow-up PRU appointments. Their reports of his sexological history were mutually confirmatory: sexually he was very low key. He did not talk or boast about sex with friends, male or female. His first of three steady relationships began when he was 27. None of them lasted.

When he was seen at age 19:6, he said, comparing himself with other teenagers, "I am interested in the girls, but not all the girls. I'm not girl happy like the others are. I might find somebody nice someday." The tenor of his sex life for the next 10 years and beyond was set in this declaration. When he was 24, he said he'd had a sexual relationship and later confessed it was a lie so that he would appear normal. He was not prudish or lacking in knowledge—just indifferent to sex in general, including masturbation and homosexuality. At age 28:2 he responded to a sex history interview. He spoke of Ruby, with whom he would not have a sexual relationship—"Well, not that way, because I like the girl too much to get involved with her; you know I don't believe in it when it's a person that you love."

He gave a none too convincing account of his having first experienced sexual intercourse with his second steady girlfriend, Jean, at her bidding. She wrote a heartbreak love letter, which he showed, begging to see him again. "I don't really have any feelings for her," he said. "I think she's not ready for real love because she doesn't know the fact of it, because she's been kept in the house so long, because her mother doesn't let her out of the house. . . . She hanged on to me too long, you know. You don't like to be tied down with a person you know."

His third girlfriend, Kitty, met him at the bar and asked him out. She said she liked him and wanted to prove it in bed. "I didn't want to, but she did," he said, and so they did. Afterwards, "I didn't feel happy. It was just fun, you know. It was different." After a month, he broke up: "because I didn't think she was ready for a real relationship, because she was calling other people up at the time."

How often he would like to have sex would depend on whether he was married or not, he said. If he were married, the frequency would be up to his wife. He would never push sex on her. Maybe once or twice a month would be all right.

He was astonished to hear that some males masturbate even more often than once a day, instead of "once every other week or only once in a while." He rated hismelf as not very driven by sex: "I don't think I have to be," he said. "What do you do when a girl comes on strong to you, though," he asked, "to have sex? Like you really don't want to, but she's all over you? To all guys it's all relative, is it?" He was 31 when he posed these questions. There were no such questions applicable to other of his life's activities. Apathy was specific to sexual function alone.

Formulation: After the first 3 months of life, the baby's attachment to his mother was precipitously canceled by her death in an auto accident.At age 3, every other positive attachment he had to family members was destroyed and converted into abuse, as the stepmother blackmailed the sibilngs and her husband into augmenting her own abusive torture and deprivation of the child for the ensuing 13 years.

Since rescue at age 16, two principles of the effects of extreme abuse have been manifest. One is the principle of addiction to abuse, evidenced as the provocation of those in authority, for example the police, to become abusive. The other is the principle of appeasement which evokes loyal parenting and abolishes abusive parenting. In this case, even in childhood, establishment of protective nurturance, as in parent-child pairbonding, preempts the establishment of lover-lover, sexuoerotic pairbonding for which no prototype was experienced in childhood insofar as childhood social isolation and deprivation were extreme. In adulthood, an incipient love affair is experienced as alien. Erotic attachment is liable to undergo the same fate as the attachments of early infancy, so it atrophies before that happens.

R53Am

Lovemap: Hypophilic; diffident about dating; one girlfriend relationship only, discontinued; sporadic masturbatory genital arousal.

Development Data: At the age of 11:7, this patient, the fourth of 13 children, had the dimensions and developmental age of a 5-year-old. After only 15 weeks in a children's rehabilitation center, he had gained 3 inches and 16½ pounds. His mother refused to have him return home, ever, even to visit. No record was kept of the sexological history prior to the onset of puberty at age 15. At age 16, his responses were that he had experienced ejaculation and the masturbation frequency was, maybe, 3–4 times a week. The content of dreams and daydrams might include "meeting girls and wondering if they're still going to go with me," though less often than wondering about ever seeing his family again. By age 18:5, his only dating history had been meeting a girl from a nearby town. They wrote and talked by phone, but he did not consider himself in love with her.

A high school drop-out, he hoped to work and save enough to go far away and find another job, but not before first meeting his natal family. His mother's response to a case-worker's home visit was: "Tell him that you tried to find his family, but they had moved; and that you asked at the school, and they told you the children and parents are well." Thereafter, he did go away and could not be traced for follow-up.

Formulation: He had close bonds of attachment and loyalty to those 2 or 3 of his siblings who also were victims of maternal deprivation and cruelty. The effect of his being rescued was abrupt and permanent separation and loss, no different than if he had been kidnaped, or had been the sole survivor of a catastrophe which wiped out his entire family. One long-term sequel of this trauma was, by inference, a functional deficiency for the establishment of new bonds of attachment and loyalty, including the pairbondedness of lover with lover.

Hyperphilic Rating (N=1)

In the absence of a measure with a fixed zero, there is no fixed unit of measurement with which to determine what constitutes too much or too little, sexuoerotically. At least implicitly, there is always a comparative rating scale involved. Near the midpoint of the scale ratings may justifiably be criticized as being arbitrary, whereas at the extremes, as in the present case, they escape criticism.

W65Lf

Lovemap: Hyperphilic; madonna/whore paradox.

Developmental Data: Sexual data entered the patient's history at age 11, after the onset of puberty. Her foster mother requested help because "with boys, she throws herself around in front of them, swings her hips around, wants to wear bright makeup, and wants to go out with them." The defined purpose of her PRU interview was "to learn about sex." She defined her experiences with boys as "kissing, hand-holding, and bike riding." She had refused her foster brother when he called her into the bedroom and asked her did she "want to fuck," she said.

From the foster family she was transferred to a residential institution for adolescents. In the first 6 months there, from ages 11:10 to 12:4, a social worker reported, she had sex with 4 or 5 different boys; and with her special boyfriend "she had an attachment deeper than he had for her." She was given professional advice about the use of contraceptive cream and condoms.

She was 13 when she became pregnant, after having herself removed the IUD with which she had been fitted, and 14:4 when the baby, a girl, was born and given up for adoption. Among visitors to her friends in the residential care facility where she continued to live, she met a boy of her own age. Two years later he became her boyfriend. Another year later, when she was 17, they went to live in the home of his parents who welcomed them as a cohabiting couple. They married when she was 18.

According to their own account, they were enraptured of one another even to the point of excess. He expected her to answer the phone whenever he called to declare his love several times every working day. The first time each day was from a pay phone at the bus stop where he transferred from one bus route to another on the way to work.

The husband rated their sex life as good, and said that the frequency was usually every night. They reciprocated in oral sex. She claimed to have multiple orgasms, 3 or 4, but "I've always wondered whether she really does," he said. She took the pill as a contraceptive until they decided on a pregnancy. She was 18 when her second child, a girl, was born.

Three months before this granddaughter's third birthday, the baby's grandmother phoned to report that her daughter-in-law (who would be 21 the next day) had recently been depressed, not talking much and, with her husband, drinking again, until she had run away with a new boyfriend. With him, she was back into taking drugs—"speed, coke, and maybe heroin." The daughter-in-law, her husband, and her boyfriend had all three ended up in different institutions for detoxification.

The husband remained psychiatrically hospitalized indefinitely. His mother had custody of the baby. His wife and her new boyfriend had found her natal parents who did not want them. They had no permanent address, and she was "running around with several different men."

Formulation: Hyperphilic repetitiousness and compulsivity is virtually pathognomonic of paraphilia, so what appears as hyperphilia alone may mask an unrecognized paraphilia. In any case, the subjective sexuoerotic data were too sparse to permit any conclusion about paraphilia. It is possible that the case may represent a paraphilic instance of negative to positive: what was earlier in life an erotically negative sexual experience (not entered in this patient's early records) becomes subsequently transformed into being erotically positive, and compulsively repeated. Metaphorically, the interlude in which the lusty harlot gave way to the loving madonna (wife and mother) was terminated by the return of the lusty harlot.

Paraphilic Rating (N=5)

As in the case of hyperphilia, so also in paraphilia there is an ideological issue of who should have the right or the power to define what is normal, sexually, and what variations might and might not be socially tolerated. In the present instance, a rating of paraphilic was not given to minor and playful oddities of sexual interaction. It was restricted to those anomalies of pairbonding expressed in imagery and ideation and/or in performance that were reiteratively obsessional and compelling, and that had in some degree the preemptive power of a monomania, and the unyielding resistance of an encapsulated paranoia to logical reasoning. According to ordinary social criteria they were unorthodox, and they encroached upon the inviolacy of the partner and the ultimate welfare of the self.

There are 40-odd named paraphilias classifiable into seven categories or grand stratagems: sacrificial/expiatory; marauding/preda-

tory; mercantile/venal; fetishistic/talismanic; stigmatic/eligibilic; so-
licitational/allurative; and understudy/subrogational.

In the present study, 2 of the 5 paraphilias are in the sacrificial/
expiatory category. One is paraphilic masochism and the other is sadistic bondage and coercion. Two others are in the stigmatic/eligi-
bilic category and are related to age eligibility (chronophilia), one
being gerontophilia, and one being pedophilia. The fifth is in the
mercantile/venal category, and is bisexually convoluted. The data
on each of these 5 cases, though abridged, are more extensive than
in the preceding 6 cases.

S68Jf

Lovemap: Paraphilic (sacrificial/expiatory type fused with mer-
cantile/venal type); masochism enhanced by the unpredictable dangers and excitements of a constant change of partners in street-corner
prostitution, begun as a career at age 19. Her ideal customer had
a big penis and was, unlike herself, black "because they are more
aggressive." She disliked being paid by those who agreed to "slap
on me," because it didn't seem right to receive payment for the intense pleasure (rated 10 on the "Richter" orgasm scale) that she obtained from being slapped around, independently of genital contact.
Sometimes while being slapped around she would be thinking back
to age seven "to where my mother was standing there in a black
negligee, and my father was screaming at her, calling her a bitch,
and getting ready to hit her, and it looked sexual, to me."

Developmental Data: When she was a girl of 9, her mother
discovered that her husband had another woman. Intoxicated and late
home one night, he fell into a drunken sleep. In a jealous rage his
wife poured gasoline over him and ignited it. The 3 children were
bystanders to the crisis, with fire, police, and ambulance officials, and
the removal of their dying father's body. Subsequently, the patient
"had always felt that his death was because of something I had done."

After the mother's trial and sentencing, the girl was sent to stay with friends. Their 16-year-old son "sexually abused me," she said. "He would come to my room. He'd grab ahold of me, and force me to have intercourse with him. . . . He would slap on my face, punch me on the arm, make me take off all my clothes."

When she was 10, there was a girl, a neighbor, who would force her to undress, and would slap her face and burn her with a cigarette while the boys she brought with her watched. The neighbor girl would also kiss her lips and genitals, and require her to reciprocate. She was required also to watch the neighbor girl petting and kissing the boys. Once "she thought I had peed, and she made me lick it up."

There were twin boys, aged 11, in the foster home where the patient was placed at age 13. They would "kick me, punch me, and slap me all the time." At age 16, when she was living with her grandmother, her older brother would slap her, to which the grandmother's response was that "men are supposed to hit on women when they do something wrong." It was at this age that the girl first realized that pain was erotically arousing to her.

She became pregnant at age 20. Having no accommodation other than a motel room with a pimp, she took up residence in a halfway house where she gave the baby up for adoption. She was referred for a sexological evaluation and counseling and talked forthrightly except to those who responded judgmentally. Her agenda was to resume her career as a prostitute, and by the end of the year to become pregnant again by a black man, so that she would have a baby to love and to love her.

Formulation: The polarity of negative and positive became reversed, in a manner typical for paraphilia, so that the aversiveness of sexual coercion and injurious pain became transformed into the addictiveness of soliciting sadistic slapping and orgasmic masochistic ecstasy.

G60Wm

Lovemap: Paraphilic (sacrificial/expiatory type); late onset sadistic bondage and coericon, age not specific. The long-term effects of parental abuse, neglect, and victimization had left this boy socially ostracized, ridiculed, and unemployable in adulthood. At age 18, he and a 24-year-old woman incapacitated with arthritis met in a home for the handicapped. Both received disability payments and eventually were able to set up a housekeeping and cohabitation relationship in their own apartment. They considered it wrong to use birth control or, being unmarried, to have a baby; so they engaged only in mutual oral sex, except for penovaginal sex on one occasion. By the time he was 26, his partner lost interest in having sex, he said, but he could not explain why. He forced her to participate on two occasion by tying her up. When she screamed, he gagged her. The upshot was that they separated.

People of all ages razzed and tormented him because of social gaffes and mistakes at the street market where he tried to pick up odd jobs. One particular culprit was a girl, aged around 11, who teased him, calling him "mentally retarded, crazy." He thought he "would tie her up, fuck her, and gag her if she screamed." This thought kept returning as a way of "getting back at everybody else who had picked on me." His mother was included. She would have nothing to do with him.

He had no home. He had not known his father. His stepfather had disappeared. His grandmother was the only family member to whom he could talk. He asked her what to do about his obsession with forcing sexual intercourse on a young girl. Having noticed him rub the thigh of her 11-year-old daughter, his grandmother took him at his word, and sent him to the Johns Hopkins emergency room to request the treatment (with Depo-Provera) that she had heard about in a television program on sex offenders. He was seen on an emergency basis in the PRU where he had been followed as a child and, since age 14, had had two follow-up visits. Detailed arrangements for transportation and personal follow-up and treatment notwith-standing, he failed to keep subsequent appointments.

Developmental Data: He was removed from the home of maternal abuse from ages 3 to 9. He was 7 and his brother 6 when his foster mother discovered them in sex play together and with her own daughter. She had them removed to another foster home. At age 11, he chased girls, trying to kiss them. His sisters retaliated by slapping him. At 12, he told about having a crush on a girl and of how much he loved her. He was always thinking about her, and about kissing her, and going to bed with her. He cried when saying that he "played with his privates" and said he was afraid of being punished. He was able to ejaculate. He dreamed about love stories, and of women and men together, kissing, holding each other closely, and often going to bed. He said he did not know what went on next. Until updated in a PRU interview, his formal sex education had been neglected, except that at age 12 he knew his mother was pregnant. In adulthood, he revealed that at age 13 he had been forced by an older male into receiving anal intercourse. He had no erotic attraction towards boys or men.

At age 27, he said that the only time he had had vaginal intercourse was once with his crippled friend. He thought that his interest in coercing sex on a young girl would be curtailed if he could reestablish a stable relationship. Meanwhile, he had never enacted his sadistic fantasy with a young girl.

Formulation: The imagery and ideation of sadistic coercion may have had roots in his own experience of sexual coercion at age 13— and perhaps even earlier in experiences associated with child abuse, the specific memories of which were not retrieved. However, there was a reversal of roles and sex: the coerced boy became the coercing man, and in imagery, the child was female, not male. Stigmatization and rejection in adulthood were precipitating, but not sufficient causes.

S67Tf

Lovemap: Paraphilic (stigmatic/eligibilic type, chronophilic sub-type); nonexclusive gerontophilia; specifically and explicitly a love-smitten attraction to her foster father at first sight, from the time of foster placement at age 10 to the present and, from age 13 onwards, naively and overtly avowed as a fantasy of sexual intercourse.

Developmental Data: The record begins with the child's transfer from the home of origin at age 7 because of extreme growth retardation, but lacks data about neglect and abuse which was not, at that time, professionally known and recognized as a part of the syndrome. Chatting in connection with drawing a house, she said that the father in it "is a mean man; he hits me all the time." Thus, it was construed as paradoxical that the child was "very coquettish with males."

Following diagnosis and the onset of catchup growth, the child returned to her home state and did not return to the clinic until, at age 14, there was a problem of irregularity of the menses which had begun at age 12. She had been in the same foster home since age 10. She was critical and jealous of her foster mother, but idolized her foster father. At age 12, she told him she wanted to marry him some day. When around him, she was unabashedly flirtatious, as she was also with other males, and in particular with one of her doctors. She was 15 when she had the first of a series of crushes on younger males of advanced high school age.

At 17, she allowed that her attachment to her foster father "could be called a love affair," but added that she realized that "he likes me as a daughter." He was quite aware that "she has a very strong feeling of sexual attaction toward me. She would like to make love to me." At age 21, she herself was quite explicit about having erotic dreams involving him, and fantasies of "just being with him, and having sex with him; just spending time with each other." She had a relationship with one young male that included oral sex, exclusively, and with another that excluded all sexual contact. Her one and only experience of penovaginal intromission had been with the boyfriend, aged 24, of her natal mother. Though she considered that she had not consented to intercourse, the two of them had been fully involved in heavy kissing, and she knew that she had been flirting with him very seductively.

Formulation: It is likely that in the unretrievable history of childhood, prior to age 7, there are data pertaining not only to paternal meanness and beating but also to illicit sexual stimulation initiated by an older male. It would at age 7 have been aversive on the criterion of the sexual taboo, even if not on the criterion of coercive threat and harm. According to the paraphilic principle of the reversal of polar opposites, erotic aversion would have become erotic attraction to an older male. It is likely that the full intensity of genital lust might not be able to find expression with a younger, agemated male.

I63Tm

Lovemap: Paraphilic (mercantile/venal type); homosexually an exploiting hustler with superimposed episodic capitulation to males; heterosexually a self-appointed victim with superimposed episodic retaliation.

Developmental Data: The boy's diagnosis at 6:8 was "psychosocial (emotional deprivation) dwarfism" without reference to child abuse. At the time abuse had not yet been recognized as a determining factor. He recalled and first revealed abuse during the course of a psychiatric admission: he had been beaten with the buckle end of a belt and kept locked in a closet, and left, hungry and thirsty, with nothing more than the smell of food cooking downstairs. He dimly recalled an image of what he construed as sexual abuse, namely of his mother lying down naked, with him "on top of her, in back of her knees."

So as to confirm the diagnosis by demonstrating the possibility of catchup growth, the boy was taken into protective custody and placed in an institution run by a religious charity where he lived from age 7 until 14. Except for a notation that he had girlfriends from an early age, the institution kept no records of sexual behavior. Its bureaucracy was extremely defensive and restrictive when, in the course of an IQ outcome study, a member of the PRU attempted to get a sex history from the boy, then aged 13, and to impart some sexual education.

A year later, at age 14, he ran away from the institution—the first episode of dromomania which would be repeated episodically until the present age of 26. At age 19, his retrospective account was that after running away at age 14, and while "living on the street," he was sitting on a park bench when he was picked up by "a crazy old man—He blew me, you know, for $20." He stayed briefly with this man who introduced him to Harry, aged 19 and also gay. Ostensibly, Harry got clearance through the religious charity to take the boy to live with him at his home in a nearby city. There he was introduced to an older man, Ray, who "was into S and M" (sadomasochism). All this happened, the patient said, "when I was 14, and still didn't know." Even though he met men by introduction and had no need to go back to the street, he referred to himself as being, at that time, "a male prostitute."

There was no substantiating validation of his story, and it was obviously not complete insofar as, at age 14, he was placed in an institution for behaviorally disturbed youth from which, on weekends, he was "big-brothered" into the home of a police officer and his wife. That arrangement terminated following two charges of forced entry of the couple's home and robbery while they were away at work.

These two incidents coincided with being not quite 15 years old, with having no money, with having a 13-year-old lover who was pregnant, and not knowing where to turn. He brought his girlfriend to the PRU where the staff initiated the requisite counseling and planning to no avail, as the two of them disappeared instead of keeping the next appointment.

As a consequence of the robberies, the boy spent a month in the state's correctional institution for juveniles, and then was released on probation, permanently separated from his girlfriend and future child. During the ensuing year and a half, his places of residence were transient, and at least once he ran away again, on this occasion out of state. At the age of 16½, he was assigned to a foster family with whom he remained associated for 10 years in a relationship so bizarre that, had he been the only informant, his story would have been dismissed as confabulatory. But it was authenticated, and raised unanswerable questions regarding behind-the-scenes conspiratorial collusion.

The new foster father was wealthy, philanthropic, and influential in local politics. In the community, it was known that he had once been charged and acquitted in a case involving adolescent male sexual attraction, which, it was widely understood had not abated. The patient discovered that his role was, in effect, to be an adolescent replacement for a predecessor, now a young adult man, who had been with the family since age 15, and had been legally adopted. This young man perceived his new foster brother as a rival—not for his adopted father's sexual attention in which he had no further interest, but for his share of the inheritance. The threat of disinheritance became a crisis when, with the acquiescence if not the connivance of her father, the foster father's daughter and only child had an affair with the patient. Her father arranged a lavish wedding. Bride and bridegroom were both 17. The rivalry between the older adopted son and the younger, new son-in-law culminated in an ambush and shoot-out staged by the adopted son, in which, by luck, no one was injured.

The bride's father was unstinting in providing financial and material support to his son-in-law and daughter. Like her mother, the young wife knew about, but overlooked, her father's sexual affair with her husband. Their male-male sexual encounters were restricted to mutual masturbation. For the younger man, they were perfunctory and were avoided, except insofar as they could be exploited for money—sometimes as much as a thousand dollars.

A pattern evolved. Once every 3 to 6 months, the patient would experience a mounting degree of agitated distress which he could not explain. Its relief required trading off sex for money. With the money in his wallet, he would run away from home to the striptease bars in the city. He would sit at a bar for hours maudlinly seeking attention and affection without lust, and squandering hundreds of dollars on selected bar girls, provided they would sit and listen to him as if they were a mother, until he had no money left. Then he would make a phone call to his wife and tell her to come and take him home. Alternatively, in suicidal despair, he would ask for help from the staff at the charitable agency where he had been known since childhood. On three occasions, the outcome was psychiatric hospitalization.

Recovery proved always to be followed by a relapse. The cycle repeated itself until the age of 21. By then he had become too much of an adult in physique and appearance to appeal to an ephebophile. Consequently, his former tactic of getting money from his father-in-law to squander on bar girls was no longer effective. Nonetheless, the obsession recurred.

To quiet the state of agitated distress that accompanied the return of the squandering obsession, he obtained money to squander on bar girls by trading sex for money not in person, but through a surrogate, namely his wife. He conscripted her to pick up men as a bar girl, herself, and to charge them for sexual services. She was under a strict injunction to perform only manual or oral sex, however, and never to allow vaginal intromission. When he heard bar-girl gossip that she might be having intercourse with some customers, he became violent and beat her up. Then he was overcome with remorse and could not explain his behavior to himself. The marriage survived this crisis for only a few chaotic months until the wife made a permanent separation and sued for divorce.

Yet once again he sought psychiatric treatment, and yet once again he ran away, out of state, and ostensibly found shelter in the home of two gay men of his acquaintance. Subsequently, in times of crisis, he would make a telephone call to the PRU and request an appointment which he did not keep. In one call he said he was remarried to a woman 14 years his senior. Her special appeal was that "she hugs me as if she were my mother." The dilemma of his sex life was not resolved, however. Recently, once again he ran away and, suicidal, reported to the emergency room of a county hospital.

Formulation: In this case, as is pathognomonic in paraphilia, there was a divergence between the expression of erotic lust, on the one hand, and pairbonded affectionate love, on the other. The affectionate lover-lover pairbond was unattainably equated with the affectionate mother-infant pairbond that, in earliest life, the patient had been deprived of. Thus, the marriage was foredoomed to be deficient in the pairbondedness of affectionate love. Whereas erotic lust was intact, it was by itself alone too exploitative and one-sided, not only in the nonpromiscuous heterosexuality of marriage, but also in the promiscuous homosexual trading of sex as a commodity. In one homosexual serial transaction, the commodity received as payment was, quite literally, a wife.

The genesis of paraphilia in this boy's case may have originated in early-life sexual experiences not retrieved in the written record. It may have been augmented by the sequence of events that ensued from age 14 onward, following the achievement of heterosexual success which was manifested as the pregnancy of the early adolescent girlfriend. These events were: not revealing his girlfriend's pregnancy; breaking and entering so as to have money in order to run away with her; being caught and incarcerated; becoming a runaway again and making money by being picked up as a teenaged male hustler; and being placed in foster care in a family in which the head of the household was a homophilic ephebophile who lavishly provided material wealth.

P62Mm

Lovemap: Paraphilic (stigmatic/eligibilic type; chronophilic sub-type); pedophilia, documented in adolescence but subsequently disavowed.

Developmental Data: When he was 7 years old, 4 years after he had been rescued from parental abuse, this patient's foster parents complained of his sexual behavior and had him removed from their home. Three complaints were briefly noted. He called his foster parents animals, and presumably had been either eavesdropping or spying on their sexual activity. They suspected "his attentions" to their 2-year-old daughter who had stopped talking in the course of 6 weeks and was crying more frequently. They heard him tell people he'd take off all their clothes and cut their wee wee off.

There was no further record of sex-history data until the boy was 13 and already pubertal. The then foster father had observed him "handling himself in the backyard when he thought no one was looking." He said the boy's sex education was from himself, school, and books from church, and that the sex information interview in the PRU had made the boy angry because "he knew it all."

It was not feasible to accept, prima facie, all that the foster parents reported. Foster care was their trade. Over the years, there were always a dozen or more foster children in the house. It is quite likely that the patient was correct when, as an adult, he said that he was not one of their favorites, and that he was excessively subjected to disciplinary deprivation and punishment. He adopted the family name as his own, and lived in the home until he became independent in young adulthood.

Sexual data reappeared in the record when the boy was 16½ and, according to the foster father, wanted to wear the underwear of the younger boys [there were always a dozen or more foster children in the home]. The foster mother said that she had seen the patient fondle the leg of an 8-year-old girl and he had an erection. This girl said he had fondled her genitals on half a dozen occasions while she was in the bathtub, and had fingered her vagina. He might, perhaps, have attempted intercourse. Once he was found in the girl's bedroom with his pants down. He acted as though nothing had happened, but he said he was sorry and would not do it again. He was defensive when brought into the PRU, and protested that he didn't want to talk about it. He dismissed sex-education books, saying, "I don't read none of that trash." About masturbation, he claimed, "I don't do that; never have." He claimed also to have no interest in having a girlfriend, and it was confirmed by his foster parents that he did not have one.

Ten years later, when the incident at age 16½ was alluded to, he became indignant and protested that he had never had sex with younger children. "I love kids," he said, "and I always try to do anything I can to help them, not hurt them. It hurts me when I get the name of child molester." He declared that his sex life was "normal," and that he had several girlfriends, but that "sex don't interest me as much as it should." No further details were forthcoming, and it was obvious that further inquiry would not be tolerated.

The same intolerance applied to inquiry about three arrests and imprisonment. The only information obtained was that he had beat his girlfriend's other boyfriend with a baseball bat; that he was drunk in a barroom and hit a police officer; and that he had been charged with attempted murder. Short and slight of build, he did not have the appearance of being a likely candidate for such charges.

On the day after his follow-up interview at age 26, he made an unexpected phone call asking if he might, while still on vacation from his construction job, bring his girlfriend to meet the PRU staff. An early appointment was scheduled, but it was not kept.

Formulation: There are too many gaps in the data to permit a formulation of paraphilia other than that the sexuoerotic manifestations of adolescence were, by age 16½, pedophilic, and that there has been no clearcut evidence in the ensuing ten years that they have either lessened or increased. Rather, the evidence of adulthood indicates an insufficiency of age-matched, reciprocal pairbondedness, which is compatible with an age-discrepant pedophilic disposition.

Discussion

This report is phenomenological and classificatory. It is not etiological, although, insofar as they are developmental, the findings do disclose the possibility of dynamic relatedness between events at two or more different phases of the lifespan. It is on the basis of divergent developmental histories that some conjectures concerning divergent outcomes can be formulated, as in what follows.

A comparison of cases with a normophilic instead of a hypo-, hyper-, or paraphilic outcome allows a conjecture that a normophilic outcome is contingent on a developmental history in which, despite conditions of deprivation and abuse, the genital organs are exempted (perhaps during a critical phase of lovemap development) from abusive injury, humiliation, or threat, and from coerced sexuoerotic involvement with another person.

A comparison of the three anomalous sexological outcomes with one another allows a conjecture, also tentative, as to the antecedent history of the three outcomes. Thus, in hypophilia, the developmental history is one of a period of abuse with total deprivation of pairbonded attachment. Subsequently, there may or may not be some degree of attachment to the less abusing parent, or to a substitute. Also, subsequently, there is an insufficient degree of catchup growth in social age, including sociosexual age. In adulthood, filial affection usurps the place of erotic affection, and genital sexual intercourse is dysfunctional and not pleasurable.

In hyperphilia, the conjecture is of an antecedent history that is explicitly genital and erotically pleasurable, but threateningly dangerous in its consequences if disclosed or discovered. According to the principle of opponent-process (Solomon, 1980; Money, 1986a) whereby the polarities of negative and positive change places, the negatively dangerous activity becomes positively erotized, and, as in addictive gambling, for example, is performed repetitiously, episodically, and compulsively, irrespective of adverse consequences.

In paraphilia, the conjecture regarding the developmental history of deprivation and abuse is that, regardless of its duration, by the age of eight or perhaps later, the genitals become explicitly involved in anomalous and unorthodox sexual activity that will eventually be represented in the paraphilia. Although the activity is initially aversive, aversion becomes repolarized into attraction, according to the principle of opponent-process. No longer avoided, the activity becomes episodically and addictively repeated. Paraphilias differ in degree of intensity and harmfulness. They exist in imagery and ideation as dreams and fantasies, from which they may be transposed into actual performance. They embody a Jekyll-and-Hyde split between affectionate love and purity (Dr. Jekyll) and dirty, carnal lust (Mr. or Ms. Hyde). Love and lust require different partners—the madonna or the provider for Jekyll,and the whore or playboy for Hyde.

The transition from Jekyll to Hyde is not a voluntary choice, but an altered state of consciousness that operates, like a temporal-lobe epileptic seizure, on its own timetable. Nosologically, it is classified as a paraphilic fugue (Money, 1986a) and belongs in the general category of dissociative disorders. It is related to the dissociative phenomenon known as multiple personality, a pathology recently recognized as a not infrequent outcome of traumatizing abuse in childhood.

In addition to having an interface with epileptiform seizures and dissociative disorders, paraphilic fugue has an interface also with bipolar disorders. There is an intrinsic bipolarity in the duality of two personalities (Jekyll and Hyde) which alternate episodically. The paraphilic interface with the manic-depressive bipolar disorders is more inclusive, however, insofar as in some paraphiles, if not all, bipolarity of mood synchronizes with bipolarity of personality change —from quiescent, plodding, and sex-dormant or tranquil Dr. Jekll, to irritable, hyperkinetic, and sex-agitated or manic Mr. Hyde. In some cases of synchronous bipolarity of sexuality and mood, treatment with lithium carbonate beneficially affects both (Money, unpublished data; Cesnik and Coleman, 1989) when used either alone or together with an antiandrogenic hormone (Money, 1987).

There are sporadic cases in which paraphilia manifests an interface with schizophrenic disorder of the ruminative obsessive type with eidetic paraphilic imagery that verges on hallucination. There are also cases in which ideation in defense of the paraphilia constitutes an idée fixe which is not quite a circumscribed delusion—similar to that seen, for example, in so-called erotomania, also known as Clérambault-Kandinsky syndrome.

In a small number of the 40-odd named paraphilias, such as paraphilic rape, sadistic assault, lust murder, voyeurism, and exhibitionism, the paraphilic act is defined as a crime. It may be indubitably antisocial. A criminal or antisocial act is not nosologically equivalent to a criminal or antisocial personality disorder, however. Nosologically, a paraphilia is not a manifestation of another disorder, shared interfaces, notwithstanding. A paraphilia is a syndrome in its own right.

The foregoing followup data could not have been predicted during the childhood years. They demonstrate the essentiality of long-term followup in order to ascertain the delayed-onset symptoms of the syndrome (as, indeed, of any syndrome) and of its treatment. They demonstrate also that, in some instances, the foster home to which some of the children were transferred exacerbated rather than ameliorated the behavioral sequelae of the syndrome; and that even the best of foster care could not fully undo the damage that had previously been done by neglect and abuse in interfering with healthy development of mind as well as body.

22

Nonjudgmentalism

The syndrome, multifariously named by multifarious authors quoted in the preceding chapters can now, in the final chapter, claim its own name, the Kaspar Hauser syndrome. This name properly recognizes that it is not a syndrome simply of maternal deprivation, but of abusive deprivation, neglect, torture, and tyranny.

There are syndromes that spread catastrophe in the family pedigree by being carried on the human genome. As the cases of Chapter 21 demonstrate, the Kaspar Hauser syndrome also spreads catastrophe in the family pedigree, from one generation to the next, and the next, and the next again, indefinitely, but not on the genome. If there were a science of environmentics, as there is a science of genetics, then it could be said that the Kaspar Hauser syndrome is an environmentic syndrome, and that it spreads catastrophe in the family pedigree environmentically. The prevention of environmentic transmission of catastrophe within the family pedigree equals in importance the prevention of genetic transmission.

In public health, the incubation time for the spread of an epidemic is, for the most part, measured in hours, days, or possibly weeks.

In the Kaspar Hauser syndrome, by contrast, the incubation time is measured in generations. The child diagnosed with the syndrome is the index case, or proband, from whom it may be possible to trace, in retrospect, the environmentic catastrophe that traumatized one or both parents, and even the grandparents. But further back in the pedigree, the retrospective data will almost certainly be lost to today's science. Prospectively, it may be possible to keep track of the offspring of the proband, although the chance of being lost to followup is high. The fact is that medical science is not geared to keeping track of epidemics that spread with very slow velocity, from one generation to the next, unless there is already strong presumptive evidence of genetic transmission. Environmentic transmission has not yet been incorporated into epidemiological theory.

Instead of being conceptualized as a link in a chain of environmentic transmission, the Kaspar Hauser syndrome is, in today's practice, conceptualized as a one-shot transmission by parents whose role as agents of transmission is likely to be construed as criminal instead of pathological, or possibly as both. A crime, by law, requires punishment. Imprisoning or otherwise punishing the parents of a child with the Kaspar Hauser syndrome does not, however, break the chain of transmission. Thus, the epidemic continues unabated. Moreover, public policy formulates no plan of research on how to intervene and stop it. The victims of abuse become, in turn, victimizers who then become the recipients of a second round of abuse.

Victimology is a forensic specialty. Its practitioners serve the law, either overtly, or covertly as undercover agents in the guise of providing health care. It is in the very nature of their practice to pass judgment— to find not a patient, but a perpetrator, and to provide evidence of guilt. Those being judged must beware of self-incrimination. Without the legal protection of confidentiality, they must censor what they say. Deprived of data that are censored, scientific investigation and the advancement of knowledge on the origins of maternal abuse and neglect, paternal collusion, and the etiology, treatment, and outcome of the Kaspar Hauser syndrome are doomed.

Mandatory reporting of child abuse and neglect became legislated at a time when parents rights allowed too much societal indifference to parental brutality and injurious punishment of their children. Physicians were reluctant to report suspected abuse, even with photographic evidence of lacerations, burns, and bruises, and radiographic evidence of bone fractures. In the absence of witnessed or photographed acts of abusive brutality, in court it was not the parents, but the physician who was, in effect, put on trial to prove that the injuries were not accidental, as claimed by the defense. For this very same reason, even today, suspicions of abusive violence and neglect are under-reported in comparisons with suspicions of sexual abuse.

As compared with reports of suspected brutal abuse and neglect, reports of suspected sexual abuse bring immediate action from the child protection authorities. They take over from the physician or other healthcare professional who initiates the action. Even if the suspicion is flimsy or patently contrived, as in some divorce and custody battles, the suspect is arrested without delay. Accusation of child sexual abuse has become so much of an industry that the sexual abuse of children is now a legal and criminological specialty, shut off from impartiality and nonjudgmentalism which are prerequisites of scientific investigation.

The very fact that mandatory reporting exists may, however, be put to effective use in the diagnosis of certain suspected cases of Kaspar Hauser syndrome. These are cases in which the parents view the medical profession as their adversary, intent on taking their child from them and "putting it away" in an institution. They become threatening and litigious. Instead of being incited to manifest further irrationality, they may be kept rational by being told that the medical role is not the judicial role. It is not the doctor's role to blame them for their child's failure to grow, but to find out how to get the child to begin growing again. That will require not putting the child away, but "the real-life test of a good, old-fashioned rest cure." This idiom makes more acceptable the period of separation necessary to establish the diagnosis. It must be accepted, however. Otherwise the doctor would be obliged, by law, to report the parents for criminal neglect. By cooperating on the real-life test, the parents thus enter into a safe position from which to align themselves with the medical profession against a common enemy, namely the child's syndrome. Each parent needs a caseworker, psychotherapist, or pastoral counselor with whom, as trust develops, to reveal the actual history of abuse and neglect and, eventually, to establish ways of circumventing it—even if that might involve long-term separation from the child.

Before patients can develop trust to reveal self-incriminating evidence, professional nonjudgmentalism is a categorical imperative. It is not easily achieved, for in the vocabulary and idiom of the English language is embodied a religious and legal philosophy of extreme antiquity that postulates free will, voluntary choice, and moral responsibility for the entirety of one's own behavior, and hence blameworthiness for wrong doing. This philosophy has its own epistemology and psychology whereby behavior is teleologically explained in terms of motivation. Thus, simply by asking, "Why did you do it?" and expecting an answer that begins with "Because," one surreptitiously, by implication, passes judgment. The nonjudgmental question would be, "How did it happen?" The answer would begin not with the causality contained in a sentence that begins with "Because," but with the pragmatics of a step by step account analogous to a play by play sportscaster's account of a game.

To avoid the pitfalls of motivationistic psychology, I have turned not to the robot-like explanations of stimulus-response behaviorism, but have instead, conceptualized order out of chaos by formulating five universal exigencies of being human. These five exigencies do not cause anything. They are five great galaxies of reasoning. Among them are distributed all the explanations, some already found, many more still sought, regarding causality and human existence, irrespective of which science they are claimed by. These five universal exigencies have been briefly summarized as follows (Money, 1984).

Pairbondage (or Pairbondship)

Pairbondage means being bonded together in pairs, as in the parent-child pairbond, or the pairbond of those who are lovers or breeding partners. In everyday usage, bondage implies servitude or enforced submission. Though pairbondage is defined so as not to exclude this restrictive connotation, it has a larger meaning that encompasses also mutual dependency and cooperation, and affectional attachment. Pairbondage has a twofold phyletic origin in mammals. One is mutual attachment between nursing mother and her feeding baby, without which the young fail to survive. The other is mutual attraction between males and females, and their accommodation to one another in mating, without which a diecious species fails to reproduce itself.

Male-female pairbonding is species specific and individually variable with respect to its duration and the proximity of the pair. In human beings, the two extremes are represented by anonymous donor fertilization versus lifetime allegiance and copulatory fidelity.

Troopbondage (or Troopbondship)

Troopbondage means bondedness together among individuals so that they become members of a family or troop that continues its long-term existence despite the loss or departure of any one member. Human troopbondage has its primate phyletic origin in the fact that members of the troop breed not in unison but asynchronously, with transgenerational overlap, and with age-related interdependency. In newborn mammals, the troopbonding of a baby begins with its pairbonding with its mother as the phyletically ordained minimum unit for its survival and health. After weaning, it is also phyletically ordained for herding and troop-bonding species that isolation from and deprivation of the company of other members of the species or their surrogate replacements is incompatible with health and survival. Nonhuman primate species are, in the majority of instances, troopbonders like ourselves.

Abidance

Abidance means continuing to remain, be sustained, or survive in the same condition or circumstances of living or dwelling. It is a noun formed from the verb, to abide (from the Anglo-Saxon root, *bidan,* to bide). There are three forms of the past participle, abode, abided, and abidden.

In its present usage, abidance means to be sustained in one's ecological niche or dwelling place in inanimate nature in cooperation or competition with others of one's own species, amongst other species of fauna and flora. Abidance has its phyletic origin in the fact that human primates are mammalian omnivores ecologically dependent on air, water, earth, and fire, and on the products of these four, particularly in the form of nourishment, shelter, and clothing, for survival. Human troops or individuals with an impoverished ecological niche that fails to provide sufficient food, water, shelter, and clothing do not survive.

Ycleptance

Yclept is an Elizabethan word, one form of the past participle of to clepe, meaning to name, to call, or to style. Ycleped and cleped are two alternative past participles. Ycleptance means the condition or experience of being classified, branded, labeled, or typecast. It has its phyletic basis in likeness and unlikeness between individual and group attributes. Human beings have named and typecast one another since before recorded time. The terms range from the haphazard infor-mality of nicknames, that recognize personal idiosyncracies, to the highly organized formality of scientific classification of medical diagnoses that prognosticate our futures. The categories of ycleptance are many and diverse: sex, age, family, clan, language, race, region, religion, politics, wealth, occupation, health, physique, looks, temperament, and so on.

We all live typecast under the imprimatur of our fellow beings. We are either stigmatized or idolized by the brand names or labels under which we are yclept. They shape our destinies.

Foredoomance

Doom, in Anglo-Saxon and Middle English usage meant what is laid down, a judgment, or decree. In today's usage it also means destiny or fate, especially if the predicted outcome is adverse, as in being doomed to suffer harm, sickness or death. A foredoom is a doom ordained beforehand. Foredoomance is the collective noun that, as here defined, denotes the condition of being preordained to die, and to being vulnerable to injury, defect, and disease.

Foredoomance has its phyletic origins in the principle of infirmity and the mortality of all life forms. Some individuals are at greater risk than others because of imperfections or errors in their genetic code. Some are at greater risk by reason of exposure to more dangerous places or things. All, however, are exposed to the risk, phyletically ordained, that all life forms, from viruses and bacteria to insects and vertebrates, are subject to being displaced by, and preyed upon, by other life forms.

Foredoomance applies to each one of us at first hand, in a primary way, and also in a derivative way insofar as it applies also to those we know. Their suffering grieves us; their dying is our bereavement.

In the Kaspar Hauser syndrome, questions of causality are associated primarily with pairbondship, its failure, and sequelae. Secondarily, they are associated with ycleptancy, that is, with the typecasting of the person with the syndrome in medicine, in the family, and in society at large.

The typecasting of the original Kaspar Hauser in society at large has been a topic of fascination for chroniclers, scholars, humanists, and literary artists ever since he first appeared at the Haller Gate in Nuremberg in 1828. The literary representation and significance of Kaspar Hauser have undergone transformations with the passage of time. Examples from four distinct genres—the chronicle, poetry, drama, and the novel—are examined in Part III.

PART III

KASPAR HAUSER IN LITERATURE

JOSHUA KENDALL, M.A.

23

Chronicle and Controversy:
Kaspar Hauser and Human Nature

From the day he appeared at Nuremberg's Haller Gate in 1828 (see Chapter 1), Kaspar Hauser created nothing short of a public sensation. Within two years he achieved what would today be called celebrity status. His fame was spread in newspaper articles and books. This first body of writing on Hauser was essentially phenomenological and reportorial. It addressed the interrelated tasks of documenting Hauser's bizarre life and solving the mystery of his birth. It thrived even beyond Hauser's murder in 1833. It was so widely disseminated that Hauser eventually earned the moniker, "das Kind von Europa," the child of Europe. The German literary critic Jochen Hörisch (1979), in a comprehensive compilation of source materials on Hauser's life, reprinted several examples of the early publications. In his own concluding essay, Hörisch (p.269) cites the 1833 edition of the *Brockhaus Conversations-Lexikon der neusten Zeit und Literatur*, which is translated as follows.

There is hardly a town in Germany or a city in the neighboring countries where the name of this orphan and something about his life history is not known. This widespread reputation is a consequence partly of the odd events and crimes that are connected to his person and have been shrouded in darkness and partly of the enthusiastic attention which many excellent men have directed toward him.

Later on in this entry from the *Lexikon*, there is also a reference to the uncertainty of many of the facts about Hauser's life. In particular, it is noted that many widely circulating rumors impeded the search for the truth about his origins.

The authors for whom Hauser's past and present provided an array of interpretive puzzles can be classified as those who empathized with his tragic life, and those who considered him a fraud. The impetus to discredit Hauser stemmed from two sources, the first the age-old reluctance to accept the horror of child abuse, and the second the logistics and political expediency of a cover-up. Those responsible for Hauser's internment clearly had a vested interest in casting doubts on the veracity of his story. Because of their ties to the ruling prince, this group wielded considerable influence. In fact, they controlled the very engines of the press. The authority of the state included the absolute right of censorship. This was the era preceding the unification of Germany in 1871.

The most widely circulating book discrediting Hauser appeared in 1830, *Caspar Hauser, nicht unwahrscheinlich ein Betrüger* (*Kaspar Hauser, not Unlikely a Fraud*), written by the retired Berlin police official Johann Friedrich Karl Merker. Merker had originally published his allegations in the criminology journal of which he was editor, *Beiträge zur Erleichterung des Gelingens der praktischen Polizei* (*Contributions to the Facilitation of the Success of Practical Police Work*). Unlike most of the other authors of this genre, Merker had never met Hauser. He based his conclusions on his interpretation of the reporting of others. Particularly outraged by the fund-raising efforts to support Hauser, led by the Berlin criminologist Julius Edward Hitzig, Merker initiated the effort to discredit Hauser. Lacking any concrete evidence to substantiate his claims, however, he engaged in innuendo. His book is but a series of attempts to spread his suspicions. The following passage (Hörisch, p.221) is typical.

> Should my remarks, however, not be fully refuted, there would thus arise a sufficient reason to subject the foundling and his fairy tales to a more careful scrutiny.

Merker set the stage for the later, more famous Hauser detractors such as Lord Stanhope and Julius Meyer, who spun more elaborate narratives in the debate that ensued after Hauser's murder.

Contravening Merker's character assassination of Hauser, the widely respected judge and legal scholar, Anselm von Feuerbach, rallied to his defense. The president of the appellate court in Ansbach, von Feuerbach met with Hauser as early as 1828 (just six weeks after Hauser's first appearance in Nuremberg) and took a personal interest in his welfare. Von Feuerbach published (1833,1983) his personal account of Hauser's development since his captivity under the title, *Beispiel eines Verbrechens am Seelenleben des Menschens (An Example of a Crime against the Human Soul)*. This book appeared in Boston in translation the following year as *Kaspar Hauser. An account of an individual kept in a dungeon, separated from all communication with the world, from early childhood to about the age of seventeen*. Modelled on Itard's famous case history of Victor of Aveyron written some thirty years earlier, von Feuerbach's book is remarkable in several respects. It retains its status to this day as the most authoritative account of Hauser's socialization. It served as the primary source for Jakob Wasserman's 1908 novel, *Caspar Hauser oder die Trägheit des Herzens (Caspar Hauser or the Indolence of the Heart)*, for Peter Handke's 1967 play, *Kaspar,* and for Werner Herzog's 1974 film, *Jeder für sich und gegen alle (Everyman for himself and God against all)*. Von Feuerbach's book is also a literary chef-d'oeuvre characterized by a concise and artful prose. Resonating throughout is von Feuerbach, the powerful advocate for humanity, rooted firmly in the ideals of the German Enlightenment. Von Feuerbach demonstrates an uncannily modern sensibility vis-à-vis the devastation of traumatic suffering and the human capacity to rebound from such devastation. (Bance, 1974/75)

In his judicial career dating back to the 1790s, von Feuerbach had earned a reputation as *der Wohltäter der Menschheit* (the caretaker of humanity) through his devotion to the law. Working within the intellectual framework of the Enlightenment, von Feuerbach was devoted to the rule of law, both as a just means to punish criminals, but also as a means to protect citizens from the arbitrary use (or abuse) of royal authority. This concern manifests itself in the title of his book on Hauser, namely in the term, *Verbrechen* (crime). Midway through his detailed documentation of Hauser's first days of freedom, von Feuerbach spells out his charges. He accuses those responsible for Hauser's incarceration of *Seelenmord* (soul murder). Von Feuerbach was the first to use this term that has since been borrowed by subsequent authors, both literary and scholarly, to characterize the mental consequences of torture. The psychoanalyst, Leonard Shengold, for example, titled his 1989 clinical and literary study of child abuse *Soul Murder: The Effects of Childhood Abuse and Deprivation.*

In tracing the history of the concept of soul murder, Shengold begins with von Feuerbach, then mentions Henrik Ibsen and August Strindberg before referring to the famous twentieth century case of soul murder, that of Daniel Paul Schreber, whose *Denkwürdigkeiten eines Nervenkranken (Memoirs of My Nervous Illness)* (1903/1955), Freud analyzed (Freud, 1953-1974, vol.12). Using concepts anticipating those used by contemporary writers on child abuse, von Feuerbach (1983, p.53) specifically defined the soul murder of Kaspar Hauser as, "the withdrawal of all means of spiritual development and education, the unnatural holding back of a human soul in a completely irrational, animal-like state." Von Feuerbach's achievement was to accept the murdered soul and empathize with the cruelty it had undergone.

Von Feuerbach's case history describes Hauser's triumph over adversity. Hauser's near-complete assimilation into German society represents for von Feuerbach the power of nurture over nature. He concludes his book by noting that Hauser has been transformed from the abnormal to the normal (p.110):

> His life-style is now entirely the normal one of other men.
> . . . There is no longer anything extraordinary about him other
> than the extraordinariness of his fate and his undescribable
> goodness and affectionate nature.

Von Feuerbach doubtless exaggerates his claims somewhat, for the scars of Hauser's incarceration left their mark on many aspects of his life. As von Feuerbach himself documents, Hauser's development from his disoriented state in 1828 is certainly nothing short of miraculous. At least intellectually, his catch up growth was beginning to put him on a par with his peer group. Even by the end of his life, however, his access to the full range and appropriate expression of human emotions remained limited. His continued inability to understand his own sexuality is a case in point. Hauser did confide in von Feuerbach his plan to marry, but von Feuerbach noted soberly (p.105):

> By a wife he understands nothing else but a female head
> of household or maidservant, whom one keeps, only as long
> as she is necessary, and sends away again, whenever she has
> too often salted the soup, not mended the shirts and cleaned
> the clothes properly and so forth.

Nevertheless, Hauser's adaptation to the prevailing cultural norms, ranging from Protestantism to the German taste for sausages, was for von Feuerbach unambiguous. It represented a triumph, both for

Hauser and German *Kultur*.

According to the general consensus among contemporary scholars (see for example, Tradowsky, 1983), von Feuerbach was also the person responsible for solving the intricate mystery of Hauser's birth. Von Feuerbach's account appeared not in the 1832 case history, but in another 1832 text, not published until 1852, referred to as the *Memoire*. Subtitled *Wer möchte wohl Kaspar Hauser sein?* (*Who might Kaspar Hauser be?*), the *Memoire* was actually a letter von Feuerbach sent to Queen Caroline of Bavaria. Through an impressive chain of deductive reasoning, von Feuerbach concluded that Kaspar Hauser was in fact, as rumors had alleged since 1830, an heir to the throne of Baden, and a nephew of Queen Caroline. Hauser was first kidnapped so as to make way for the accession of his half-brothers to the throne. He was incarcerated and not murdered, because he was deemed more valuable as a potential source of embarrassment to his uncle.

Von Feuerbach's own untimely death signifies the high and perilous stakes faced by the authors of the historical discourse on Hauser. He who aimed to uncover the forces of intrigue and crime in Hauser's past himself became a victim of the same forces. Von Feuerbach died in May of 1833, five months before Hauser's murder. As his descendants claim, he was most likely poisoned as a result of his discoveries about Hauser's past. The *Memoire* also suffered a premature death. Shortly after von Feuerbach's son, the influential philosopher Ludwig Feuerbach, succeeded in publishing it for the first time in 1852, it was withdrawn from circulation. The royal censors were quick to invoke their privilege. As Hermann Pies (1925) pointed out, the debate on Hauser's origins was carried on with passion on both sides well into the 1870s. The central question framing the controversy was the same as during Hauser's lifetime, *Erbprinz oder Betrüger?* ("Heir to the throne or fraud?"). In Pies' assessment, it was only after the major players in Hauser's tragedy were dead that the necessary historical scholarship could proceed, unimpeded by threats and further intrigue.

24

Poetry: The Romanticized Hauser

Whereas efforts to write about Kaspar Hauser during his brief life took the form of chronicles, after his murder, a distinct generic shift in the writing on Hauser took place. Hauser was quickly transformed into a literary figure, who became the subject of lyric poetry. As Jochen Hörisch (1979) noted, "Kaspar Hauser's death clearly set up the possibility of his being poeticized (p. 294)." Poets who took up the subject of Hauser no longer had to concern themselves with accurately representing the details of his life. Freed from the constraints of historical reporting, they were able to focus on those particular aspects of Hauser's life story that were striking to them. Put another way, each poet personalized Hauser's tragic life. Each poet put his personal stamp on the figure of Hauser. Through their portrayals of Hauser, they all address concerns relevant to their own lives and their own particular historical moments. In what follows, three prominent examples of this lyric poetry are reprinted and discussed.

DAS UNGELÖSTE RÄTSEL VON NÜRNBERG
ANONYMOUS (1834)

Könntet Leute, ihr doch sagen,
Wer dieses Kind, wer Kaspar Hauser war!
Laßt euch alle, alle fragen,
Damit die Untat werde offenbar!

Wer war's, die er Mutter nannte?
Wenn dieses Weib man Mutter nennen darf,
Das den eignen Sohn verbannte
Und ihn in den finstern Kerker warf.

Pfingsten traf das arme Wesen
In Nürnberg anno 28 ein,
Trug 'nen Brief, darin zu lesen,
Daß Schwolisché er gerne wollte sein.

Ach, so viel man sich auch mühte
Um den Findling, der so blaß und stumm war,
Traurig blieb er im Gemüte,
Wenn er auch durchaus nicht stumpf und dumm war.

Flüsternd sprach man, daß seine Stirne
Bestimmet sei für einer Krone Zier,
Doch mit teuflischem Gehirne
Macht man aus diesem Knaben fast ein Tier.

Später stach ein ungenannter
Kerl in Ansbach unsern Kaspar tot.
Er starb als ein Unbekannter,
Sein blaues Blut färbt dort die Erde rot.

Hat kein Fürst 'ne Trän' vergossen,
Durch die vielleicht der Menschheit werde klar,
Weshalb denn dieses Blut geflossen,
Und wer der arme Junge wirklich war?

Fünfundzwanzig Silbergroschen
Gern zahl ich dem, der mir den Namen nennt,
Doch andere werden Gold für geben,
Daß keiner jenen Kaspar Hauser kennt.

THE UNSOLVED RIDDLE OF NUREMBERG (TRANS. J. KENDALL, 1991)

My countrymen, if you could only say,
Who this child, who Kaspar Hauser was!
All of you, you must never stop questioning,
So that the crime will be exposed!

Who was it, whom he called mother?
If one can actually call such a woman mother,
Who banished her own son
And threw him into a dark prison.

In the year of '28 the poor creature
Entered Nuremberg on Whitsunday,
Carrying a letter, in which it could be read,
That he wanted to be in the Light Cavalry.

Let everyone be aware
That this foundling, so pale and speechless,
Piteous and full of sadness,
Was by no means dull and stupid.

It was whispered that his head
Was to be decorated by a crown,
But diabolical scheming practically
Transformed this boy into an animal.

Later an unnamed ruffian
Stabbed our Kaspar to death in Ansbach
He died as an unknown man,
His blue blood coloring the earth red.

Has no prince shed a tear
By which it could become clear to humanity
Why this blood had to flow,
And who the poor youth really was?

Twenty five silver pennies would I gladly
Pay to someone to name the name,
But others will surely give gold,
So that no one knows the identity of Kaspar Hauser.

This anonymous ballad from 1834 (Hörisch, p.255) is the earliest poem to revolve around the figure of Kaspar Hauser. The central riddle, alluded to in the title, is the identity of Kaspar Hauser. The poet also addresses the riddle of the identity of Hauser's parents and the riddle of his incarceration and murder. The poetic purpose is political. Through the act of writing, the poet intends to promote the resolution of these riddles and to bring to justice the perpetrators of the evil wrought on Hauser. The poem constitutes more, however, than an attempt to denounce and expose those aristocrats who conspired to torment and kill Hauser. It incorporates Hauser's tragedy into a broad-based critique of the predominant feudal hierarchy.

Hauser's victimization, in short, symbolizes a more widespread political victimization. In the last stanza, the poet mentions that he would gladly pay 25 silver pennies to find out Hauser's true identity. He finally realizes the futility of that hope as he notes that there are others who would part with gold to maintain the Hauser cover-up. In the eyes of the anonymous poet, Kaspar Hauser is a symbol for the large segment of the population subject to the whims and manipulations of a corrupt aristocracy. The poem falls into the tradition of political protest poetry. In this case, the system under attack is an oppressive feudalism.

*   *   *

GASPARD HAUSER CHANTE PAUL VERLAINE (1873)

Je suis venu, calme orphelin,
Riche de mes seuls yeux tranquilles,
Vers les hommes des grandes villes:
Ils ne m'ont pas trouvé malin.

A vingt ans un trouble nouveau,
Sous le nom d'amoureuses flammes,
M'a fait trouver belles les femmes:
Elles ne m'ont pas trouvé beau.

Bien que sans patrie et sans roi,
Et très brave ne l'étant guère,
J'ai voulu mourir à la guerre:
La mort n'a pas voulu de moi.

Suis-je né trop tôt ou trop tard?
Qu'est-ce que je fais en ce monde?
O vous tous, ma peine est profonde:
Priez pour le pauvre Gaspard!

GASPARD HAUSER SINGS
(TRANS. J. MONEY, 1991)

I have come a reticent orphan
Enriched only by my quiescent vision
Of the big city people
Who do not find me very clever.

At age twenty a new disturbance
Kindled by the flames of love
Sent me in search of pretty women
Who did not find me attractive.

Although without country or sovereign
And lacking much bravery,
I have wanted to die in war:
But death has not claimed me.

Was I born too soon or too late?
What am I supposed to do in this world?
Attend everyone to the depth of my pain
And pray for a destitute Gaspard!

The French symbolist poet Paul Verlaine invokes the figure of Hauser in order to portray his own personal oppression at the hands of the authorities over him. Verlaine's poem entitled "Gaspard Hauser chante" appeared in the collection *Sagesse* in 1881 (Hörisch, p.257). Verlaine composed the poem in 1873 from his cell in the prison of Petits-Carnes in Brussels.

Verlaine had been convicted of shooting his lover, the adolescent French poet Arthur Rimbaud. Isolated and scorned by society, Verlaine clearly identified with Hauser. He stresses his connection to Hauser by writing the poem in the first person. Though ostensibly written from the point of view of Hauser, the poem's statements and rhetorical questions pertain to Verlaine himself as well. Some statements even seem to be much more relevant to Verlaine's life experience than to Hauser's. For instance, in the second stanza, the poet comments on his discovery of his passion for women at the age of twenty and his plight of unrequited love. Hauser was unable to consummate sexual relations with women, but the particular resonance of this stanza seems rather to capture Verlaine's discovery of his own homosexuality. The "disturbance" might also refer to the conflict Verlaine experienced as he acknowledged and attempted to pursue his own homoerotic feelings. Under the guise of addressing Hauser's rejection by women, Verlaine poeticizes his own rejection by men, most notably, by Rimbaud.

Verlaine's poem highlights Hauser's status as the ultimate social outcast. Ostracized, Hauser has no place in society. In all the areas in which men typically establish their identity, Hauser suffers nothing but humiliating rejection. Besides being rejected by women, Hauser is ridiculed by "the big city people" as a dummy. As a man "without country or sovereign," Hauser is denied the right to die in combat. Even death rejects him. As is typical of the poets who romanticize Hauser's rejection by society, Verlaine also romanticizes Hauser's incarceration. He presents Hauser as a Rousseauean noble savage who suffers at the hands of civilization represented by the modern city. In such portrayals, Hauser's childhood deprivation is viewed not as a tragedy, but as a liberating experience since it occurs outside of society. Verlaine's poem aroused widespread interest, particularly in Germany. The German poet Stefan George, who met with Verlaine in Paris, published a translation in 1905. George eventually became most famous for being at the center of his own literary movement, the so-called "George-circle." Richard Dehmel, a less well-known contemporary of George, and a poet who wrote in the expressionist vein, also published a translation of Verlaine's poem, in 1906.

✿   ✿   ✿

KASPAR HAUSER LIED
GEORG TRAKL (1913)

Er wahrlich liebte die Sonne, die purpurn den Hügel hinbstieg,
Die Wege des Walds, den singenden Schwarzvogel
Und die Freude des Grüns.

Ernsthaft war sein Wohnen im Schatten des Baums
Und rein sein Antlitz
Gott sprach eine sanfte Flamme zu seinem Herzen:
O Mensch!

Stille fand sein Schritt die Stadt am Abend:
Die dunkle Klage seines Munds:
Ich will ein Reiter werden.

Ihm aber folgte Busch und Tier,
Haus und Dämmergarten weisser Menschen
Und sein Mörder suchte nach ihm.

Frühling und Sommer und schön der Herbst
Des Gerechten, sein leiser Schritt
An den dunklen Zimmern Träumender hin.
Nachts blieb er mit seinem Stern allein;

Sah, daß Schnee fiel in kahles Gezweig
Und im dämmernden Hausflur den Schatten des Mörders.

Silbern sank des Ungebornen Haupt hin.

KASPAR HAUSER SONG
(TRANS. F. SHARP, 1981)

He verily loved the sun which, purple, descended the hill,
The paths of the wood, the singing blackbird
And the joy of the green.

Earnestly he lived in the shadow of the tree
And his countenance was pure.
God spoke a soft flame to his heart:
O Man!

Silently, his step found the city in the evening;
The dark lament from his mouth:
I want to become a rider.

But bush and animal beset him,
House and dusky garden of white men
And his murderer sought him out.

Spring and summer and beautiful the fall
Of the just one, his quiet step
Past the dark rooms of dreaming ones.
Nights he remained with his star alone;

Saw that snow fell into bare branches
And in the hall's half-light, the shadow of the murderer.

Silver, the head of the unborn one sank away.

The Austrian poet Georg Trakl, a central figure in the development
of German Expressionism, also took up the figure of Kaspar Hauser
to symbolize his own feelings of helplessness. Trakl's "Kaspar Hauser
Lied" was written in 1913 (Sharp, pp.125–126), but appeared post-

humously in 1915. Trakl died in 1914, and there is some speculation that he may have committed suicide. Trakl was particularly oppressed by his work as a pharmacist in the German army. In a letter written in 1912, he confided in a friend his frustration with his assignment in Innsbruck and remarked, "Why the vexation? I will, in any case, always be a poor Kaspar Hauser (cited in Sharp, 1981, p. 123)." Trakl had been influenced by the French symbolists and was familiar with both Verlaine's Hauser poem and Stefan George's German translation. But it was Jakob Wassermann's 1908 novel that exerted the most direct influence over Trakl's literary treatment of Hauser. Some of the central images in Trakl's poem have direct antecedents in passages from Wassermann's novel.

Like Verlaine, Trakl romanticizes Hauser's experience of isolation in his cellar. Unlike Verlaine, Trakl makes this notion explicit. He devotes the first two stanzas of "Kaspar Hauser Lied" to detailing Hauser's existence outside of society in a place reminiscent of Eden. The poetic transformation of a childhood of torture and loneliness into one of joy and emancipation is here in its complete form. In this paradise, Hauser enjoys an almost symbiotic relationship with nature. In the first seven lines, Trakl portrays Hauser's communion with both nature and God, who addresses him directly in line seven with the appellation, "O Man!" For Trakl, as for Verlaine, Hauser's peaceful existence is threatened once he enters the city, the symbol of the alienating modern social order. Only when he crosses the threshold into society, does Hauser become conscious of his aloneness. Various dangers lurk, most notably, the man who is to murder him. In the poem's last line, Trakl refers to Hauser at his death as "the unborn one." Trakl seems to suggest that Hauser is unborn because unlike other men, he never found his own place in society. Trakl is attempting to present Hauser's plight as both unique and common at the same time. The fate of humankind, despite each individual's particular niche in the social nexus, is to resemble Hauser in that all must confront unbearable feelings of isolation.

25

Drama:
Kaspar, The Prisoner of Language

In the very year in which Johns Hopkins pediatric endocrinologists published their ground-breaking scientific papers defining what was to become the Kaspar Hauser syndrome (Powell et al., 1967a,b), the Austrian playwright and novelist Peter Handke published a radically new literary reinterpretation of the Hauser story. Handke's play, *Kaspar,* opened to enthusiastic reviews in Frankfurt in 1968, earning a nomination as "play of the year" from *Theater Heute,* the influential German theater journal. The play soon appeared in English translation in a volume entitled *Kaspar and Other Plays* (1969). The well known British director Peter Brook brought *Kaspar* international renown through productions in Paris, London, and New York in the early 1970s. It debuted to critical acclaim in the United States at the Brooklyn Academy of Music in 1973.

Born in Austria in 1942, Handke was profoundly influenced by the most famous German playwright of the twentieth century, Bertolt Brecht. Though he did not share Brecht's orthodox Marxism, Handke

229

also approached the theater with a commitment to political engage-
ment. He sought to carry on Brecht's rebellion against the realist
tradition in Western theater. Like Brecht, Handke wanted to strip
away the illusion of the theater. His aim was to make the audience
conscious that it was witnessing a play, not a representation of
something outside the theater. Thus, his portrayal of Kaspar Hauser,
although based on events in Hauser's life recorded in his autobiographical writing, is not so much an attempt to tell the story of Hauser's
life as an attempt to stage it as a theatrical event. His Hauser is not
the historical figure of the 19th century, but rather a contemporary
version of the historical Hauser.

As a cultural and political radical of the 1960's, Handke incorporates
Brecht's *Verfremdungseffekt* (alienation effect) into his generation's
fight against alienation per se: what it perceived as the oppressive
conditions of Western society in toto. For Handke, the literary artist,
at the core of the abuses of authority and power is a predominant
linguistic violence. In an interview in 1969, Handke outlined his politics,
in general, and the politics of Kaspar, in particular, as follows (Joseph,
1969, pp.38-39).

> In Kaspar no concrete social model is being critiqued (neither
> the capitalist nor the socialist) but rather, by abstracting modes
> of speech from their grammatical foundations, the forms of
> linguistic alienation, here and now, are made clear.

Handke's work of this period is steeped in the social theory of the
1960s in which the concepts of linguistics are applied to an examination
and critique of social relations. Led by such French scholars as the
historian Michel Foucault, the social theorists of this era saw language
as a primary means by which an abhorrent status quo both constituted
and perpetuated itself. Through the figure of Hauser, Handke under-
lines and explores the significant role that language and linguistic
convention perform in the formation or deformation of the individual.
For Handke, modern man and woman are in a perpetual state of

spiritual alienation as a direct result of linguistic alienation. As he puts it (Joseph, p.39):

> The people, who are alienated from their language and their speech, are like the workers who are alienated from their products and also the world.

As opposed to the hard-line Marxists, Handke stresses the primacy not of economic alienation, but of linguistic alienation.

In his depiction of Kaspar, Handke traces the identity and development of an individual through his changing relationship to language. The historical Hauser, whose remarkable linguistic progress is chronicled by von Feuerbach, is transformed by Handke into a generalized stand-in for the modern everyman. Handke is fascinated by Hauser's bizarre use of language. Upon his release from his cellar, it was reported, Hauser could formulate only one sentence: "A schöner Reiter möcht i wörn, wie Vater aner gween is" (I would like to be a gallant horseman like my father) and used it in diverse contexts. He uttered it, regardless of what he was feeling, be it joy, pain or hunger, and went so far as to use it to address inanimate objects.

Handke portrays the process by which Hauser leaves the as-if psychotic cosmos of his all-purpose sentence and enters into the conventionalism of the bourgeois relationship to language. For Handke, the bourgeois socialization of Hauser represents a loss, a tragedy. True, Hauser gains a new understanding of himself and the world around him, but for Handke, his madness is preferable to conventional sanity and the mode of conceptualization he assimilates. Foucault's *Madness and Civilization* (1961/1973) had indelibly marked Handke and others of his literary generation by shattering the traditional understanding of severe psychopathology. From Foucault, Handke assimilates what might be called a romantic posture toward madness. Armed with only one sentence, Hauser is, in Handke's eyes, in a horrifying state of isolation and madness, but at least, it is a state uniquely his own.

Through the character of Kaspar, Handke dramatizes an individual's developmental arrest and his subsequent effort at recovery. As documented in the preceding chapters in this volume, the eponymous Kaspar Hauser syndrome is characterized by developmental retardation in three spheres: the statural, behavioral, and intellectual. Handke's play faithfully captures all three. In the introductory stage directions, Handke explicitly states that Kaspar "must not be big" (p.12). As the play unfolds, Handke draws a direct parallel between Hauser's physical development and his ability to conceptualize the world around him. The Kaspar of the all-purpose sentence at the beginning of the play is physically uncoordinated, has a bizarre gait and is often seen stumbling around, if not actually falling down, on stage. As he learns to speak in conventional sentences, he begin to stand up straight on stage and move about in a relatively free-wheeling way.

The central focus of Handke's dramatized case history is Kaspar's impaired intellectual development and the process by which he attempts to overcome the traumatic residue of his years of incarceration. For the purposes of his dramatic presentation, Handke highlights Kaspar's acquisition of language that, in essence, lays the foundation for his intellectual development. As Kaspar works his way out of his one sentence world, he hones his ability to use concepts. According to the empirical work of developmental psychologists, the foundation for conceptualization and abstraction is usually laid by the second year of life (see, for example Ainsworth 1962b, p.59). Handke dramatically recreates Kaspar Hauser as he regains his dormant symbolic functions. For Handke, the benefits of Kaspar's recovery of his intellectual powers are dubious. In regaining his symbolic functions, Handke's Kaspar merely undergoes another imprisonment. Only now his prison is the one shared by the majority of his fellow men. It is what the late nineteenth century German philosopher Friedrich Nietzsche, called "the prison house of language," when in his famous formulation often cited by contemporary literary critics (Jameson, 1972), he wrote: "We have to cease to think if we refuse to do it in the prison house of language."

In Handke's dramatic world, all socialization is an inherently brutalizing process. The brutality stems not so much from the abuses of particular agents (such as parents, politicians or bureaucrats) as from the impersonal indoctrination into the realm of language. To dramatize this indoctrination, Handke creates a group of characters who never appear on stage, but whose utterances figure prominently in the play. He labels them with the neologism *Einsager*, meaning literally, in-sayers, but with the metaphorical implication of indoctrinators. The entire play revolves around the relationship or conflict among the *Einsager*, Kaspar, and his doubles. In the middle of the play, Handke introduces multiple Kaspars to accentuate Kaspar's automaton-like existence. No other characters appear on stage. The *Einsager* are faced with the task, as Handke puts it, of "bringing Kaspar to speech through speech" (p.15). At the beginning of the play, the audience observes Kaspar as he relates to the entire world with his only utterance transformed by Handke into, "I would like to be somebody just like another once was" (p.13). The *Einsager* attempt to coerce Kaspar into relinquishing his sentence in favor of prevailing linguistic norms. Their effort and its ultimate failure constitute the dramatic tension of Kaspar. Their coercive discourse is so horrifying that, as Handke mentions in a note, "the play might also have been called Speech Torture" (p.7). Yet Handke is not presenting a torture unique to Kaspar. The *Einsager* represent the impersonal, ubiquitous torturers who routinely warp the ability of developing human beings to conceptualize themselves and their world.

Not only is Handke's Kaspar a radical departure from previous literary representations of Kaspar Hauser, but it is also highly innovative in its dramatic form. Handke's text does away with a wide range of dramatic conventions. Handke lists no dramatis personae, and he divides the play not into acts and scenes, but into paragraphs. Furthermore, he writes the dialogue not sequentially, but in two vertical columns, one for Kaspar on the left, and the other, on the right, for the *Einsager*. He organizes the text in this way so as to indicate

that Kaspar and the *Einsager* are sometimes speaking simultaneous-
ly. Handke's text also includes copious stage directions. Some of the
play's sixty-five paragraphs consist of nothing but stage directions.
The formal properties of the play reflect the influence of the French
absurdist tradition. Handke is following in the tradition of Samuel
Beckett and Eugene Ionesco whose plays dramatizing existential
themes first received international renown in the 1950s.

To summarize the dramatic action, the play opens with the
symbolic birth of Kaspar. After his emergence on stage, the audience
witnesses Kaspar as he learns how to control his body and walk.
In stage directions, throughout the play, Handke stresses the
importance of Kaspar's body movements and gesticulations. At first,
he wears a mask so that his face expresses continual astonishment
and perplexity. Later on, after the *Einsager* have bullied him into
accepting their linguistic and conceptual order, his mask expresses
satisfaction. Punctuated by the dimming of the stage lights in the
play's first sixteen paragraphs, which can be said to constitute the
first scene, Kaspar repeatedly utters his all-purpose sentence. As he
utters the sentence with more and more conviction, he proceeds to
knock over all of the stage props that consist of, among other items,
a table, rocking chair and wardrobe. The initial response of the
Einsager is to reassure Kaspar of the usefulness of his sentence. As
Kaspar wreaks havoc on stage, the *Einsager* sarcastically retort: "You
have a sentence, with which you can bring every state of chaos into
order" (pp.18-19).

As Kaspar learns to put together an "orderly sentence," to borrow
Handke's phrase from the notes, he goes about putting the stage in
order. As Kaspar straightens up one stage prop after the other, the
Einsager blurt out a series of generalizations about order that resemble
fascist slogans. For example they declare, "The order of objects creates
all presuppositions for happiness. . . . You were not put on this world
for your pleasure. (p.41). Once Kaspar completes this task (end of
paragraph 25), he sets about perfecting the art of articulating complete
sentences. By the end of paragraph 27 (midway through the play),

Kaspar has mastered the conventional use of language.

The second half of the play portrays Kaspar's rebellion against the *Einsager*. Though he now wears the mask of satisfaction, he gradually begins to express greater and greater dissatisfaction with their mode of conceptual order. The rebellion begins slowly, but culminates in Kaspar's complete rejection both of the *Einsager* and the world itself. At the end of the play, Kaspar and his doubles commit a symbolic suicide as they allow themselves to be knocked over like bowling pins and swept up by the curtain as it closes.

Before this inevitable denouement, Kaspar's relationship with the *Einsager* has gone through a series of seemingly contradictory stages. In order to emancipate himself from them, Kaspar must first go through the stage in which he fully identifies with them and parrots their harsh maxims. The shift occurs when, after barking out a string of statements concerning table manners, Kaspar begins to express doubt. "What have I just said?" Kaspar questions. "If I only knew what it is, that I have just said!" This speech (paragraph 64) signals that Kaspar has begun to perceive the meaninglessness both of conventional language and of life itself under the tyranny of such conventions. By the time of his death, Kaspar is once again removed from the world of conventional language. In the final paragraph, he is reduced to producing grating noises and uttering nonsense words. Like Beckett and Ionesco, Handke aims to highlight the arbitrariness of all linguistic communication. For Handke, the final cacophony that emanates from Kaspar is no more nonsensical than any of his previous utterances.

In his interpretation of the Kaspar Hauser story, Handke redefines von Feuerbach's concept of the soul murder carried out against Kaspar Hauser. For von Feuerbach, Hauser's soul was murdered as a result of his years of physical and emotional isolation. For Handke, the soul murder took place not during Hauser's incarceration, but after. Handke attributes the murder of Hauser's soul precisely to what von Feuerbach characterizes as Hauser's recovery. For Handke, the soul murder of Kaspar Hauser does not represent a unique case of extreme childhood deprivation. Instead soul murder is a universal experience.

It is the sine qua non of the developmental experience of all men and women. Put another way, in his Kaspar Hauser story, Handke attempts to challenge, if not undermine some of the standard conceptual tools of psychology. Inspired by such nineteenth-century humanists as von Feuerbach, modern psychology has attempted to map out a framework in which the paired concepts of trauma and recovery, pathology and normality and even sickness and health stand in a relation of binary opposition to one another. In the world of Kaspar, these distinctions all unravel. Kaspar's recovery is, in fact, traumatic, his return to so-called normality and psychological health a descent into a new form of madness that leads to his death.

Handke employs a particularly striking device to illustrate his desire to turn upside down the conventional understanding of madness. As noted above, at a crucial juncture in the play, Handke introduces multiple Kaspars. These characters look exactly like the original Kaspar. They are essentially copies of him, who appear wearing the same mask. Their appearance comes just at the point where the original Kaspar has made a significant breakthrough. He has just officially entered into a conventional relation to language and the world, as reflected in his newly discovered sense of identity. For the first time, he experiences himself as his own person with his own thoughts and perceptions and the ability to articulate them. Kaspar reveals his new identity by thrice repeating the sentence, "I am who I am" (p.56). In the very next scene, one by one, the multiple Kaspars make their entrance. Their presence highlights the dubious nature of Kaspar's developmental achievement. In Handke's play, Kaspar's new identity does not signal the completion of the therapeutic process of psychic integration. Instead, Kaspar's new identity marks the beginning of a new life as a non-entity. A new splitting takes place. He has been transformed into an automaton. The multiple Kaspars all endure the same, meaningless existence. The new splitting does not entail the fragmenting of an individual's psyche. Rather Kaspar splits into a series of individuals, all of whom are interchangeable.

Handke's play is essentially antipsychological. From the standpoint of some contemporary psychologists, psychic splitting or dissociation is a common defense against traumatic abuse and/or deprivation suffered in childhood (see, for example, Shengold, 1989). For Shengold, traumatic experiences are split off from the child's conscious awareness. The splitting or dissociation, though initially a life-saving mechanism, eventually leads to chronic self-destructive or destructive behavior in adulthood. The psychological cure involves bringing the unbearable experiences into awareness. Ostensibly, this brings about psychic integration. For Handke, such a cure is worse than the disease. Both the integration of a developing individual's psyche and the subsequent integration of the individual into society come at a terrible price. They rob the individual of a meaningful existence as a unique human being. The traumatized Kaspar at the outset of Handke's play is in a state of constant suffering. Yet, precisely because his psyche is, by Handke's criterion, unintegrated, he is a unique individual. This Kaspar has no doubles. There is no one else exactly like him. As opposed to the Kaspar who is cured, the traumatized Kaspar has carved out a meaningful existence for himself. For Handke, as long as Kaspar feels compelled to repeat his wish "to be somebody, just like another once was," he has a powerful reason to go on living. Once his wish is granted, once he becomes a somebody just like everyone else, his life loses its meaning.

26

The Novel: Kaspar Hauser, Symbol of Isolation and Deprivation in The Big City

Like Handke, the contemporary New York novelist Paul Auster revives the Hauser legend to symbolize what he perceives as the coercive process whereby all human beings achieve the status of individuation. However, whereas for Handke the coercive force is the structure of language itself, for Auster it is interpersonal in nature. Auster's scholarship reflects the rediscovery and widespread significance of child abuse that has emerged progressively since the mid 1960s.

Auster incorporates his rewriting of the Kaspar Hauser story into all three novels of his *New York Trilogy* (1990), though only the first novel, *City of Glass*, contains direct allusions to Hauser (p.41):

> Not long after these disclosures, Kaspar was murdered by
> an unknown man with a dagger in a public park. . . . If
> Stillman was the man with the dagger, come back to avenge

239

himself on the boy whose life he had destroyed, Quinn wanted
to be there to stop him.

City of Glass was first published in 1985. The second novel, *Ghosts,*
appeared in 1986, as did the third novel, *The Locked Room.* All
three novels were reissued in one volume under the title *The New
York Trilogy* in 1990.

The protagonist of *City of Glass* is a detective writer, Dan Quinn.
He is familiar with "the cases of cruel and sadistic parents who locked
up their children, chained them to beds, beat them in closets, tortured
them for no reason other than the compulsions of their own madness"
(p.40). Through his protagonist, Auster recognizes such cases as extreme manifestations of pathological aggression. At the same time,
he avoids isolating the victims. In fact, he goes so far as to represent
them as the prototypes of the contemporary or post modern city-
dweller. Much as the French student radicals of 1968 identified with
the helpless victims of Nazi aggression and chanted: "We are all
German Jews," Auster intones: "We are all Kaspar Hausers."

Though themes of deprivation and isolation pervade the entire
New York Trilogy, it is in *City of Glass* that Auster directly reinvokes
the historical and literary Hauser. He turns the phenomenological
reporting of the 1830s upsidedown. Instead of a police-blotter "who-
dun-it," Auster follows in the footsteps of the famous American
detective writers of the 1930s and 1940s, Raymond Chandler and
Dashiell Hammett, and creates a spell binding detective novel about
a modern Kaspar Hauser whose life is in imminent danger. In exacting
clinical detail, Auster portrays the New Yorker Peter Stillman, Jr.
as an abused dwarf with a Hauser-like history. For nine years, from
age three to twelve, Stillman was locked in a bedroom by his father
Professor Peter Stillman, Sr. Peter, Jr. lived his entire childhood in
isolation and darkness. His father even covered up the windows. His
only human interaction consisted of receiving food and occasional
beatings from his father. Like the patients in the studies represented
in this present volume, Peter, Jr. is eventually rescued and placed

in a hospital. After eleven years in the hospital and two years in the care of his former speech therapist, who becomes his wife, Peter, Jr. makes a partial recovery. Nonetheless, the effects of his devastating trauma remain still palpable. As Auster describes him (p.28):

> Peter stood up. Or rather, he began the sad, slow adventure of maneuvering his body out of his chair and working his way to his feet. At each stage there were relapses, crumplings, catapults back, accompanied by fits of immobility, grunts, words, whose meaning Quinn could not decipher.

Auster accurately captures the fracturing of mind and body that typically results from prolonged isolation and abuse.

Auster's suspenseful narrative is set in motion by a threat to Peter, Jr.'s life. His deranged father is about to be released from a Westchester psychiatric hospital and Peter, Jr., who has been receiving threatening letters from his father, fears that his father, upon his release, will murder him. Unlike the historical Hauser who is murdered by an unknown assailant, Peter, Jr. is threatened by the same person, his father, who violently abused him in the first place.

Peter, Jr. decides to hire a detective to protect himself. Through a complex series of misidentifications characteristic of Auster's fiction, Peter, Jr.'s wife, Virginia, hires not a detective, but a down-and-out writer of detective novels, Dan Quinn. Quinn's assignment is to tail the older Stillman as he travels to New York City, presumably to carry out his threats against his son. After months of staking out Peter, Sr. who settles in a flea-bag hotel on the Upper West Side of Manhattan, and after three personal encounters with him, Quinn loses track of his prey. This failure, superimposed on an already abiding sense of isolation and purposelessness, topples Quinn into madness. He first becomes a homeless street person. As he deteriorates, he seeks shelter in a garbage dumpster. He then lives for a time isolated in a dark room in his client's vacated apartment, recreating Peter, Jr.'s early life experience. As the novel ends, though, Quinn is nowhere to be found. He, too, has become a contemporary version of Kaspar Hauser. The Kaspar Hauser legend lives on, Auster is suggesting, in all New Yorkers, in all of us.

Before his lapse into total despair and madness, the thirty-five-year-old Quinn had carved out a successful literary career and possessed a bright future. Like his creator, Paul Auster, Quinn had established himself as a distinguished writer of poetry and criticism and as a translator. Tragedy then befell Quinn in the form of the sudden deaths of his wife and son, whose given name was the same as his future client's, Peter. As a consequence, Quinn became a recluse. His major solace was to lose himself in labyrinthine walks around Manhattan. The threat to his sense of self posed by his personal losses manifests itself in a distinct shift in his mode of literary production. At the outset of Auster's novel, Quinn resigns himself to writing only mystery novels. He adopts the pseudonym of William Wilson. In Auster's fictional world, names always have echoes. As Auster makes clear, Quinn's pen name links him directly to two other William Wilsons: the character in the 1839 Edgar Allan Poe story, "William Wilson" and an actual New York Mets outfielder, William Wilson, of the 1980s, whose exploits Quinn follows closely. Poe's Wilson, haunted by a split personality, inspired Robert Louis Stevenson to create literature's most famous split personality, Dr. Jekyll and Mr. Hyde. As William Wilson, Quinn writes novels chronicling the career of the detective Max Work. Auster describes Quinn's fractured identity (p.7). In the triad of selves that Quinn had become, Wilson serves

> as a kind of ventriloquist, Quinn himself was the dummy, and Work was the animated voice that gave purpose to the enterprise. . . . If Wilson did not exist, he nevertheless was the bridge that allowed Quinn to pass from himself into Work.

This psychic splitting works; it allows Quinn to engage in productive work. Isolated behind his psychological defense mechanism, Quinn resembles both Kaspar Hauser upon his appearance in Nuremberg, and Kaspar Hauser at the beginning of Handke's play. He is little more than a dummy.

Quinn's life history is essentially Kaspar Hauser's in reverse. Hauser's life consists of three phases. He proceeds from prisoner isolated in a cellar to dummy or mere object of curiosity, his initial status upon discovery, to literate bourgeois capable of articulate self-expression. Quinn takes the opposite course. When last seen in Auster's novel, he has completed his descent from literate bourgeois to dummy to prisoner. He has entered his cellar. After giving up his hunt for Peter, Sr., who, as he eventually learns, has committed suicide by jumping off the Brooklyn Bridge, Quinn installs himself in Peter, Jr.'s mysteriously vacated Upper East Side apartment. Naked, he camps out in a six-by-ten room, the darkest in the apartment. Day after day, hour upon hour, he does little else, but lie on his back and stare at the ceiling. Miraculously, each day, upon awakening, he finds a tray of food beside him. As opposed to Hauser's diet of dark bread and water, Quinn is served gourmet meals, including carafes of red wine and linen napkins. Quinn's only activity during this period is to write in his red detective notebook. The longer he endures this isolation, the less he is able to write. Eventually the notebook runs out of pages and Quinn is reduced to a state akin to the complete prelinguistic isolation of Hauser in his cellar.

Though Auster, unlike Handke, does not frame Hauser's tragedy in terms of some abstract mode of linguistic oppression, he still connects his Hauser story to the problem of linguistic representation. Whereas Handke's Hauser is the victim of an abstract force, the *Einsager*, who rob him of any meaningful identity, Auster's Hauser figure, Peter, Jr. is terrorized by a distinct human agent: his father. Yet language still plays a pivotal role in Auster's tale. Peter, Sr., a one-time tenured professor of religion at Columbia, in fact, justifies his cruel abuse of his son by way of his own peculiar ideas about language and linguistic signification. Steeped in Protestant theology, Peter, Sr. develops a notion that equates the fall of man with the fall of language. In particular, he interprets the arbitrariness of the sign, that lack of an essential correspondence between words and things, as a concrete manifestation of human evil. Auster is here inserting into the Peter, Sr.'s theological speculations the central premise of structuralist linguistics that has proven so pivotal to the intellectual formation of his generation. The 1960s and '70s saw, in literary and academic circles, a renewed interest in the often overlooked work of the early-twentieth-century Swiss linguist, Ferdinand de Saussure. For Auster, born in 1947, and his contemporaries, Saussure's structuralist linguistics with its emphasis on the arbitrariness of language posed an endless aesthetic and philosophical problem.

Though Peter, Sr., in his academic career, struggled also with the ramifications of linguistic indeterminacy, he comes out on the opposing side of the debate. Unlike the post-modernists and post-structuralists who revel in this indeterminacy, Stillman viewed it as a threat to be overcome. He interpreted the arbitrariness of language as a moral, if not theological, issue: the arbitrariness of the names that human beings of all cultures assign to things serves as proof of man's baseness.

In order to fully appreciate the warped mind of his prey, Quinn reads Peter, Sr.'s tenure book, *The Garden and the Tower: Early Visions of the New World.* In his book, Peter, Sr. views America as the new Eden, the land where both man and language can be restored. Auster devotes chapter 6 of *The City of Glass* to a detailed summary of this fictional book. He concludes this chapter by detailing Peter, Sr.'s prophecy toward which the book builds (p.59).

> In the year 1960 . . . the new Babel would begin to go up,
> its very shape aspiring toward the heavens, a symbol of the
> resurrection of the human spirit. History would be written
> in reverse. What had fallen would be raised up; what had
> been broken would be made whole.

After reading Stillman's book, Quinn makes an essential connection: 1960 is the very year that Stillman locks up his son. In his determined effort to "save" Peter, Jr. from the twin evils of worldly life and language, Peter, Sr. brutalizes him.

Auster does more than merely transport the Kaspar Hauser story to American soil: he suggests a parallel between the life history of Kaspar Hauser and the history of America. This implied comparison comes to the surface in the chapter where Auster summarizes Stillman's theological treatise. In his treatise, Stillman recounts the diametrically opposing views that the European explorers adopted toward America's indigenous inhabitants. In the sixteenth century, Europeans tended to think of America as an example of a pure state of nature. In their chronicles of this era, to which Stillman devotes the first half of his book, they portrayed native Americans as alternatively prelapsarian innocents or as heathen cannibals, even devils. In the phenomenological reporting of the 1830s, the same categories were often applied to Kaspar Hauser. Having spent the formative years of his childhood outside of the constraints imposed by society, Hauser was falsely regarded by many of his contemporaries as having grown up in a state of nature. In fact, Hauser's isolation from society constituted a perverted form of socialization, marked by brutality and extreme neglect. Likewise, the public perception of Hauser often oscillated between the extremes of noble savage and malicious fraud. Both perspectives precluded recognizing Hauser as human.

In Auster's view, the conceptual framework put forward in Peter Stillman's theological treatise is dangerous because of its utopianism. Stillman seeks to bring about paradise on earth. His aspirations include creating a perfect society, a perfect language and a perfect son. Through his portrayal of Peter, Sr., Auster highlights the vicious underbelly of utopian idealism. It is precisely utopian idealism that lurks behind Peter, Sr.'s cruel treatment of his son. To aspire to something perfect, Auster cautions, is to open the floodgates to endless aggression. Such a messianic vision can legitimate violence toward anything that is thought to stand in its way. In his re-writing of the Kaspar Hauser story, Auster stresses the perils of a blind faith in absolutist moral principles. Only by fully recognizing and accepting the humanity of all human beings, no matter how odd or foreign, can we adopt a morally responsible attitude towards others.

In the second and third volumes of *The New York Trilogy,* entitled respectively *Ghosts* and *The Locked Room,* Auster takes up new self-contained narratives, yet the specter of Kaspar Hauser still looms large. Both of these short novels focus on the literal and figurative isolation of the various New Yorkers who populate them. *Ghosts* revolves around the mutual spying that two Brooklynites engage in from rented rooms across the street from one another. From the vantage point of their respective windows, the main characters, Blue and Black, stare at each other for months on end. Before ending in a brief, violent flurry of action, the novel chronicles Blue's thoughts and actions as he attempts to understand both the purpose of his assignment and Black. The very title of the third volume, *The Locked Room,* captures the defining life experience for Kaspar Hauser as well as for all the contemporary Kaspar Hauser figures portrayed in the pages of Auster's trilogy. In *The Locked Room,* the protagonist is another literary detective, who is faced with the task of tracking down a missing writer, who happens to be a childhood friend. In typical Auster fashion, both the protagonist and his prey end up undergoing long periods of self-inflicted physical and emotional confinement.

Though neither Blue nor Black is a writer, in *Ghosts,* Auster seems to be emphasizing the experience of confinement as central to the identity of all human beings, but especially, the writer. This notion once again turns upside-down the Hauser legend. During his confinement, Hauser himself was denied access to language. Hauser's own work as a writer began only after his rescue when he began to recall his earlier life in the cellar. In one of the few meetings between the two detectives, Black and Blue, Black tells Blue of the life of one of America's most famous nineteenth-century writers, Nathaniel Hawthorne (p.208).

Take Hawthorne, says Black. A good friend of Thoreau and probably the first real writer America ever had. After he graduated from college, he went back to his mother's house in Salem, shut himself up in his room and didn't come out for twelve years.

As Auster sees it, America's "first real writer" needed to confine himself in order to define himself as a writer. For Hauser himself, learning how to write by writing and rewriting his autobiography, provided access to selfhood. By contrast, for Hawthorne as for Dan Quinn in *City of Glass*, the act of writing required the loss of selfhood. As Auster has Black say, "Writing is a solitary business. It takes over your life. In some sense, a writer has no life of his own. Even when he's there, he's not really there" (p.209). In *Ghosts*, as in *City of Glass*, writers are portrayed as of necessity isolated from both the world and themselves. In Ghosts, Auster suggests that writers are condemned not to lives as dummies, as was Dan Quinn, but to lives as ghosts.

The protagonist of *The Locked Room*, the narrator, is a young magazine writer, entrusted with the literary estate of his boyhood friend, Fanshawe, who has disappeared mysteriously and is given up for dead. Though Auster spins an entirely new yarn, in typical Auster fashion, a few of the characters from *City of Glass* actually appear in its pages, including a detective named Quinn who, this time, remains at the periphery of the action. As it turns out, Fanshawe is not dead. He has, in fact, inexplicably withdrawn from society in favor of the cold predictability of a self-enforced isolation. In his life, Fanshawe undergoes two different kinds of isolation experiences: one in which he begins to define himself as a writer and establishes his selfhood, and one that marks his lapse into madness. Before his disappearance, Fanshawe had established himself as a mature writer during a one-year stint of isolation in a French farm house where, as the narrator notes, he is "alone for the whole time, barely seeing anyone, barely even opening his mouth" (p.327). Auster clearly differentiates Fanshawe's literary initiation from Hawthorne's, as referred to in *Ghosts*. For Fanshawe, as opposed to the young Hawthorne, according to the narrator, "solitude became a passageway into the self, an instrument of discovery" (p.327). This is no longer the case after Fanshawe, having shadowed his friend, the novel's narrator, for a while in New York, locks himself in a cabin on a ship and then in the cellar of an old house in Boston.

Fanshawe's isolation at the end of *The Locked Room* resembles Quinn's at the end of *City of Glass:* he sees no one, and a woman, whom he never sees or talks to, comes twice a week to bring him everything he needs from the outside world. From his cellar in Boston, Fanshawe lets it be known that he never goes above the ground floor. He produces a manuscript, which he hands over to the narrator before committing suicide. The manuscript is incomprehensible to the narrator, Fanshawe's best critic. In the final gesture of the novel, he tears up its pages and throws them into the wind. During this second period of self-inflicted isolation, Fanshawe loses both his own psychic and literary self. Even though he has written a novel, he has lost his ability to communicate with others. Like Hauser in his cellar, Fanshawe in his cellar is isolated in his own private linguistic cosmos.

Both the narrator and Fanshawe are obsessed by stories of enforced isolation. The narrator who, although he undergoes his own experience of isolation on a trip to Paris, eventually returns to society, is particularly fascinated by how easily a life, any life, can slip into isolation and despair. For example, he quotes the case of a young writer (not unlike Dan Quinn) who spoke like a Shakespearean actor, only to fall prey to alcoholism and homelessness. He quotes also the example of Goffe and Whalley, two of the judges who help to condemn the British monarch Charles I to death. They immigrate to the New World where they spend the rest of their lives in a cave. The third example is that of the Russian literary critic and philosopher, Mikhail Bakhtin, who has received renewed attention from the current generation of post-structuralist literary critics. During the German invasion of his homeland during World War II, in an act of desperation, Bakhtin smokes the pages of his magnum opus. One by one, he rolls cigarette tobacco into them.

In one of his notebooks, Fanshawe describes in some detail the following scene of confinement experienced by Peter Freuchen, the famous Artic explorer (pp.300-301).

> Alone, his supplies dwindling, he decides to build an igloo and wait out the storm. . . . Because of the particular weather conditions outside, his breath was literally freezing to the walls, and with each breath the walls became that much thicker, the igloo became that much smaller, until eventually there was no room left for his body. . . . For surely, a man cannot live if he does not breathe. But at the same time, he will not live if he does breathe.
>
> Curiously, I do not remember how Freuchen managed to escape his predicament. But needless to say, he did escape.

For Auster, Freuchen's predicament is Hauser's predicament, and also the essential predicament of not only the writer but also of all human beings in contemporary society. In all cases, life forces us to accept almost unbearable conditions. In order to stay alive in his cellar, Kaspar Hauser is forced to become a dummy and retreat into an as-if psychosis where the only thought that he utters is to idealize the one responsible for his torture ("I want to be a gallant horseman like my father"). Similarly, writers like both the famous Nathaniel Hawthorne and the popular mystery writer of Auster's fiction, Dan Quinn, must endure a symbolic death in order to write. In Auster's literary cosmos, life in New York resembles Freuchen's life in the igloo: each breath that the New Yorker takes to affirm his selfhood, in fact, brings him closer to annihilation. Yet Auster avoids lapsing into complete despair. Needless to say, like Freuchen, Hauser did escape. That is, he escaped the cellar only to face a murderous assault five years later. Yes, escape is possible; but it is only temporary, until one is confronted with the next life threatening confinement.

Epilogue

The decoding of Kaspar Hauser's biographical history comes in two versions. The version espoused during his lifetime and subsequently by his supporters in the world of scholarship and literature, is that he did, indeed, experience years of abuse, isolation, and neglect in childhood which left their mark permanently inscribed on his subsequent development. By contrast, the version espoused during his lifetime by his detractors in the criminal justice system is that this experience was all a figment of the imagination, and a hoax.

The juxtaposition of fact against fantasy is an early precursor of an antithesis that would, from 1897 onward, haunt twentieth-century psychiatric theory. It was in 1897 that Freud relinquished his incest and seduction theory in favor of a purely endopsychic theory of the Oedipal fantasy of incest. Kaspar Hauser himself was not destined to play any part in the antithesis in psychiatric theory of history as fact versus history as fantasy. The syndrome that would eventually be named after him was, however, destined to play a role, although unrecognized at the time, by way of the theory of maternal deprivation. As applied in American child psychiatry from 1940 onward, maternal

251

deprivation theory was incompatible with Freud's purely endopsy-chic and Oedipal theory of the origin of psychopathology. Maternal deprivation paved the way for the restoration of seduction theory or, to be more precise, the theory that psychopathology may originate in childhood in traumatically generated external events, rather than in internally generated fantasies.

Freud's early theorizing about the origins of neurosis drew a distinction between actual (*aktuell*) neurosis and psychoneurosis. The German term *aktuell* signifies "present day in origin," not, as in ver-nacular English, "involving acts or actions." In characterizing the *aktuell* neurosis, Freud was influenced by the theory of semen conservation, despite its great antiquity and lack of scientific credentials. After its revival by Tissot (1832/1974) in the eighteenth century, semen-con-servation theory held immense popularity in nineteenth-century medicine until eventually displaced by germ theory after 1870. Loss of semen, the most potent of the vital fluids, according to semen-conservation doctrine, resulted in degeneracy, disease, and death. Freud attributed *aktuell* neurosis to the actual practice of mastur-bation, to which he added coitus interruptus and, for good measure, prolonged continence. Two forms of *aktuell* neurosis were identified nosologically, namely neurasthenia and anxiety neurosis.

In the history of Freudian theory the counterpart of *aktuell* neurosis is psychoneurosis. There are two meanings of psychoneurosis. In one, psychoneurosis is a synonym for neurosis, hysteria, and hysterical neurosis. In the other it is the nosological category that comprises hysterical neurosis and obsessional neurosis. In early usage, psycho-neurosis in the form of hysteria was said, as was *aktuell* neurosis, to be sexually derived, but with a major difference, namely that its sexual origins lay in past events rather than present ones. These origins Freud would eventually attribute to sexual seduction and incest in the earliest years of childhood.

Breuer, with whom Freud collaborated in publishing *Studies in Hysteria* in 1895, recognized the significance of sex in his patients' neuroses. "I do not think I am exaggerating," he wrote, "when I assert that the great majority of severe neuroses in women have their origin in the marriage bed" (Sulloway, 1979, p.78). Breuer wrote circumspectly, but he and Freud both knew that the origins of neurosis in some instances long antedated the marriage bed. This was so in Freud's 1883 case of "the daughter of the innkeeper on the Rax" whom he named Katharina in the *Studies in Hysteria* (Masson, 1985, p.81). This girl, Katharina, had revealed to Freud at the age of thirteen or fourteen, that she had been nocturnally subjected to a sexual violation. In the account published in the 1895 edition of the *Studies*, the male responsible was said to be her uncle. In the 1924 edition, however, Freud admitted that the responsible person was not her uncle, but her father.

In his 1896 paper, "The etiology of hysteria" (reprinted as Appendix B of Masson's book), Freud expounded his newly formulated theory of the origin of hysteria, attributing it to "infantile sexual scenes" and "sexual intercourse" in childhood. The words he used to characterize the sexual scenes were: rape, abuse, seduction, attack, assault, aggression, and trauma. From among these terms, in English translation, seduction was the one by which Freud's new theory would enter history as the "seduction theory" of neurosis. Of it Freud wrote:

All the singular conditions under which the ill-matched pair conduct their love-relations—on the one hand the adult, who cannot escape his share in the mutual dependence necessarily entailed by a sexual relationship, and who is yet armed with complete authority and the right to punish, and can exchange the one role for the other to the uninhibited satisfaction of his moods, and on the other hand the child, who in his helplessness is at the mercy of this arbitrary will, who is prematurely aroused to every kind of sensibility and exposed to every sort of disappointment, and whose performance of the sexual activities assigned to him is often interrupted by his imperfect control of his natural needs—all these grotesque and yet tragic incongruities reveal themselves as stamped upon the later development of the individual and of his neurosis, in countless permanent effects which deserve to be traced in the greatest detail (Masson, pp.283–84).

Freud's satisfaction with his seduction theory was shortlived. It was scarcely a year old when, in the fall of 1897, he abandoned it. Possibly he had been insidiously influenced by the skepticism of fellow professionals of whom he wrote to his friend Wilhelm Fliess as follows.

A lecture on the etiology of hysteria at the Psychiatric Society [April 26, 1896] met with an icy reception from the asses and from Krafft-Ebing the strange comment: It sounds like a scientific fairy tale. And this after one has demonstrated to them a solution to a more than thousand year old problem, a source of the Nile! They can all go to hell (Masson, p.9).

Irrespective of insidious influence, it was nonetheless inherent in the very nature of seduction theory itself that Freud would become dissatisfied. The theory was conceptually too constricting. It failed to account for the development of neurosis in the absence of a history of sexual seduction in childhood. It relied too heavily on the fortuity of a unique event in the ontogeny of individual development, at the expense of universal regularity in the phylogeny of species development. Its causality was extrinsic to the organism, not intrinsic to it.

Freud might have resolved his dissatisfaction with seduction theory by keeping it paired with hysterical neurosis in a taxonomical system in which, as in the case of *aktuell* neurosis, each neurosis would have its own etiology. This would have rescued the long-term manifestations of traumatic experiences in childhood from the professional neglect that became their fate for more than half a century.

The route by which Freud resolved his dissatisfaction with seduction theory was not by taxonomy, but by new theorizing. He postulated that, in psychoneurosis, the revelations of traumatic seduction pertained not to the history of behavioral acts, but to the history of mental imagery and ideation in fantasies and dreams, and in the unconscious. By universalizing this postulate, infantile seduction fantasies became the basis of a comprehensive theory that would be both phylogenetic and endopsychic in origin. In other words, it would be applicable to all members of the human race, and its principles would be consistently of the mind or, in German, of the soul (*Seele*). It would explain mental health as well as pathology. It would become not just the theory of the Oedipus complex, but in its widest scope the entire psychoanalytic theory of all of human nature. Although its constructs would resemble those of the Biblical theory of human nature, it would be, above all, a secular alternative to theological theories of human nature. Being secular, psychoanalytic theory would have immense popularity among the erudite of a scientifically secular twentieth century. It would also invite attack. Its Achilles' heel would prove to be the very seduction theory that it had set aside. Insofar as there was no setting aside of the actualities and the sequelae of seduction and trauma in the lives of some children, seduction theory would eventually be recycled.

It is only with the knowledge of hindsight that one recognizes that the recycling of seduction theory began, without fanfare, in the 1940s. This was the era when child psychiatrists and psychologists working in child guidance began to pay attention to the long-lasting psychopathological sequelae of prolonged maternal deprivation in infancy, also known as institutionalism and hospitalism (see Chapter 4).

Maternal deprivation is a far cry from sexual seduction, but the two share in common their origin in social traumas in childhood, mediated through the senses, not in endopsychic traumas which spontaneously unfold in fantasy. Although maternal deprivation theory did not officially repudiate orthodox psychoanalytic theory, it transformed Freudianism into neo-Freudianism. Developmentally, as for example in object-relations theory, more attention was focused on an infant's transactions with the world of people and things. One legacy of the term, maternal deprivation, was that mothers, and to a lesser degree fathers, became scapegoats for psychopathology in a child's development—witness the term, schizophrenogenic mother, for instance. The resurrection of seduction theory was not, however, a legacy of neo-Freudianism until after the battered child syndrome had been rediscovered in the 1960s.

The distinction between discipline and abuse has historically been a hazy one in Western culture, insofar as the social order is posited on the axiom that punishment produces conformity. Parents, like school teachers, are vested with the power of corporal punishment of children on the presupposition that they have a moral obligation to use that power with discretion. Historically, another axiom, that of the sanctity of the family and of parenthood, has been incompatible with the very idea that parents might abuse their own children. When particularly brutal cases came to public attention, as from time to time they did, an alibi was invoked: the child, like Cinderella, had a cruel stepmother, the mother was mentally retarded, the father was a drunkard, or the parents were foreign immigrants. True Americans did not abuse their children!

A particularly scandalous case of parental child abuse was brought before the New York Supreme Court in 1874 (Williams, 1980), and received much attention in the press. The child, Mary Ellen Wilson, aged nine, was probably an illegitimate offspring of her stepmother's deceased first husband. She was confined to a bedroom, sometimes tied to a bed, inadequately clothed and fed, and forbidden to have playmates or to talk with outsiders. Every day she was beaten or whipped. She bore a scissors wound on the forehead, inflicted for having wrongly held a quilt which her stepmother was cutting. Her rescue was brought about by a church worker who was visiting a terminally ill neighbor. There were no charitable institutions that would intervene. However her case did prompt the intervention of a Mr. Henry Berg. He was a social activist, and a prominent member of the Society for the Prevention of Cruelty to Animals (SPCA). Mary Ellen's case led Mr. Berg to found the Society for the Prevention of Cruelty to Children (SPCC) that same year, 1874.

With the forming of the SPCC, public outrage was appeased. In the absence of legislative action, however, the Mary Ellen Wilson case had no long-term influence on the prevention of child abuse. This practice continued to be a well-hidden item on the public and legal agenda for nearly a century, until 1962. In that year, C. Henry Kempe and associates from Colorado published "The Battered-Child Syndrome" in the Journal of the American Medical Association, with a summary as follows (p.17).

> The battered-child syndrome, a clinical condition in young children who have received serious physical abuse, is a frequent cause of permanent injury or death. The syndrome should be considered in any child exhibiting evidence of fracture of any bone, subdural hematoma, failure to thrive, soft tissue swellings or skin bruising, in any child who dies suddenly, or where the degree and type of injury is at variance with the history given regarding the occurrence of the trauma. Psychiatric factors are probably of prime importance in the pathogenesis of the disorder, but knowledge of these factors is limited. Physicians have a duty and responsibility to the child to require a full evaluation of the problem and to guarantee that no expected repetition of trauma will be permitted to occur.

In the aftermath of this and other publications, state legislatures took up the issue of child abuse and passed laws to set up child protection agencies to investigate reported or suspected cases of child abuse. Although the focus of attention was initially on abusive brutality and neglect, insidiously it shifted to sexual abuse.

A precedent for this shift had been set as early as 1873, a year before the Mary Ellen Wilson trial, by the self-appointed police czar of obscenity and sexual vice, Anthony Comstock. Of him there is suspicious evidence that he was a child abuser who abusively confined and brutalized his own daughter (Money, 1985, p.110). He found

venomous satisfaction in making arrests and suppressing advertise-
ments and publications pertaining to contraception, obscenity, and
female nudity. To this end, he persuaded Congress in 1873 to pass
what we still know as the Comstock Laws. Later that same year,
he persuaded Congress to appoint him as United States Postal Inspector, and to confer on the office unlimited power of censorship
over all incoming and outgoing mail. The Comstock Laws and the
Postal Inspector between them established federal policy and provided
authority for the enforcement of antisexualism in perpetuity. Thus,
a century later, with the power of antisexual enforcement already
in place, child abuse would become focused not on brutality, but
on sexual molestation. Inadvertently, history had set the legal stage
to be ready for the revival of Freud's early seduction theory. The
trauma of sexual molestation in childhood would soon be held responsible for the delayed emergence of mental pathology later in life.

The lid of Pandora's box had been well and truly lifted by the
end of the 1970s. The first wasps escaped in the guise of a reexamination
of Freud's famous analysis of Judge David Paul Schreber's autobiographical *Memoirs of My Nervous Illness* (see Chapter 23). In
1973, Schatzmann published *Soul Murder: Persecution in the Family;*
and in 1974 Niederland published *The Schreber Case: Psychoanalytic
Profile of a Paranoid Personality.* Schatzmann in particular paid attention to Schreber's childhood history of postural harnesses, constraints, and physical training exercises strictly imposed by his physician father. Ostensibly, the child experienced these procedures as
abusive. Their symbolic transformation became the delusions of psychosis in adulthood.

In 1984, Jeffrey Masson, Sanskrit scholar, psychoanalyst, and,
briefly, director of the Freud Archives, let loose his broadside on
psychoanalytic orthodoxy. He accused psychoanalysis of failing to
unmask what he considered Freud's error, if not fraudulence, in
abandoning the seduction theory. In 1985 he published *The Assault
on Truth: Freud's Suppression of the Seduction Theory.* This book
repopularized seduction theory and reinvigorated its new lease on

life. Masson wrote from the vantage point of being the champion of females who had been victims of sexual abuse, especially by their fathers. The sequelae were no longer diagnosed as hysteria or psychoneurosis, but as posttraumatic stress syndrome, borderline personality disorder, dissociative or multiple personality disorder, or possibly depressive disorder. The revival of seduction theory fitted hand in glove with the change in focus from brutality to sexual molestation among child advocates in what rapidly evolved into a new professional specialty of victimology.

Victimology received a certain amount of endorsement from militant extremists of the women's movement. A century earlier, women had fought for emancipation from the domination of men and the right to vote. The price was the renunciation of female sexuality. Otherwise the emancipated woman would have been identified as a harlot. The proper Victorian lady renounced even contraceptive family planning as irreligious and immoral, lest it convey an implication of sexual licentiousness. Then after a hundred years came the time for revenge, and male sexuality was denounced by being equated with power, violence, brutality, rape, child molestation, and pornography.

Misery acquaints a man with strange bedfellows, according to Shakespeare. So also does vengeance. Thus did militant feminists and ultraright religious fundamentalists bed together in their attack on men's sexuality, particularly their attack on men's pornography. The hidden agenda of the ultraright, however, was an attack on women's emancipation itself. The attackers demanded the return of women to their preexistent status quo of vulnerability to the depredations of other men, and subservient dependence on their ultraright fathers or husbands to protect them.

Victimology does not have a theory by which to explain the origin of sex offending in the one branded as perpetrator. In victimological doctrine, according to the terminology currently in vogue, the concept of sexological pathology exists epistemologically only as a social construction. It is, therefore, subject to being both deconstructed and

reconstructed. In victimology, sexual child abuse is socially deconstructed as a phenomenon of pathology, and socially reconstructed
as a phenomenon of criminology. In other words, sexual child abuse
is not viewed as sickness, but as sin.

Speaking of sex offenders in a recent interview, Judith Herman,
a Harvard psychiatrist and specialist in sexual abuse, said: "They are
just evil. They do it because they want to and it gives them satisfaction"
(Hawkins, 1991, p.50). In the course of the past decade or so, a new
trend has emerged whereby child sexual abusers are classified not
only as evil, but also as practitioners of satanism. Attempts to link
sexual child abuse to the rituals of satanic cults, although popular
in the sexual abuse industry, have not been authenticated (Waterhouse,
1990). Nonetheless, they wreak sexological havoc with public opinion
and intensify the frenzied societal hysteria of contemporary antisexualism.

For conservatives of the ultraright, denial of equal rights for women
was only one item in a more comprehensive program of sexual counterreformation mounted in response to the sexual reformation (more
popularly known as the sexual revolution) of the 1960s and 1970s.
Other items on the counterreformation list were, and still are, as follows.

Censorship of explicit sex education materials and courses, including those specifically designed for self-protection against AIDS,
irrespective of age—even for adults, in the case of gay males.

Official orchestration (in U.S. law enforcement there is a "Child
Exploitation and Obscenity Section") of a crusade against pornography
in the electronic and print media based on the ideological dogma
that explicit depiction of genital nudity and erotic behavior exploits
and harms women and children.

Legislative extension, in 1984, of the age of childhood in America
from sixteen to eighteen, and criminalization of the private possession
or showing of genital nudity of anyone below age eighteen in any
medium, including works of art and family snapshots of a nude infant
bathing.

Official entrapments and arrests, on charges of pedophilia, by undercover agents using decoy mail.

Judicial and administrative discrimination against lesbians and gays, for example, for military service, security clearance, and, until very recently, for U.S. entry permits.

Selective restriction of access, at home and abroad, to contraceptive technology, or abortion, to regulate population density or personal family size.

Statistically indiscriminate pathologization of teenaged pregnancy and unwed parenthood.

Statistical inflation of the incidence of survivors, so called, of rape and sexual abuse, by extending the definitions of rape and abuse to include, respectively, acquaintance rape, "bad touch," and even seeing a parent naked.

Fabrication and treatment of a new disease, sexual addiction, the counterpart of nineteenth-century spermatorrhea.

Proscription of selected categories of sex research, officially justified on grounds of illegality (e.g., childhood sexuality), invasion of privacy (e.g., a new Kinsey survey), and personal sensitivity (e.g., clinical sexological histories).

The sexual counterreformation has been aided and abetted by the shift in focus from brutality to sexual molestation as the primary manifestation of child abuse, and by the inclusion of sexual abuse under the jurisdiction of criminology and victimology. Victimologists are caught in the bind of being unable to serve both Hippocrates and Hammurabi at the same time. The outcome is that they become, in effect, undercover agents in the service of the health police. Their first allegiance is to tlf orensic agency that employs them, not to the individual they investigate. They do not use the medical terminology of patients or clients, nor even the courtroom term, accused, but the prison term, perpetrator; and not plaintiff, but victim. Similarly, syndrome and relapse are replaced by offense and recidivism.

Child sexual abuse at its most gruesome includes torture and murder. To classify it only as evil, satanic, or criminal, is the adversarial way of the Inquisition and the criminal code that leads, possibly, to the elimination of individual abusers in the gas chambers or the electric chairs of the prison system. But it does not lead to the elimination of sexual child abuse as an epidemiological problem in public health. It is a problem that exists in each new generation and may well increase exponentially as a function of the adverse side effects of society's antisexual attitude and practices in childhood. Elimination of the problem of sexual child abuse will require a knowledge of the developmental etiology of abuse in those children who grow up to become abusers. Attainment of that knowledge is predicated on medical and scientific sexological research, and on the study of abusiveness as pathology, not solely as crime.

One of the unplanned defects of the perpetrator-victim approach to sexual child abuse is that it lacks checks and balances against false accusations of abuse and their disastrous effects on both the accused and the ostensible victim. A second unplanned defect is the paradox that efforts to warn and protect children against exposure to abuse may backfire and themselves be traumatizing (Krivacska, 1990). A third unplanned effect is that sexological research of childhood and adolescence has been effectively halted. There is no pediatric sexology, and no developmental science of sexual health. Thus ignorance is virtually guaranteed for the foreseeable future—ignorance of how to ensure normal sexological development in childhood, and ignorance of how to prevent sexological abnormality, in adolescence and adulthood.

Pretend for a moment that those who became acquainted with the case of Kaspar Hauser when he made his appearance at the Haller Gate of Nuremberg in 1828 would today be given a reincarnated glimpse into what has been discovered regarding the profound developmental sequelae of childhood abuse and neglect in the Kaspar Hauser syndrome. Perhaps they would be amazed that it took so long, over a century and a half, to discover what is still incomplete. Perhaps also they would be even more amazed at how little effort has been expended on discovering the cause and prevention of parental abuse and neglect of children. They would have recognized, in this respect, that nothing much has changed since 1828. They would be indisputably familiar with the policy that abuse and neglect of children, if not condoned, is classified as a crime, is attributed to voluntary choice, and is treated by punishment, in some cases by imprisonment. They would perhaps be nonplussed by the continued vitality of this policy, despite no evidence whatsoever of its success in preventing or reducing abuse and neglect of children. They would scarcely be able to believe the evidence of their senses that, to maintain this policy in the scientific twentieth century, it has been necessary to have recourse to medieval ideas of satanism and satanic cults of child abusers, especially child sexual abusers. Surely they would also wonder what on earth the twenty-first century might have to offer—more of the same, or something new?

Bibliography

Abramson, L. Facial expressivity in failure to thrive and normal infants: Implications for their capacity to engage in the world. *Merrill-Palmer Quarterly*, 37:159–182, 1991.

Ainsworth, M.D. Deprivation of maternal care: A reassessment of its effects. *Public Health Papers*, no.14, World Health Organization, Geneva, 1962a.

———. Reversible and irreversible effects of maternal deprivation of intellectual development. In *Maternal Deprivation*. New York, Child Welfare League of America, 1962b.

Asher, R. Munchausen's syndrome. *Lancet*, 1:339–41, 1951.

Auster, P. *The New York Trilogy: City of Glass, Ghosts, The Locked Room.* New York, Penguin, 1990.

Bakwin, H. Loneliness in infants. *American Journal of Diseases of Children*, 63:30–40, 1942.

———. Psychologic aspects of pediatrics: Emotional deprivation in infants. *Journal of Pediatrics*, 35:512–521, 1949.

Bakwin, H., and Bakwin, R.M. *Clinical Management of Behavior Disorders in Children*, 2nd ed. Philadelphia, W.B. Saunders, 1960.

Bance, A.F. The Kaspar Hauser legend and its literary survival. *German Life and Letters*, NS 28:199–210, 1974/1975.

266   BIBLIOGRAPHY

Barbero, G.J., and Shaheen, E. Environmental failure to thrive: A clinical view. *Journal of Pediatrics*, 71:639–644, 1967.

Bartolome, J.V., Bartolome, M.B., Daltner, L.A., Evans, C.J., Barchas, J.D., Kuhn, C.M., and Schanberg, S.M. Effects of beta-endorphin on ornithine decarboxylase in tissues of developing rats: A potential role for this endogenous neuropeptide in the modulation of tissue growth. *Life Sciences*, 38:2355–2362, 1986.

Bayley, N. Consistency and variability in the growth of intelligence from birth to eighteen years. *Journal of Genetic Psychology*, 75:165–196, 1949.

———. On the growth of intelligence. *American Psychology*, 10:805–818, 1955.

Bowlby, J. Maternal care and mental health. *Bulletin of the World Health Organization*, 3:355–535, 1951.

———. Some pathological processes engendered by early mother-child separation. In *Problems of Infancy and Childhood: Transactions of the Seventh Conference*, March 23–24, 1953, New York, NY. New York, Josiah Macy, Jr. Foundation, 1954.

Bovard, E.W. The effects of early handling on viability of the albino rat. *The Psychological Review*, 65:257–271, 1958.

Breuer, J., and Freud, S. *Studien über Hysterie.* Leipzig and Vienna, Franz Deuticke, 1895.

Capitanio, M.A., and Kirkpatrick, J.A. Widening of the cranial sutures. A roentgen observation during periods of accelerated growth in patients treated for deprivation dwarfism. *Radiology*, 92:53–59, 1969.

Casler, L. Maternal deprivation: A critical review of the literature. *Monographs for Research in Child Development*, 26:3–64, 1961.

Chapin, H.D. Are institutions for infants necessary? *Journal of the American Medical Association*, 64:175–177, 1915. Facsimile reprinted in *Infant Asylums and Children's Hospitals: Medical Dilemmas and Developments 1850–1920; an Anthology of Sources* (J. Golden, ed.). New York, Garland Publishing, 1989.

Chesney, R.W., and Brusilow, S. Extreme hypernatremia as a presenting sign of child abuse and psychosocial dwarfism. *The Johns Hopkins Medical Journal*, 148:11–13, 1981.

Clarke, A.D.B., and Clark, A.M. Some recent advances in the study of early deprivation. *Child Psychology and Psychiatry*, 1:26–36, 1960.

Coid, J., Allolio, B., and Rees, L.H. Raised plasma metenkephalin in patients who habitually mutilate themselves. *Lancet,* 2:545–546, 1983.

Coleman, R.W., and Provence, S. Environmental retardation (hospitalism) in infants living in families. *Pediatrics,* 19:285–292, 1957.

Cornell, E.L., and Armstrong, C.M. Forms of mental growth patterns revealed by reanalysis of the Harvard Growth Data, *Child Development,* 26:169–204, 1955.

Davis, K. Extreme isolation of a child. *American Journal of Sociology,* 45:554–565, 1940.

———. Final note on a case of extreme isolation. *American Journal of Sociology,* 52:432–437, 1947.

Dearborn, W.F., and Rothney, J.W.M. *Predicting the Child's Development.* Cambridge, MA, Sci-Art Publishers, 1941.

Dennis, W. *Children of the Créche.* New York, Appleton Century-Crofts, Educational Division, Meredith Corporation, 1973.

D'Ercole, A.J., Underwood, L.E., and Van Wyk, J.J. Serum somatomedin-C in hypopituitarism and in other disorders of growth. *Journal of Pediatrics,* 90:375–387, 1977.

Drash, P.W., Greenberg, N.E., and Money, J. Intelligence and personality in four syndromes of dwarfism. In *Human Growth: Body Composition, Cell Growth, Energy, and Intelligence* (D.B. Cheek, ed.). Philadelphia, Lea & Febiger, 1968.

Elmer, E. Failure to thrive: Role of the mother. *Pediatrics,* 25:717–725, 1960.

Engel, G.L., and Reichsman, F. Spontaneously and experimentally induced depression in an infant with a gastric fistula—a contribution to the problem of depression. *Journal of the American Psychoanalytic Association,* 4:428–452, 1956.

Evans, S.L., Reinhart, J.B., and Succop, R.A. Failure to thrive: A study of 45 children and their families. *Journal of the American Academy of Child Psychiatry,* 11:440–457, 1972.

Ferholt, J.B., Rotnem, D.L., Genel, M., Leonard, M., Carey, M., and Hunter, D.E.K. A psychodynamic study of psychosomatic dwarfism: A syndrome of depression, personality disorder, and impaired growth. *Journal of the American Academy of Child Psychiatry,* 24:49–57, 1985.

Feuerbach, A. von. *Kaspar Hauser. An account of an individual kept in a dungeon, separated from all communication with the world, from early childhood to about the age of seventeen* (H.G. Linberg, trans.). Boston, Allen & Ticknor, 1833. (Originally published, 1832).

———. *Kaspar Hauser: Beispiel eines Verbrechens am Seelenleben des Menschen* (P. Tradowsky, ed.). Dornach, Rudolf Geering, 1983.

Field, T.M., Schanberg, S.M., Scafidi, F., Bauer, C.R., Vega Lahr, N., Garcia, R., Nystrom, J., and Kuhn, C.M. Effects of tactile/kinesthetic stimulation on preterm neonates. *Pediatrics,* 77:654–658, 1985.

Fischer, L.K. Hospitalism in six-month-old infants. *American Journal of Orthopsychiatry,* 22:522–533, 1952.

Fischoff, J., Whitten, C.F., and Pettit, M.G. A psychiatric study of mothers of infants with growth failure secondary to maternal deprivation. *Journal of Pediatrics,* 79:209–215, 1971.

Foucault, M. *Madness and Civilization: A History of Insanity in the Age of Reason* (R. Howard, trans.). New York, Vintage Books, 1961/1973.

Freud, A., and Burlingham, D. *Infants Without Families: Reports on the Hampstead Nurseries 1939–1945.* New York, International Universities, 1973.

Freud, S. Psycho-analytic notes on an autobiographical account of a case of paranoia (Dementia Paranoides). In *The Standard Edition of the Complete Psychological Works of Sigmund Freud,* vol. XII, pp.3–79 (J. Strachey, ed.). New York, Basic Books, 1953–1974.

Fried, R., and Mayer, M.F. Socio-emotional factors accounting for growth failure of children living in an institution. *Journal of Pediatrics,* 33:444–456, 1948.

Gesell, A. *Wolf Child and Human Child.* London, Scientific Book Club, 1942.

Gesell, A., and Amatruda, C.S. *Developmental Diagnosis: Normal and Abnormal Child Development. Clinical Methods and Practical Applications.* New York, Paul B. Hoeber (Medical Book Dept. of Harper & Bros.), 1941.

Glaser, K. and Eisenberg, L. Maternal deprivation. *Pediatrics,* 18:626–642, 1956.

Goldfarb, W. Effects of psychological deprivation in infancy and subsequent stimulation. *American Journal of Psychiatry,* 102:18–33, 1945.

Gordon, H. Mental and scholastic tests among children, physically defective, canal boat and gipsy children, and backward children in ordinary elementary schools. *Educational Pamphlets,* No. 44. London, His Majesty's Stationery Office, 1923.

Green, W.H. Psychosocial dwarfism: Psychological and etiological considerations. In *Advances in Clinical Child Psychology,* vol.9 (B.B. Lahey and A.E. Kazdin, eds.). New York, Plenum, 1986.

Guilhaume, A., Benoit, O., Gourmelen, M., and Richardet, J.M. Relationship between sleep stage IV deficit and reversible HGH deficiency in psychosocial dwarfism. *Pediatric Research,* 16:299–303, 1982.

Hamill, P.V.V., Drizd, T.A., Johnson, C.L., Reed, R.B., and Roche, A.F. *NCHS growth curves for children birth–18 years, United States. Vital and health statistics data from the national health survery,* Series 11, Number 165, USPHS National Center for Health Statistics. Washington, U.S. Government Printing Office, 1977.

Handke, P. *Kaspar.* Frankfurt am Main, Suhrkamp, 1967.

———. *Kaspar and Other Plays.* M. Roloff, trans. New York, Farrar, Strauss and Giroux, 1969.

Hawkins, J. Rowers on the River Styx. *Harvard Magazine,* vol.93, no.4, pp.43–52, 1991.

Hern, N. *Peter Handke.* New York, Fredrich Ungar, 1978.

Herrenkohl, E.C., and Herrenkohl, R.C. A comparison of abused children and their nonabused siblings. *Journal of the American Academy of Child Psychiatry,* 18:260–269, 1979.

Hörisch, J., ed. *Ich möchte ein solcher werden wie . . . : Materialien zur Sprachlosigkeit des Kaspar Hauser.* Frankfurt am Main, Suhrkamp, 1979.

Honda, Y., Takahashi, K., Takahashi, S., Azumi, K., Irie, M., Sakuma, M., Tshushima, T., and Shizume, K. Growth hormone secretion during nocturnal sleep in normal subjects. *Journal of Clinical Endocrinology and Metabolism,* 29:20–29, 1969.

Howse, P.M., Rayner, P.H.W., Williams, J.W., Rudd, B.T., Bertrande, P.V., Thompson, C.R.S., and Jones, L.A. Nyctohemeral secretion of growth hormone in normal children of short stature and in children with hypopituitarism and intrauterine growth retardation. *Clinical Endocrinology,* 6:347–359, 1977.

Hufton, I.W., and Oates, R.K. Nonorganic failure to thrive: A long-term follow-up. *Pediatrics,* 59:73–77, 1977.

Hunter, W.M., and Rigal, W.M. Plasma growth hormone in children at night and following a glucose load. (Abstract). *Acta Endocrinologica*, Suppl. 100, 121, 1965.

Itard, J.M.G. *The Wild Boy of Aveyron* (G. Humphrey and M. Humphrey, trans.). Englewood Cliffs, NJ, Prentice-Hall, 1962.

Jameson, F. *The Prison House of Language: A Critical Account of Structuralism and Russian Formalism*. Princeton, NJ, Princeton University Press, 1972.

Jordan, H.W., and Howe, G. De Clérambault syndrome (erotomania): A review and case presentation. *Journal of the National Medical Association*, 72:979–985, 1980.

Joseph, A. *Theater unter vier Augen: Gespräche mit Prominenten*. Berlin, Kiepenheuer und Witsch, 1969.

Jungmann, O. *Kaspar Hauser: Stoff und Problem in ihrer literarischen Gestaltung*. Würzburg, Konrad Triltsch, 1935.

Kanner, L. Autistic disturbance of affective contact. *The Nervous Child*, 2:217–250, 1943.

Kehoe, P., and Blass, E.M. Behaviorally functional opioid systems in infant rats: II. Evidence for pharmacological, physiological, and psychological mediation of pain and stress. *Behavioral Neuroscience*, 100:624–630, 1986.

Kelly, D.D., ed. *Stress-Induced Analgesia*. Annals of the New York Academy of Sciences, vol. 467. New York, The New York Academy of Sciences, 1986.

Kempe, C.H., Silverman, F.N., Steele, B.F., Droegemueller, W., and Silver, H.K. The battered-child syndrome. *Journal of the American Medical Association*, 181:17–24, 1962.

King, J.M., and Taitz, L.S. Catch up growth following abuse. *Archives of Disease in Childhood*, 60:1152–1154, 1985.

Krieger, I. Food restriction as a form of child abuse in ten cases of psychosocial deprivation dwarfism. *Clinical Pediatrics*, 13:127–133, 1974.

Krieger, I., and Mellinger, R.C. Pituitary function in the deprivation syndrome. *Journal of Pediatrics*, 79:216–225, 1971.

Krivacska, J.J. *Designing Child Sexual Abuse Prevention Programs: Current Approaches and a Proposal for the Prevention, Reduction and Identification of Sexual Misuse*. Springfield, IL, Charles C Thomas Publisher, 1990.

Lane, H. *The Wild Boy of Aveyron*. Cambridge, MA, Harvard University Press, 1976.

Leonard, M.F., Rhymes, J.P., and Solnit, A.J. Failure to thrive in infants: A family problem. *American Journal of Diseases of Children,* 111:600–612, 1966.

Lewis, V.G., Money, J., and Bobrow, N.A. Idiopathic pubertal delay beyond age fifteen: Psychologic study of twelve boys. *Adolescence,* 12:1–11, 1977.

Levy, D.M. *Maternal Overprotection.* New York, Columbia University Press, 1943.

Levy, D.M. Maternal overprotection and rejection. *Archives of Neurology and Psychiatry,* 25:886–889, 1931.

———. Primary affect hunger. *American Journal of Psychiatry,* 94:643–653, 1937.

———. *New Fields in Psychiatry.* New York, W.W. Norton, 1947.

Lowrey, L.G. Personality distortion and early institutional care. *American Journal of Orthopsychiatry,* 10:576–585, 1940.

Magner, J.A., Rogol, A.D., and Gorden, P. Reversible growth hormone deficiency and delayed puberty triggered by a stressful experience in a young adult. *The American Journal of Medicine,* 76:737–742, 1984.

Malson, L. *Wolf Children and the Problem of Human Nature.* With complete text of *The Wild Boy of Aveyron* by J.M.G. Itard (E. Fawcett, P. Aryton, J. White, trans.) New York, Monthly Review Press, 1972.

Masson, J.M. *The Assault on Truth: Freud's Suppression of the Seduction Theory.* New York, Penguin, 1985.

McClelland, W.J. Differential handling and weight gain in the rat. *Canadian Journal of Psychology,* 10:19–22, 1956.

Meyer-Bahlburg, H.F.L. Psychosocial management of short stature. In *The Clinical Guide to Child Psychiatry* (D. Shaffer, A.A. Ehrhardt, and L.L. Greenhill, eds.). New York, Free Press, 1985.

Money, J. *The Destroying Angel: Sex, Fitness and Food in the Legacy of Degeneracy Theory, Graham Crackers, Kellogg's Corn Flakes and American Health History.* Buffalo, Prometheus Books, 1985.

———. *Gay, Straight, and In-Between: The Sexology of Erotic Orientation.* New York, Oxford University Press, 1988.

———. *Lovemaps: Clinical Concepts of Sexual/Erotic Health and Pathology, Paraphilia, and Gender Transposition in Childhood, Adolescence, and Maturity.* New York, Irvington, 1986.

———. Paleodigms and paleodigmatics: A new theoretical construct applicable to Munchausen's syndrome by proxy, child-abuse dwarfism, paraphilia, anorexia nervosa, and other syndromes. *American Journal of Psychotherapy*, 43:15–24, 1989.

———. The syndrome of abuse dwarfism (psychosocial dwarfism or reversible hyposomatotropinism). *American Journal of Diseases of Children*, 131:508–513, 1977.

Money, J., and Annecillo, C. IQ change following change of domicile in the syndrome of reversible hyposomatotropinsim (psychosocial dwarfism): Pilot investigation. *Psychoneuroendocrinology*, 1:427–429, 1976.

Money, J., Annecillo, C., and Hutchison, J.W. Forensic and family psychiatry in abuse dwarfism: Munchausen's syndrome by proxy, atonement, and addiction to abuse. *Journal of Sex and Marital Therapy*, 11:30–40, 1985.

Money, J., Annecillo, C., and Kelley, J.F. Abuse-dwarfism syndrome: After rescue, statural and intellectual catchup growth correlate. *Journal of Clinical Child Psychology*, 12:279–283, 1983a.

———. Growth of intelligence: Failure and catchup associated respectively with abuse and rescue in the syndrome of abuse dwarfism. *Psychoneuroendocrinology*, 8:309–319, 1983b.

Money, J., Annecillo, C., and Werlwas, J. Hormonal and behavioral reversals in hyposomatotropic dwarfism. In *Hormones, Behavior and Psychopathology* (E.J. Sachar, ed.). New York, Raven Press, 1976.

Money, J., and Needleman, A. Child abuse in the syndrome of reversible hyposomatotropic dwarfism (psychosocial dwarfism). *Pediatric Psychology*, 1:20–23, 1976.

Money, J., and Werlwas, J. Folie à deux in the parents of psychosocial dwarfs: Two cases. *Bulletin of the American Academy of Psychiatry and the Law*, 4:351–362, 1976.

———. Paraphilic sexuality and child abuse: The parents. *Journal of Sex and Marital Therapy*, 8:57–64, 1982.

Money, J., and Wolff, G. Late puberty, retarded growth and reversible hyposomatotropinism (Psychosocial dwarfism). *Adolescence*, 9:121–134, 1974.

Money, J., Wolff, G., and Annecillo, C. Pain agnosia and self injury in the syndrome of reversible somatotropin deficiency (psychosocial dwarfism). *Journal of Autism and Childhood Schizophrenia*, 2:127–139, 1972.

Montagu, M.F.A. The sensory influences of the skin. *Texas Report of Biological Medicine*, 11:291–391, 1953.

Mulinos, M.G., and Pomerantz, L. Pseudo-hypophysectomy: A condition resembling hypophysectomy produced by malnutrition. *Journal of Nutrition*, 19:493–504, 1940.

Niederland, W. *The Schreber Case: Psychoanalytic Profile of a Paranoid Personality*. New York, Quadrangle/New York Times Book Co., 1974.

Patton, R.G., and Gardner, L.I. *Growth Failure in Maternal Deprivation*. Springfield, IL, Charles C Thomas, 1963.

———. Influence of family environment on growth: The syndrome of "maternal deprivation." *Pediatrics*, 30:952–962, 1962.

Perry, J.H., and Freedman, D.A. Massive neonatal environmental deprivation: A clinical and neuroanatomical study. In *Early Development*, Research Publication of The Association for Research in Nervous and Mental Disease, vol. 51. Baltimore, The Association for Research in Nervous and Mental Disease, 1973.

Pies, H. *Kaspar Hauser: Augenzeugenberichte und Selbstzeugnisse*. Stuttgart, Robert Lutz, 1925.

Powell, G.F., Brasel, J.A., and Blizzard, R.M. Emotional deprivation and growth retardation simulating idiopathic hypopituitarism. I. Clinical evaluation of the syndrome. *New England Journal of Medicine*, 276:1271–1278, 1967a.

Powell, G.F., Brasel, J.A., Raiti, S., and Blizzard, R.M. Emotional deprivation and growth retardation simulating idiopathic hypopituitarism. II. Endocrinologic evaluation of the syndrome. *New England Journal of Medicine*, 276:1279–1283, 1967b.

Powell, G.F., Hopwood, N.J., and Barratt, E.S. Growth hormone studies before and during catch up growth in a child with emotional deprivation and short stature. *Journal of Clinical Endocrinology*, 37:674–679, 1973.

Reinhart, J.B., and Drash, A.L. Psychosocial dwarfism: Environmentally induced recovery. *Psychosomatic Medicine*, 21:165–172, 1969.

Ribble, M.A. *The Rights of Infants: Early Psychological Needs and Their Satisfaction*. New York, Columbia University Press, 1943.

Saenger, P., Levine, L.S., Wiedemann, E., Schwartz, E., Korth-Schutz, S., Pareira, J., Heinig, B., and New, M.I. Somatomedin and growth hormone in psychosocial dwarfism. *Pëdiatrie und Pädologie*, suppl. 5:1–12, 1977.

Sassin, J.F., Parker, D.C., Mace, J.W., Gotlin, R.W., Johnson, L.C., and Rossman, L.G. Human growth hormone release: Relation to slow-wave sleep and sleep-waking cycles. *Science*, 165:513–515, 1969.

Schanberg, S.M., and Field, T.M. Sensory deprivation stress and supplemental stimulation in the rat pup and preterm human neonate. *Child Development*, 58:1431–1447, 1987.

Schanberg, S.M., and Kuhn, C.M. The biochemical effects of tactile deprivation in neonatal rats. In *Perspectives on Behavioral Medicine*, vol.2 of *Neuroendocrine Control and Behavior* (R.B. Williams, Jr., ed.). New York, Academic Press, 1985.

Schatzmann, M. *Soul Murder: Persecution in the Family*. New York, New American Library/Signet, 1973.

Schreber, D.P. *Denkwürdigkeiten eines Nervenkranken*. Leipzig, Oswald Mutze, 1903.

———. *Memoirs of My Nervous Illness* (I. Macalpine and R.A. Hunter, trans.). London, William Dawson and Sons, 1955.

Sharp, F.M. *The Poet's Madness: A Reading of George Trakl*. Ithaca, NY, Cornell University Press, 1981.

Shengold, L. *Soul Murder: The Effects of Childhood Abuse and Deprivation*. New York, Fawcett Columbine, 1989.

Silver, H.K., and Finkelstein, M. Deprivation dwarfism. *Journal of Pediatrics*, 70:317–324, 1967.

Silverton, R. Social work perspective on psychosocial dwarfism. *Social Work in Health Care*, 7:1–14, 1982.

Simon, N. Kaspar Hauser. In *Traumatic Abuse and Neglect of Children at Home* (G.J. Williams and J. Money, eds.). Baltimore, Johns Hopkins University Press, 1980.

Singh, J.A.L., and Zingg, R.M. *Wolf-Children and Feral Man*. New York, Harper & Bros., 1941.

Skeels, H.M. *Adult Status of Children with Contrasting Early Li e Ex* periences: A follow-up study. [Monographs of the Society for Research in Child Development, Serial No. 105, vol.31, no.3.] Chicago, University of Chicago Press, 1966.

Skeels, H.M., and Fillmore, E.A. The mental development of children from underprivileged homes. *Pedagogical Seminary and Journal of Genetic Psychology*, 50:427–439, 1937.

Skuse, D. Extreme deprivation in early childhood. I. Diverse outcomes for three siblings from an extraordinary family. *Journal of Child Psychology and Psychiatry,* 25:523–541, 1984a.

———. Extreme deprivation in early childhood. II. Theoretical issues and a comparative review. *Journal of Child Psychology and Psychiatry,* 25:543–572, 1984b.

Solomon, R.L. The opponent-process theory of acquired motivation. *American Psychologist,* 35:691–712, 1980.

Sontag, L.W., Baker, C.T., and Nelson, V.L. *Mental growth and personality development: A longitudinal study.* [Monograph no. 68 of the Society for Research in Child Development, vol. 23, no. 2.] Lafayette, IN, Purdue University Child Development Publications, 1958.

Southall, D.P., Stebbens, V.A., Rees, S.V. Apnoeic episodes induced by smothering: Two cases identified by covert video surveillance. *British Medical Journal,* 294:1637–41, 1987.

Spaziante, R., Merola, B., Colao, A., Gargiulo, G., Cafiero, T., Irace, C., Rossi, E., Oliver, C., Lombardi, G., Mazzarella, B. Beta-endorphin concentrations both in plasma and in cerebrospinal fluid in response to acute painful stimuli. *Journal of Neurosurgical Sciences,* 34:99–106, 1990.

Spitz, R.A. Anaclitic depression: An inquiry into the genesis of psychiatric conditions in early childhood, II. *Psychoanalytic Study of the Child,* 2:313–342, 1946a.

———. Hospitalism: A follow-up report on investigation described in Volume I, 1945. *Psychoanalytic Study of the Child,* 2:113–117, 1946b.

Sulloway, F.J. *Freud, Biologist of the Mind: Beyond the Psychoanalytic Legend.* New York, Basic Books, 1979.

Taitz, L.S., and King, J.M. A profile of abuse. *Archives of Disease in Childhood,* 63:1026–1031, 1988a.

———. Growth patterns in child abuse. *Acta Paediatrica Scandinavica,* Supplement 343:62–72, 1988b.

Takahashi, Y., Kipnis, D.M., and Daughaday, W.H. Growth hormone secretion during sleep. *Journal of Clinical Investigation,* 47:2079–2090, 1968.

Talbot, N.B., Sobel, E.H., Burke, B.S., Lindemann, E., and Kaufman, S.B. Dwarfism in healthy children: Its possible relation to emotional, nutritional and endocrine disturbances. *New England Journal of Medicine,* 236:783–793, 1947.

Tanner, J.M. *Growth at Adolescence.* Oxford, Blackwell, 1962.

———. Growth and endocrinology of the adolescent. In *Endocrine and*

Genetic Disease of Childhood (L.I. Gardner, ed.). Philadelphia, Saunders, 1969.

————. Letter to the editor. Resistance to exogenous human growth hormone in psychosocial short stature (emotional deprivation). *Journal of Pediatrics*, 71:317–324, 1967.

Taylor, B.J., and Brook, C.G.D. Sleep EEG in growth disorders. *Archives of Disease in Childhood*, 61:754–760, 1986.

Theoharides, T.C. Galen on Marasmus. *Journal of the History of Medicine and Allied Sciences*, 26:369–390, 1971.

Tissot, S.A. *A Treatise on the Diseases Produced by Onanism.* Translated from a New Edition of the French, with Notes and Appendix by an American Physician. New York, 1832. Facsimile reprint edition in *The Secret Vice Exposed! Some Arguments Against Masturbation* (C. Rosenberg and C. Smith Rosenberg, advisory eds.). New York, Arno Press, 1974.

————. *L'Onanisme, Dissertation sur les Maladies Produites par la Masturbation.* Lausanne, Glasset, 1781.

Waterhouse, R. The making of a Satanic myth: Adult 'survivors' tell horrific tales of ritual child abuse but the evidence is missing. *The Independent on Sunday* (U.K.), August 12, 1990, p.8.

Wetzel, N.C. *The Treatment of Growth Failure in Children: An Application of the Grid Technique.* Cleveland, NEA Service, Inc., 1948.

Whitten, C.F., Pettit, M.G., and Fischhoff, J. Evidence that growth failure from maternal deprivation is secondary to undereating. *Journal of the American Medical Association*, 209:1675–1682, 1969.

Williams, G.J. Cruelty and kindness to children: Documentary of a century, 1874–1974. In *Traumatic Abuse and Neglect of Children at Home* (G.J. Williams and J. Money, eds.). Baltimore, Johns Hopkins University Press, 1980.

Wolff, G., and Money, J. Relationship between sleep and growth in patients with reversible somatotropin deficiency (psychosocial dwarfism). *Psychological Medicine*, 3:18–27, 1973.

Yalow, R.S. Radioimmunoassay: A probe for the fine structure of biologic systems. *Science*, 200:1236–1245, 1978.

Yarrow, L.J. Maternal deprivation: Toward an empirical and conceptual re-evaluation. *Psychological Bulletin*, 58:459–490, 1961.

Name Index

Subject Index

DATE DUE

FEB 27 2002			
JUN 1 4 2005			

GAYLORD · PRINTED IN U.S.A.